GENDER AND THE VICTORIAN PERIODICAL

Periodicals in the Victorian era portrayed and reinforced current gender notions and ideals. Indeed, the Victorian periodical press was a critical cultural site for the representation of competing gender ideologies. This is the first full-length book to examine masculinities and femininities as defined and interrogated in these periodicals. It investigates readers, editors and journalists; and it considers the power of the press at home, in the domestic space, in metropolitan centres and at the margins of empire. The work is based on archival research into a wide range of publications from the 1830s to the *fin de siècle*; from enduring intellectual heavyweight quarterlies through more ephemeral women's and working men's magazines, to magazines for boys and girls. The study is informed by the theories and approaches of media and cultural studies and women's studies. A valuable appendix supplies information about the many periodicals of the period mentioned in the book.

HILARY FRASER is Geoffrey Tillotson chair in Nineteenth-Century Studies in the School of English and Humanities at Birkbeck College, University of London. She is the author of *Beauty and Belief: Aesthetics and Religion in Victorian Literature* (Cambridge, 1986), *The Victorians and Renaissance Italy* (1992) and *English Prose of the 19th Century* (with Daniel Brown, 1997).

STEPHANIE GREEN is Lecturer for the University Extension Program at the University of Western Australia and Marketing and Promotions Manager of Fremantle Arts Centre Press. She is a writer and has published widely on topics in nineteenth-century literature.

JUDITH JOHNSTON teaches in English, Communication and Cultural Studies at the University of Western Australia. She is editor with Margaret Harris of *The Journals of George Eliot* (Cambridge, 1998) and author of *Anna Jameson: Victorian, Feminist, Woman of Letters* (1997).

CAMBRIDGE STUDIES IN NINETEENTH-CENTURY
LITERATURE AND CULTURE

General editor
Gillian Beer, *University of Cambridge*

Editorial board
Isobel Armstrong, *Birkbeck College, London*
Leonore Davidoff, *University of Essex*
Terry Eagleton, *University of Manchester*
Catherine Gallagher, *University of California, Berkeley*
D. A. Miller, *Columbia University*
J. Hillis Miller, *University of California, Irvine*
Mary Poovey, *New York University*
Elaine Showalter, *Princeton University*

Nineteenth-century British literature and culture have been rich fields for inter-disciplinary studies. Since the turn of the twentieth century, scholars and critics have tracked the intersections and tensions between Victorian literature and the visual arts, politics, social organisation, economic life, technical innovations, scientific thought – in short, culture in its broadest sense. In recent years, theoretical challenges and historiographical shifts have unsettled the assumptions of previous scholarly synthesis and called into question the terms of older debates. Whereas the tendency in much past literary critical interpretation was to use the metaphor of culture as 'background', feminist, Foucauldian, and other analyses have employed more dynamic models that raise questions of power and of circulation. Such developments have reanimated the field.

This series aims to accommodate and promote the most interesting work being undertaken on the frontiers of the field of nineteenth-century literary studies: work which intersects fruitfully with other fields of study such as history; or literary theory; or the history of science. Comparative as well as interdisciplinary approaches are welcomed.

A complete list of titles published will be found at the end of the book.

GENDER AND THE VICTORIAN PERIODICAL

HILARY FRASER, STEPHANIE GREEN AND
JUDITH JOHNSTON

CAMBRIDGE
UNIVERSITY PRESS

CAMBRIDGE UNIVERSITY PRESS
Cambridge, New York, Melbourne, Madrid, Cape Town, Singapore, São Paulo

Cambridge University Press
The Edinburgh Building, Cambridge CB2 8RU, UK

Published in the United States of America by Cambridge University Press, New York

www.cambridge.org
Information on this title: www.cambridge.org/9780521830720

First published 2003
This digitally printed version 2008

A catalogue record for this publication is available from the British Library

ISBN 978-0-521-83072-0 hardback
ISBN 978-0-521-05457-7 paperback

To our families and friends

Contents

Plates

Preface

This book investigates the role of the periodical press in mediating gender ideologies at a time when, as the most significant organ for disseminating knowledge, information and social attitudes, it wielded considerable cultural power. The periodical press in Victoria's day had a sustained influence on the gendered assumptions of both the home and the colonial culture over which she presided. Journals and magazines became sites of intensified representations of gender and sexual identity and our evaluations and re-evaluations will, we trust, contribute to an understanding of the centrality of journalism in the construction of gender in Victorian cultural history.

We are the first to acknowledge that the scope of our study, given the many thousands of periodical titles published in the Victorian period, is too vast to enable an exhaustive coverage of the field. Indeed the variety is almost irresistible and every title has its fascinating characteristics and personalities, and is redolent with possibilities – comic, political, social and historical. However, we determined that this would be a different kind of work from the many previous excellent studies of individual titles (so invaluable to us) because it was our decision to stand back and examine the larger questions of gender rather than focus closely on particular titles. For this reason our study omits, for instance, regional journals, and we have limited ourselves to journals published for the most part in those powerful publishing centres, London and Edinburgh.

We have, except on rare occasions, avoided reviews and serial fiction in our discussions, because these have been admirably dealt with in such detail and some profusion in other publications. Only exceptionally, where an article served a particular cultural or social function, like for example George Eliot's review essay for the *Westminster* titled 'The Natural History of German Life', is it included. It has been only recently that other kinds of journalism, outside fiction, have been taken up, recognised now as of very real interest to both literary and cultural studies, as well as relevant to the study of history.

While we mention by name perhaps 120 periodical titles, we have read many more, including a significant number which began publication before the Victorian age, such as the *Gentleman's Magazine*, the *Anti Jacobin Magazine* and the *Select Magazine for the Instruction and Amusement of Young Persons*. Moreover, although no study of the periodical press could omit those dominant journals of the nineteenth century, the *Quarterly* and the *Edinburgh Magazine*, we have chosen to be judicious in our use of them, attempting to balance discussion of these with consideration of other kinds of journal. Those periodicals that continued publishing into the twentieth century were also a part of our study, so that we could gain an understanding of a press not arbitrarily restricted by a specified 'age' or a particular date, but as a continuing phenomenon which came to its zenith as part of that innately Victorian sense of a new, innovative and progressive world.

Material quoted from the various periodicals has, for the most part, retained the original spelling, grammar and punctuation. Obvious errors and misprints have been silently corrected and variant spellings likely to disrupt the reading process have been normalised. Where possible, the anonymous author of a particular article has been located through that wonderful boon to every student of the periodical press, the *Wellesley Index*, or through other means. Where such authors have been located, their publications are listed in the Bibliography under their names. Where an author has not been located, the work has been cited under the title of the article, rather than 'Anon.', for ease of reference.

At the back of the book we have included an Appendix offering brief details about the periodicals cited in this work. These notes provide, where possible, the run of the journal, the cost of the first issue, the key editor or editors, place of publication, publisher, politics, target readership and a brief general description of the contents. The studies from which the bulk of this information has been gleaned are listed at the head of the Appendix.

Acknowledgements

This book could not have been written without the generous support of the Australian Research Council, which awarded a large grant to Hilary Fraser and Judith Johnston as Chief Investigators in 1998 for a period of three years. Stephanie Green was appointed half-time Research Associate under the same grant. In the fullest sense this has been collaborative work but the major responsibility for it rests with the two named Chief Investigators. We have also received other valuable financial support. Judith Johnston was awarded an Australian Bicentennial Fellowship by the Menzies Foundation in 1998, which enabled her to take up an Honorary Visiting Fellowship at the University of Leicester Victorian Studies Centre. Stephanie Green won an institutional ARC Grant which enabled her to travel to conferences and libraries in the United States and the United Kingdom and to take up a Visiting Research Fellowship at St. Deiniol's College. We jointly convened a conference in Perth in the year 2000 under the auspices of the Australasian Victorian Studies Association, which was generously supported by the University of Western Australia and the Ian Potter Foundation. And Hilary Fraser was given a year's study leave by the University of Western Australia during which she was able to complete the book as a Visiting Fellow at Clare Hall, Cambridge. We give our warm thanks to the individuals, institutions and funding bodies who have enabled the project to go ahead in this way.

Thanks are due to Professor Joanne Shattock, Director of the Victorian Studies Centre at the University of Leicester, who was unfailingly helpful regarding the initial periodical research carried out at the University of Leicester Library. Thanks are also due to the Library staff for their cheerful assistance and to the Librarian for permission to publish illustrations 4, 5, 7 and 8. For permission to publish illustrations 1, 2 and 3 we thank the British Library. We acknowledge with gratitude the assistance of Sten Christensen, Humanities Librarian, the University of Sydney Library in obtaining the image for illustration 6 and thank the Library for permission to publish.

For permission to publish extracts from the letters of Mary Howitt, held in the Department of Manuscripts and Special Collections, the University of Nottingham, we thank the Keeper, Dorothy B. Johnston, and gratefully acknowledge the help that she and the Assistant Keeper, Caroline Kelly, gave us during this research period. Kate Perry, Archivist at Girton College, Cambridge, provided, as always, invaluable assistance.

Our book is a collaborative enterprise, not only because it is co-authored, but because so many friends and colleagues have had a significant input. Over the past four years we have all given papers related to the project in both local and international forums: work-in-progress seminars and a dedicated 'Gender and Victorian Journalism' seminar at the University of Western Australia; the aforementioned Australasian Victorian Studies Association Conference on the theme of 'Victorian Mediations: Gender, Journalism and the Periodical Press'; the British Association of Victorian Studies Conference; invited papers at the Universities of Cambridge, Oxford, Exeter and Aberystwyth. It is impossible to acknowledge the input of all those who asked probing questions and made helpful suggestions in these and other contexts over this period, but we would like to single out some who have helped us to clarify the issues we are confronting, and given us the benefit of their own knowledge of Victorian gender issues and the periodical press. We are particularly grateful to Gillian Beer, Laurel Brake, Patrick Brantlinger, Marysa Demoor, Kate Flint, Regenia Gagnier, Lyn Pykett, Valerie Sanders and Joanne Shattock for their generous contributions to our project. Alex Tyrrell generously gave us access to his article on Samuel Smiles before publication, and our indebtedness to other scholars in the field will be evident from the range of our critical references.

Monica Anderson and Victoria Burrows, as Research Assistants at various periods, made an important contribution to the project, not least the extensive wealth of information uncovered by Monica for the material located in the Appendix from which we were able to construct what we trust is useful information on the journals referred to throughout this work. Our colleagues in the Discipline of English, Communication and Cultural Studies, the University of Western Australia, have also supported the project in various ways both intellectual and practical. In particular we would thank Daniel Brown, Kieran Dolin, Gail Jones, Andrew Lynch and Bob White for their unfailing interest and enthusiasm. We would also like especially to thank Sue Lewis and Jocasta Davies for their cheerful administrative support.

Finally, we wish to thank Linda Bree at Cambridge University Press for her encouragement of the project from its beginnings, and the anonymous reader of the earlier chapters we submitted to the press for his or her astute comments and wise advice, which have helped shape the final book.

Introduction

In an anonymous article of 1868 in the *Saturday Review*, part of its notorious series on 'Modern Women' which introduced the 'Girl of the Period' phenomenon, Eliza Lynn Linton takes as her topic 'Mistress and Maid on Dress and Undress'. Responding to a letter in the *Pall Mall Gazette* purporting to be from a 'Clergyman's Wife' which indignantly laments 'the present disgraceful style of dress among female servants' (262) and proposes the adoption of suitable uniforms for women below stairs, Linton makes it the occasion for a disquisition on the sartorial morals of the fashionable women who are their employers. Linton's caustically witty piece nicely illustrates a number of the themes that will emerge in this study. It demonstrates, first of all, that the journalism of the periodical press was a fundamentally provocative and reactive medium, initiating dialogue on topics of the day, and demanding a response; that important debates about gender and class were often displaced into discussions relating to the apparently trivial and ephemeral world of fashion; and that ideologies of gender and class were always connected, always competing and always under construction in writing for the periodicals. It also shows how embedded such debates were in the commercial and consumerist culture of Victorian publishing. Linton criticises the rival *Pall Mall Gazette* for its contradictoriness in carrying in the same number as the 'Clergyman's Wife's' recommendation that servants be guided by their mistress's standards of dress a report on the latest Paris fashions which shows the lady of fashion to be morally delinquent, in a way that also draws attention to the multivalency of the periodical press, another question that will be further explored. The article similarly exemplifies the variety of competing voices to be found in periodical writing, including, as it does, the female (but anonymous) professional journalist, an amateur contributor (the 'Clergyman's Wife') to a letters' page and a male fashion writer. It is an article that insistently raises questions about gender that will be probed in the chapters to come. What is the gender of its anonymous writer and its implied reader? What does it suggest about

the tensions between the construction of Woman as a cultural category
and the diversity of women, both as they are discursively represented and
in all their materiality? What does it tell us about the contingency of their
status, as wives, maidservants, women of fashion? Broadening out from
the article to consider its author, and the series to which it belongs, what
part did they play in the articulation of the 'Woman Question' and the
associated questioning of masculine identity in the 1860s, and how did
they relate to the debates about gender of the 1830s and the 1890s? Eliza
Lynn Linton, herself a clergyman's daughter, was a woman who followed
a male profession for five decades, assumed a masculine voice in much of
her anonymous journalism and adopted a male subject position in her own
fictional autobiography, the *Autobiography of Christopher Kirkland* (1885),
at the same time as she was an anti-feminist who became infamous for her
conservative prescriptions for an essential womanhood. What effect did
her own gender instability have on her writing? And then what were the
cultural spin-offs of series of articles such as these about women? What,
finally, was the relationship between the girl of the period and the girl of
the periodical?

This book aims to address the role played by the periodical press in the
formulation and circulation of gender ideologies in Victorian Britain, and
to examine the contribution of women in particular, as editors, proprietors,
writers and readers of periodical journalism, to their dissemination. In Mary
Poovey's account of the ideological work of gender in mid-Victorian cultural
and institutional life, *Uneven Developments: The Ideological Work of Gender
in Mid-Victorian England* (1988), she argues that ideological formation is
an uneven and reciprocal process. It is our contention that the medium
that most readily articulates the unevennesses and reciprocities of evolving
gender ideologies is the periodical press, which offers material realisation,
generically and formally, of that dynamic and relational cultural process.

I

The Victorians themselves were acutely aware of the pivotal role of the
periodical press in such socially, politically and intellectually volatile times
as their own. An article of 1862, 'Journalism', in the *Cornhill* predicts that
'[j]ournalism will, no doubt, occupy the first or one of the first places in any
future literary history of the present times, for it is the most characteristic
of all their productions'. Indeed, '[i]n the state of society in which we live
at present, [good leading articles] form the greater part of the reading even

of the most educated part of the adult members of the busy classes' (52, 53). In the 'Introduction' to his new magazine *Saint Pauls*, launched in 1867, Anthony Trollope confirms this view, adding, moreover, that 'now in this year at which we have arrived, it is hardly too much to say that, – exclusive of the political and critical newspapers – the monthly periodicals afford to the reading public the greatest part of the modern literature which it demands' (1–7). Also writing at mid-century, W. R. Greg, in his article 'The Newspaper Press' (1855) for the *Edinburgh Review*, celebrates the might and power of journalism as 'the "greatest FACT" – of our times', as a culture of its own: 'Journalism is now truly an estate of the realm; more powerful than any of the other estates . . . it does all the thinking of the nation' (470, 477). Greg focusses on power, which he consistently interprets as benign. The power of journalism is, he argues, 'well-earned and richly merited' (478). While benign power, as a force for 'good' and 'truth', is naively represented in the *Edinburgh Review* by Greg, it becomes an important issue with regard to discourse, because as Foucault has argued in *The History of Sexuality*, 'where there is power there is resistance' (95). In our exploration of the British periodical press in the nineteenth century, it is the power of discourse, particularly in regard to issues of gender, which becomes the major site of either contestation or collaboration.

These were unstable and transitional times, when the old absolutist certainties were giving way to a more relativist culture which encouraged the proliferation and diversification of perspectives on the modern world. This was reflected in the generic development of the periodical press in the course of the century, from the small number of monumental quarterlies which may be said to characterise its beginnings to the vast welter of slighter and more ephemeral monthlies which typify the magazine culture of its end. Journalism is a medium in which it is not only acceptable but almost *de rigueur* to speak from a politically interested position. Whether their platform was the Liberal *Edinburgh Review* or the Tory *Quarterly*, or later the radical *Westminster Review* or the feminist *Victoria Magazine*, Victorian journalists typically employed an explicitly polemical discourse which the practice of anonymity only encouraged. Moreover, the currency of the periodical press, its ephemeral character, made it an apt mediating agency for the presentation of ideas that were constantly undergoing revision and reformulation. This was true even of such weighty publications as the *Edinburgh Review*, as a hostile critic of one of its founders and key contributors Francis Jeffrey announced in 'Remarks on the Periodical Criticism of England' in *Blackwood's Edinburgh Magazine* in 1818:

So acute a man as he is cannot conceal from himself the fact, that however paramount may be his authority among the generation of indolent and laughing readers to whom he dictates opinion, he has as yet done nothing which will ever induce a man of research, in the next century, to turn over the volumes of his Review . . . the topics which he has handled are so ephemeral, that already the first volumes of his journal have lost a very great part of their interest. (676)

Such charges might be, and indeed were levelled even more readily against the monthly and weekly magazines and the daily press later in the century. An article on 'Modern Periodical Literature' in the *Dublin Review* in 1862 histrionically declares:

A feverish clamour, the hot breath of excitement, cries out daily, Give! give! give! and the result is haste, immaturity, imperfection. Whether this excited, restless craving is the cause or the consequence originally of excessive literary activity, is not important to inquire; certain it is that both have grown together to an extent so monstrous and a growth so unhealthy that a crisis must arrive and probably soon. (277)

By contrast with such attempts to pathologise and demonise the press, some commentators viewed the changing characteristics of periodical writing as a positive sign of the times. The monthly *Metropolitan* carried an article in its first number in 1831 on 'Literature of the Day: – The New Magazine' which celebrates the new style as 'better adapted to the wants and habits of the consumer':

Compare the cumbrous periods and floundering verbiage of the very best writers of King James's day, with the snip-snap epigram style of newspaper penny-a-line men. It is the difference between a broad-wheel wagon and a railway steam carriage. The great business of a modern author is to seize his opportunity. (18, 19)

The *Metropolitan* had a stated Reform agenda, and the appeal of the new journalism was not only its modernity but also that it was a more democratic medium: 'One signal advantage which literature has gained by the modern state of things, is to be found in the downfall of authority' (18). The Reformist cause was further enhanced with the reduction of stamp duty in 1836 which, while it increased the number and circulation of periodicals on both sides of the political divide, particularly benefited the Liberal cause, as J. J. Darling's 'Liberal Newspapers – Effects of the Reduction of Stamp-Duty' in *Tait's Edinburgh Magazine* on the effects of the tax noted:

New journals are arising, and taking an active part in the great struggle between Aristocracy and Democracy which is now going on . . . The new journals are, with few exceptions, of thoroughly Liberal principles; and the increase of circulation has been almost wholly on the side of the Liberal newspapers. (685)

Both contemporary and modern commentary has tended to concentrate on the party political implications for journalism of such political moments as the First Reform Bill and such economic reforms as the reduction and eventual abolition in 1855 of the newspaper tax. Alternatively, like the technological advances which enabled the mass production and fast, cheap distribution of journals and newspapers by the beginning of Victoria's reign, and the vastly increased literacy rates among all classes which made possible a huge expansion in readership, these changes are adduced as reasons for the general growth of the periodical publishing industry in the nineteenth century. However, our own focus on the role of the periodical press in the mediation of gender ideologies, and on women's participation in the industry, leads us to inflect our interpretation of the effects of such changes in bringing about 'the downfall of authority' in ways that emphasise the implications for gender politics and for women. Our work seeks to determine the various ways in which the periodical press produced cultural meaning and then disseminated it as a form of popular culture, not only in Britain, but throughout the English-speaking world. Gender affects that discourse in crucial ways because it becomes the prime site of either critique of, or collusion with, the prevailing ideologies of the day. When Walter Bagehot wrote in 1855 of the 'age of confusion and tumult', the 'times of miscellaneous revolution' which provided the historical context for the growth of the modern periodical press in 'The First Edinburgh Reviewers', he saw the early nineteenth-century period of which he wrote as a time, fundamentally, 'when a man's own household are the special foes of his favourite and self-adopted creed' (261). The press itself was in large part responsible, of course, for this rude invasion of the paterfamilias' castle, and reciprocally a man's household, including its female members, both mistress and servant, both mother and daughter, came to have a shaping influence upon the development of the periodical press. Relations between the so-called public sphere and the private domestic sphere were considerably more intimate and dynamic than prescriptive upholders of the 'separate spheres' gender economy maintained. The periodical press, offering a liminal space between public and private domains, was a critical mediating agent between these two worlds.

Comparing modern writing for the periodical press with that of earlier ages in 'The First Edinburgh Reviewers', Bagehot invokes 'the talk of the man of the world' as 'the very model of our modern writing', by contrast with 'the lecture of a professor' which exemplified the writing of the past (256). As such an analogy would suggest, the world of journalism was a predominantly masculine one. Indeed, the very genre of the periodical in the nineteenth century was itself gendered, in ways that meant that the work of women for the press was largely obscured by the cultural identification of the 'journalist' as a signifier of masculinity. But whereas journalism was gendered masculine by those who regarded it as having a lofty status in the modern profession of letters, it was just as insistently feminised by those who denigrated periodical writing. These critics of the press, like the author of 'Modern Periodical Literature', perceived the journalist to be 'stimulated by the prospect of gain rather than by the workings of genius', to write 'in a small and smattering way' on subjects of which they only have 'superficial' knowledge (276–7). The geologist Hugh Miller, in an article of 1870 on 'Periodicalism', sees periodical writing as issuing forth 'from the closets of over-toiled littérateurs', and being responsible for 'an excited superficiality [that] creeps out upon the age' (210). And writing of the New Journalism in 1887, Matthew Arnold in 'Up to Easter' invokes the sensation novel, a sub-genre closely associated with female writers and readers, as well as listing a number of attributes conventionally gendered feminine, when he claims 'it is full of ability, novelty, variety, sensation, sympathy, generous instincts; its one great fault is that it is featherbrained' (638–9).

The language of the above quotations makes it apparent that, for some critics, journalistic writing, or some forms of it, involved a kind of intellectual emasculation. Indeed, from early in the century, when the mandarin quarterly reviews, the *Edinburgh Review* (founded in 1802) and the *Quarterly* (1809), reigned supreme, journalism was, despite its status as masculine public discourse, associated by some commentators with the feminine. The 'Confession of Faith' with which William Maginn opens the first number of *Fraser's Magazine* in 1830 makes it clear that comparisons between 'a bashful Magazine launching forth into the world, and a blushing maiden coming out in the tender prime of eighteen' were a cliché even then (1). This does not deter *Sharpe's London Magazine* in 1849 from announcing in 'To Our Readers': 'It is now two years since with timid step and down-cast eyes, we, like a bashful débutante, made our first appearance upon the stage of Literature', even if the bashful débutante has in the meantime hardened into an actress who has appeared before her readers 'in many parts' (409). By 1895, when the *Windsor Magazine* invokes the analogy in 'A Foreword', it is distinctly tired: 'Without being as nervous as a débutante at a Drawing-Room, a new Magazine which presents itself at the Court of the British public may confess to a certain fascinating timidity', a demeanour infinitely to be preferred, it seems, to that of those periodicals 'which bounce into popularity by the power of mere flourish, just as a girl whose charms are of a somewhat bold type makes a masculine circle captive to an audacious freshness' (1).

The bold and flirtatious hussy was a common alternative trope for the press throughout the nineteenth century. According to William Hazlitt, in his 1823 article on 'The Periodical Press', periodicals exemplify modern literature, which he describes as 'the directress of fashion', as 'a gay Coquette, fluttering fickle vain . . . [which] trifles with all sorts of arts and sciences . . . glitters, flutters, buzzes, spawns, dies, – and is forgotten'. 'Instead of solemn testimonies from the learned', he avers, 'we require the smiles of the fair and the polite . . . let Reviews flourish – let Magazines increase and multiply' (Hazlitt, *Complete Works*, XVI: 219). If even at this stage in the history of the nineteenth-century periodical press it was seen as a promiscuous and flighty medium, built upon the principle that ideas are as changeable and marketable as fashion, then by the end of the century the association of the magazine with fashion and hence with the feminine had become thoroughly entrenched. The later chapters of this book will examine the negotiations and contradictions surrounding *fin-de-siècle* magazine culture (and cultural constructions). The little magazines and women's fashion and other popular magazines will be read as literary texts that provide evidence of problematised constructions of gender in ways that also reflect on social status, national identity and cultural ideologies.

We are of course used to thinking about the 1890s as a time when high Victorian codifications of gender identity were irreversibly unsettled, but a reading of the periodicals of the previous six decades discloses the instability of the concept of gender as a binary category even as it was being most loudly declared. It is striking to note how often gender representation is radically transgressive in early and mid-Victorian periodicals, not only in the more liberal publications like *Chambers' Edinburgh Journal*, which runs approving articles on 'Clever Women' (281) and 'The Domestic Man' (385), but also in the conservative press. Even though gender transgression is typically mocked and reviled, its notable prominence as a topic of interest, and indeed the very fact that it is deemed necessary to police the ideological boundaries between the sexes, are telling indications that such barricades are by no means impregnable. As early as the 1830s, periodicals such as the *Lady's Magazine* and the *Lady's Museum* are to be found admonishing young men for their feminine habits and behaviour, and writing dismissively of the dandy and the exquisite. The former, for example, announces in 1831:

Dandyism is a heresy in fashionable life; it is, indeed, but the affectation of elegance.
    When a man becomes an exquisite, he converts himself into a piece of mere drawing-room furniture; a puppet, ingeniously contrived to mount a horse, seat itself in a boudoir, and even bite the head of a cane – but a thinking being! No! (February n.p.)[1]

Conversely, women are condemned for their mannish behaviour, and for cross-dressing. The *Lady's Museum*, for instance, copies a report, 'Courting Extraordinary' from the *Perth Courier*, adding its own editorial comment:

A practice has been prevalent for some time past among a few of the fair ones of the village of Methven, in assuming the garb of men, and sporting about in the gloamin, pretending that they are in love with the very toasts of the village. Such a sporting with the feelings of the fair is not at all commendable, and much less by their own sex. – [We sincerely participate in the indignation of the journalist, but we know many 'an old woman' actually united to a young and beautiful girl, constrained to the vow by the allurements of wealth, or the resistless mandate of insatiate parents. – Ed. L. M.] (241)

By the 1860s, the dandy is still not extinct and the unfeminine woman is still vexing the notion of 'distinctive womanhood'. Mary Braddon's magazine *Belgravia* in 1867, for example, carries an article on 'Swells' which considers under that general title discussions of various ambiguously gendered types: coxcombs, fops, beaux, exquisites and dandies. Of the beau, for instance, we are told:

Goldsmith considers him, anthropologically, a true though rare variety of civilised men; and being a naturalist, the Doctor's opinion is entitled to some weight. In sex he allowed him to be masculine, of which the creature's partiality to women is probably some conclusive evidence; for while such a taste would hardly have been natural to an animal strictly of the feminine gender, one of another order would have failed in winning that encouragement in which the daughters of Eve were never wanting towards him. (39)[2]

By the same token, in a signed article of 1865 on 'Woman's Mission' in *Bow Bells*, Mary Howitt declares her lack of sympathy with 'women who are always wishing themselves men':

The assumption of masculine airs or of masculine attire, or of the absence of tenderness and womanhood in a mistaken struggle after strength, can never sit more gracefully upon us than do the men's old hats, and great coats, and boots, upon the poor old gardeneresses of the English garden. (235)

Anxiety about 'mannish' women resurfaces more powerfully still in the 1890s with the emergence of the 'new woman', provoking some predictably alarmist responses in the periodical literature. Thus, the Revd. H. R. Haweis, writing for the *Young Woman*, tells the story of a typical example of 'The Mannish Girl', Clarisse, who happily gets over her youthful affectation of the masculine, loses her taste for 'all those horsey and mannish things that were fast spoiling her', and becomes engaged to a young doctor (334). And, of course, also at the end of the century Oscar

Wilde's dandified dress, adopted and displayed as a marker of resistance,[3] came to signify more radical forms of gender subversion and focussed fears about masculine deviancy which were widely articulated in the periodical press.

It is Eliza Lynn Linton, though, who time and again throughout her long writing career most memorably crystallises the convoluted and contradictory sexual politics of a binaried gender model that continually and demonstrably deconstructs itself. If the main thrust of her series of articles on 'Modern Women' for the *Saturday Review* in 1868 is that womanhood can be essentially defined, her entire strategy undermines that position, in that what she presents is a series of sketches of how women fail to measure up to that ideal, and how that failure can take many forms, including masculine ones. In her article on 'Feminine Affectations', for example, she points the finger at not only the feminine artifice of the 'excessively womanly woman', revealing gender identity as in fact a construction, but also its opposite, the equally reviled 'mannish woman':

> . . . the woman who wears a double-breasted coat with big buttons, of which she flings back the lapels with an air, understanding the suggestiveness of a wide chest and the need of unchecked breathing; who wears unmistakeable shirtfronts, linen collars, vests, and plain ties, like a man; who folds her arms or sets them akimbo, like a man . . . She adores dogs and horses, which she places far above children of all ages. She boasts of how good a marksman she is . . . [and more of the same]. All of which is affectation – from first to last affectation; a mere assumption of virile fashions utterly inharmonious to the whole being, physical and mental, of a woman. (776)

As Janet Wolff speculates in *Feminine Sentences: Essays on Women and Culture*, 'perhaps this perception of the "masculine" in women who were visible in a man's world is only the displaced recognition of women's overall exclusion from that world' (42). Linton is equally critical, though, of effeminate men, or indeed of anyone whose sexuality is ambiguous. Another type that radically unsettles the strictly defined gender categories she strives so hard to maintain is that class of what she terms, in her article on 'Pushing Women', 'amphibious beings', who not only perform a brokerage role between the East End and the West, the world of commerce and the world of fashion, but also operate, as fops and dandies – as well as, it is suggested, pimps – between genders (578). Such beings, 'half trader, half fop', like mannish women, upset the gender order by their propensity to traffic between social and sexual identities that Linton would have preferred to think of as belonging to discrete, antithetical categories.

A quarter of a century later, Linton's work is still marked by the same kind of ideological contradictions. Writing of 'The Wild Women' in 1891, against the by now rather old-fashioned depiction of the gender economy, as one in which men and women inhabit 'separate spheres', she continues to portray with unparalleled vigour and spleen both female and male forms of transgression. On the one hand, she writes of female politicians:

These insurgent wild women are in a sense unnatural. They have not 'bred true' – not according to the general lines on which the normal woman is constructed. There is in them a curious inversion of sex, which does not necessarily appear in the body, but is evident enough in the mind. Quite as disagreeable as the bearded chin, the bass voice, flat chest, and lean hips of a woman who has physically failed in her rightful development, the unfeminine ways and works of the wild women of politics and morals are even worse for the world in which they live. (79)

In 'Wild Women as Social Insurgents' such women are compared to North Country working women with '"whiskin' beards about their mou's"', 'smoking their black cutty-pipes' (597). On the other hand, men in 'Partisans of the Wild Women' are seen as emasculated: 'they are themselves like women in all essentials of mind and character' (459).

Interestingly enough, the profession of writing itself offered opportunities for a kind of higher order cross-dressing that was acceptable, whereby men might appropriate the more feminine attributes associated with their reputedly enhanced emotional and spiritual powers and women aspire to a share in men's intellectual gifts. 'Madame Elise's "Ladies" Pages' in *Bow Bells* in 1865 note without undue hostility that '[i]n poets, artists, and men of letters, par excellence, we observe their feminine trait, that their intellect habitually moves in alliance with their emotions' (139), and recommend that women writers be viewed as reversing the role of their feminised male counterparts. Whilst staunchly maintaining that there are crucial distinctions between the sexes, that '[t]he masculine mind is characterized by the predominance of the intellect, and the feminine by the predominance of the emotions', the writer warns the reader against 'too rigorous an interpretation of this statement' (139). For there is a need, it is argued, for more women writers to cultivate their masculine intellect in order to write about women's experience.

Eliza Lynn Linton, once again, offers an intriguing illustration of authorial gender trouble. She is famously intolerant of women who are not prepared to be circumscribed within the domestic circle. 'I could not accept the doctrine that no such thing as natural limitation of sphere is included in the fact of sex', she writes in volume two of *The Autobiography of Christopher Kirkland* (1885), 'and that individual women may, if they have the will and the power, do all those things which have hitherto been exclusively assigned to men' (4). She disapproves, as we have seen, equally of mannish women and feminised men:

Equal political rights; identical professional careers; the men's virile force toned down to harmony with the woman's feminine weakness; the abolition of all moral and social distinctions between the sexes; – These are the confessed objects of the movement whereby men are to be made lady-like and women masculine, till the two melt into one, and you scarcely know which is which. (2, 9)

And yet the above views are expounded by Christopher Kirkland, Linton's persona in her own fictional autobiography. And even where she is not actually masquerading as a man, in the most famous of her journalistic writing, like so many other women and men writing for the periodical press, she occupies an anonymous, and certainly an ambiguously gendered subject position whereby the masculine and the feminine may be said to 'melt into one, and you scarcely know which is which'.

In the chapters to come we will be considering the convention followed by most British magazines and reviews until the 1860s of publishing articles anonymously, and its implications for our topic. The practice of anonymous journalism enabled women to enter the field in greater numbers than was generally suspected and allowed them to address topics not generally thought of as suitable for a woman's pen, because theoretically no one except the editor knew who the author of a particular piece was. By exploring practices such as the use of anonymity, signature and cross-gendered pseudonyms, we will examine the extent to which the contribution of women challenged and helped to transform the grand narrative of gendered difference. We will also address the more general question of how a discourse which discouraged the personal and the idiosyncratic in favour of a 'house' style might have affected how journalism was gendered. We may see the effects of journalism's assimilationist aesthetic not only in the work of a woman such as Eliza Lynn Linton, whose contributions to the *Saturday Review*'s series on 'Modern Women' are not always easily distinguishable from those penned by John Richard Green, but also in the case of leading male journalists. Leslie Stephen, for example, at the turn of the century, reflecting on the history of journalism, describes his experience of reading some of his own earlier writing for the *Saturday Review* in an article entitled 'Some Early Impressions – Journalism':

I had, not long ago, to turn over the files of the paper for another purpose. Incidentally I looked for my own, and was a little startled to discover that I could rarely distinguish them by internal evidence. I had unconsciously adopted the tone of my colleagues, and, like some inferior organisms, taken the colour of my 'environment.' That, I suppose, is the common experience. The contributor occasionally assimilates; he sinks his own individuality and is a small wheel in a big machine. (432)

There is plenty of evidence to suggest that this was a common experience. Thus, for example, Leigh Hunt is said by William Beech Thomas in *The Story of the Spectator 1828–1928* to have observed that 'the paper was so well edited that all the articles seemed to have emanated from the same pen' (231).

Both the convention of anonymity and the practice of stylistic assimilation made the discourse of journalism more inclusive than forms of writing in which authorship was more commonly announced. These factors plus the opportunities for regular remuneration opened up journalism as a profession not only to star contributors, most often educated middle-class men of letters, but also to women and men from more modest social backgrounds. This was a matter of some concern to those who preferred the idea of a more exclusive press. The hostile reviewer of 'Modern Periodical Literature' in the *Dublin Review* blames the 'reward of money' for having 'tended to reduce the public writer to the level of a tradesman', and maintains that of the battalions of journalists now writing, 'a vast number, we may fairly say the majority, were never meant for authors' (276, 305):

The state of literature in the present day would almost suggest that authorship is a craft which can be acquired by practice. It would appear that many men, members of various professions and of different callings, finding their progress in such professions and callings slow, have, partly to beguile the tediousness of inactivity, and partly with a view to gain, begun to write, or rather to write and offer contributions to serial publications. At first perhaps rebuffed, after a time received and remunerated, they have bestowed additional labour on their succeeding efforts, and at last by dint of practice have acquired facility in writing short pieces either in prose or verse of moderate merit and which are received and paid for with regularity. Gradually they drop even the name of their original calling, and become professional writers. (277–8)

Mark Hampton has shown in 'Journalists and the Fragmentation of Knowledge' that this representation of entry into the profession is attested to by numerous late nineteenth-century memoirs by journalists describing their unorthodox career paths, from blacksmith or auctioneer or printer to journalist, editor or proprietor of a periodical (91–2). The press's particular role in the popularisation of specialist knowledges for the general reading public 'depended in large part upon journalists remaining "men of letters" who could write on any topic that presented itself', and this tended to perpetuate the idea of journalism as an 'open profession' rather than a closed shop. For those whose interests were served by inclusivity, '[t]he successful journalist was the one who, given a chance, could perform his duties; no *a priori* system of licensing and exclusion was compatible with the idea of journalists as the conveyors of "general knowledge"' (91). Hampton quotes the *Globe*, which argued in 1892 that:

Training in any department, would deprive journalism of what has always been its best recruiting ground – the men who have entered it because it is free and open, and imposes no condition of cost or preparation; the men who have fought their way into it; the men who have brought into it the experience and the knowledge which they have acquired in very different callings. (93)

As the gendered language of passages such as the above suggests, when journalists told stories about themselves, they were not above practising other kinds of exclusionary tactics. Notwithstanding such rhetorical strategies, the very factors that gave men 'never meant for authors' access to the profession of writing opened it up to women too, so that the periodical essay might be seen as, in Daniel Brown's words, 'the Trojan horse that allowed women writers to enter the male preserve of professional writing' (Fraser with Brown, *English Prose of the Nineteenth Century*, 21). By mid-century many of the anonymous multitude of contributors to the periodical press were indeed from the ranks of 'the fair' sex. And for many, including George Eliot, Harriet Martineau and Margaret Oliphant, periodicals were the platform from which extremely successful and high-profile professional writing careers were launched. By the 1840s women and their writing were becoming a force to be reckoned with in Victorian Britain. It is clear from articles such as George Lewes's 'The Condition of Authors in England, Germany and France' for *Fraser's Magazine* (1847), that their considerable presence in the writing scene generally was making an impact, judging from the language Lewes uses which, while humorous, nevertheless expresses considerable anxiety that writing as a profession is being invaded by 'speculators', and that the once well-trained 'army' of writers is being 'swelled and encumbered by women, children, and ill-trained troops' (285). He comically represents the profession of writing as an exclusive club of which men are the chief members, but which women are insisting on joining. In another article, 'A Gentle Hint to Writing Women', published in the *Leader* in 1850 (the year before Mary Ann Evans moved to London and began her work for the *Westminster Review*, and a decade before he was eclipsed by her fame), he further develops his argument about how '[w]e are overrun', claiming 'women have made an invasion of our legitimate domain':

They are ruining our profession. Wherever we carry our skilful pens, we find the place pre-occupied by a woman. The time was when my contributions were sought as favours; my graceful phrase was to be seen threading, like a meandering stream, through the rugged mountains of statistics, and the dull plains of matter of fact, in every possible publication. Then the pen was a profession. But now I starve. What am I to do – what are my brother-pens to do, when such rivalry is permitted? . . . How many of us can place our prose beside the glowing rhetoric and daring utterance of social wrong in the learned romances and powerful articles of Eliza Lynn, or the cutting sarcasm and vigorous protests of Miss Rigby? What chance have we against Miss Martineau, so potent in so many directions? (189)

The man who was to become George Eliot's consort declares, finally, 'My idea of a perfect woman is of one who can write but won't' (189).

II

As Lewes's articles make clear, women by mid-century had already begun to claim particular areas of writing for themselves – within journalism, not least. Women were active players in many aspects of periodical production throughout the century, often using journalism to build or even finance their careers as novelists, poets, critics, artists and historians. Some wrote with a conviction of the transformative power of the periodical press and others perceived it as a means of preserving the status quo; some became professional journalists out of financial necessity, some for the sheer pleasure of cultural engagement; some became famous as writers and public intellectuals, many more remained obscure. In the chapters to come, as well as looking at celebrated female journalists such as Eliza Lynn Linton, Harriet Martineau and George Eliot, we will be looking at some lesser known writers whose work for the press has been obscured by the ideological inflections of modern literary and cultural history. Whilst we do not see ours as a recuperative project, we do see it as an opportunity for the circulation of what Elspeth Probyn in *Sexing the Self: Gendered Positions in Cultural Studies* calls '"submerged" knowledges', for:

In reading these women writers together [with 'the Great Authors'] we can begin to trace out what is sayable at any one moment. Far from evoking a commonality, the proximity of a wealth of women writers begs the question of their differences, and hence of our own. (40)

The usefulness of drawing on some of the interdisciplinary methodologies of cultural studies, media studies and women's studies for a project such as this will be evident. Just as it seems to us to be crucial to problematise the concept of gender as a binary category, in the interests of interrogating the multivocality of the periodical press this study will also endeavour to dismantle the binaried generic classifications that have typically structured academic critique of nineteenth-century journalism – popular and cultural, domestic and public discourse, fiction and non-fiction, written text and illustration. At the outset of her book on the woman's magazine, *A Magazine of Her Own?*, Margaret Beetham underlines the connections between the 'fractured and heterogeneous' identity of the feminine and of the magazine form:

> Becoming the woman you are is a difficult project for which the magazine has characteristically provided recipes, patterns, narratives and models of the self . . . the magazine has historically offered not only to pattern the reader's gendered identity but to address her desire.
>
> This femininity has been addressed in and through a form which is itself fractured and heterogeneous. The magazine has developed in the two centuries of its history as a miscellany, that is a form marked by variety of tone and constituent parts. The relationship between the two elements in the term 'woman's magazine' has been and is dynamic. The magazine evolved as it did because from its inception it was a genre which addressed 'the feminine', but 'femininity' has also been informed by the development of print, particularly the magazine. (1–2)

The implications of Beetham's comments here may be extended in the case of our own more broadly based project. As well as the heterogeneity encompassed by the individual magazine, or even within the sub-genre of the woman's magazine, we will be addressing the awesome diversity of the periodical press more broadly conceived. As well as attending to the fractured nature of 'woman' and the feminine, we will be looking across gender and traversing sexualities to identify instances where representations of gender can be seen to construct cultural practices. If Beetham's own project was enormously ambitious, then the task we have set ourselves seems monumentally hubristic. As Lyn Pykett has observed in her suggestive essay 'Reading the Periodical Press: Text and Context', because of the vast and amorphous nature of the field, 'students of the Victorian periodical press have persistently confronted the double problem of defining the object of study, and devising an appropriate methodological framework within which to conduct that study' (100). Margaret Beetham is one critic who has tried to address the conceptual and methodological questions posed by periodical literature, opening up theoretical issues relating to the role of the magazine in the cultural production of gender.[4] However, until quite recently, scholarship on the Victorian periodical press has generally been historical and descriptive, or closely focussed on a particular journal; moreover, as Pykett notes, '[m]any students of the periodical press, apparently, aspire to the total knowledge of a past culture and seek a degree of conceptual possession of a "documentary" culture which must elude them even in relation to a living culture' ('Reading the Periodical Press', 101). Our own work benefits immeasurably from the careful and rigorous historical research of the scholars who precede us,[5] but, rather than aspiring to the kind of comprehensiveness described by Pykett as the goal of many earlier studies, it aims to meet some of the theoretical and methodological challenges she identifies. Indeed, her argument about the importance to periodical study of the 'close reading of text' together with her recommendation that 'we should think of "Text" in its Barthesian sense as a methodological field' (107) underpin our own approach, which examines the periodical as a textual field through which to engage with the production of discourse.

Our book, then, has a dual trajectory, part empirical study, giving a firm grounding in the historical specificities of nineteenth-century culture and society, and part formal and rhetorical analysis of texts, informed by the theories and methodologies of cultural, media and women's studies. We do not underestimate the difficulties of bringing together the empirical and the 'textual' in the way we envisage. They belong to quite different sites of knowledge-production. Nevertheless, it seems time to attempt such a methodological synthesis. Our argument about the importance of the relationship between gender and cultural identity in the Victorian periodical press is therefore founded on empirical examples of the periodical press in action and informed by theoretical approaches (feminism, discourse theory, theories of ideology) that enable us to foreground the journal or magazine as a site of discourse; that is, as a space in which several voices are engaged in dialogues that perform and transform the discourses of gender. To this end, our empirical research into the question of women's participation in the periodical literature of the nineteenth century will include investigating the journal and the magazine as sites of intensified representations of gender and sexual identity.

Faced with the challenge of organising and focussing our discussion of the vast and indeterminate body of material that constitutes the Victorian periodical press, we have again drawn on but significantly diverged from our predecessors in the field. Margaret Beetham, for example, as we have seen, successfully focusses her work both by delimiting her field of research to the woman's magazine and by adopting a case study methodology. Like hers, our own approach is broadly chronological, in an attempt to capture the historical specificities of particular cultural moments and to understand the self-conscious, self-referential and often intertextual development of periodical discourse as it underwent constant transformations through the course of the century. We too focus on particular journals and magazines, endeavouring to include discussion of both long-standing journals that exerted considerable cultural authority and more short-lived, marginal or culturally specific publications, but we do not organise our argument around the case study per se. Rather, we have chosen to frame our study according to a number of themes which seem to us to be crucial in the articulation of Victorian gender ideologies.

We begin with two related chapters on the gendered identity of the writing subject and the gendered positioning of the reader in periodical literature. We have suggested that the prevailing convention of anonymous or pseudonymous authorship enabled women to enter male preserves of professional writing and subject areas conventionally regarded as masculine discourses, and allowed men to enter female preserves, addressing subjects just as conventionally regarded as feminine, enabling a radical refusal of the limits of Victorian identity politics. Gender is a key factor in the construction of the public identity of the writer, but it is also important in shaping the sense that writers had of the character of their own voices and of their right of access to the magazine as medium of exchange. Chapter 1 deals with questions of the hegemony of the masculine in the field of publishing, the emergence of the woman writer in the particular area of periodical publication and the concomitant emergence of female identity as the source of a legitimate public voice. It also asks if the identity of the writing subject that emerges over time is coherent or contested, dynamic and diverse. Our second chapter, on the construction of the reader, addresses the question of both the actual and the implied reader. It examines how particular groups of periodicals position their readers, and how periodical writing functions as social discourse. In particular, it analyses the politics of reading journalism, and considers how the gendered and classed identity of the reader is textually instated through, for example, the enactment of voice and the textual construction of audience. It also suggests ways in which the writer/reader binary is collapsed in situations where readers participate, through, for example, letters to the editor, as writers and contributors.

In these first chapters we are interested in investigating the magazine's creation of a sense of a 'virtual community'. The third chapter leads on from this by raising questions about editorship and gender, and the role of the editor in determining the relationship between the journal and its audience. The concept of editorship, including the editorial policies of new journals across the century, is examined here to determine to what extent women are specifically written out of such policies, as writers and read-ers, and to assess the valorisation of particular subject matter by gender. Questions of qualifications and professionalisation are also considered. To this end we argue that a journal's house style, determined by the editor, becomes the discourse with which it attempts to woo and maintain a read-ership. Gender intersects this discourse at various points, and while we are conscious of famous examples of women editors of mainstream journals (Christian Isobel Johnstone edited *Tait's Edinburgh Magazine* from 1834 to 1846, and Marian Evans sub-edited the *Westminster Review* from 1852 to 1854) and male editors of journals designated female (most famously Oscar Wilde and the *Woman's World* (1887–9) and Arnold Bennett and *Woman* (1895–1912)), these are not closely addressed in this chapter. Rather, when we do focus on specific journals, we have chosen to consider the *Edinburgh Review*'s editorial approach to issues of gender and to examine *Eliza Cook's Journal* as an example of female editorship at mid-century. In this way we hope to demonstrate how editorial policy can determinedly reaffirm and reiterate the ideology of separate spheres or just as determinedly challenge the ideological divide.

Periodicals specifically designed to showcase writers – such as *Belgravia* (1866–99), associated with sensation novelist Mary Braddon, and *Household Words* (1850–9) and *All the Year Round* (1859–95), associated with Charles Dickens – are discussed primarily using William Makepeace Thackeray's ed-itorship of the *Cornhill*. Showcase editors had a particular effect on the jour-nals they edited, including creating an identity and a community through the magazine. This chapter also considers the long-standing journal and issues of survival, against short-lived periodicals, and whether or not the long-serving editor, or the identity of the editor (Dickens is an example), is a factor in a journal's popularity.

From the gendered politics of writing, reading and editing, we turn in the following two chapters to consider the role of the periodical press in the cultural mediation of Victorian ideologies with a particularly critical gendered inflection. Chapter 4 considers gender and the politics of home, while Chapter 5 addresses the obversely related topic of gender and cultural imperialism. The first of these is organised around an analysis of the con-nections in the periodical press between 'home', the ideologically framed private domain, and 'nation', the equally ideological public domain; and between the discourses of domestic economy and political economy. The second takes the question of nation further to look at how 'Englishness' is constructed in the periodicals, and how journalism is part of the process of imperialism, a tool of dissemination. This chapter considers to what extent editors of the mainstream periodicals, the *Edinburgh Review*, the *Quarterly Review*, *Fraser's Magazine* and so on, spoke for government policy on such issues as colonialism and migration and were instruments of propaganda promoting the migration of particular classes and national groups. The role of women in the imperialist project is of interest here, how that role is constructed by both male and female editors and journalists, and what differences their discourses reveal. By choosing a range of mainstream journals, and then a contrasting range of journals aimed at particular groups and/or topics, we investigate to what extent there was a common voice in the promotion of migration and colonisation and how gendered such promotions were. By examining early century, mid-century and late century periodicals we seek to discover whether the message changed over the century. To focus our discussion, we concentrate on writing about Australia as a colonial destination; to complicate it, we also consider how the 'empire writes back', seeking out what potential there is for such a dialogue.

Feminist writers and journals were at the forefront of discussion of the opportunities that existed for women in the colonies. Chapter 6 discusses feminism and the changing fortunes of women's presses in the Victorian period. We consider the representation of feminism in the press and the ways in which women used the periodical medium as a means of discursive intervention and as a mode of creative and political expression. Our discussion begins with the work of early feminists such as Bessie Parkes, Barbara Bodichon and the other women of the Langham Place Group in relation to the *English Woman's Journal*. This work was taken up in different ways by Emily Faithfull with the founding of the Victoria Press, producing publications directed to women. Out of this came Faithfull's *Victoria Magazine*. The importance of issues such as social justice, equity before the law, suffrage, religion, women's education and health were crucial to the emergence of publications like the *English Woman's Journal*, as they would be later in the century to the creation and demise of Florence Fenwick Miller's *Woman's Signal* (1895–9). Our study of these (and other) magazines will consider the extent to which the debates staged by feminism became blurred with other discourses – moral, national, religious – in a range of other journals such as the *Universal Review* or *Temple Bar*.

Having explored the ways in which women were constructed as readers, writers and subjects in the periodical press, in our final chapter we turn to how they were positioned as consumers in the commodity culture of the *fin de siècle*. We consider how gender becomes a discourse of consumption, and, indeed, in terms of representation, how woman became a form of commodity herself. Here we build on themes raised in earlier chapters, such as the relationship of the editor to theme and content, and the construction of the reading and writing subject – the 'Girl of the Period', the 'New Woman', and the 'New Man' – and question just how these figures might be accommodated to ongoing feminist debate. Such titles, emphasising the new and the topical, and packaging men and women as fashionable commodities, might have been transformative but rapidly come to represent high conservatism. The *Woman's World*, edited in 1888 and 1889 by Oscar Wilde, provides an interesting example of such connections. The gendered notion of the magazine as cultural ephemera, particularly the fashion magazine, and the phenomena of such journals as the *Yellow Book* are considered, by way of contrast to the *Woman's World*.

By the end of the nineteenth century the periodical press can be seen to be disseminating pleasure and desire in a way that would have disturbed all those mid-century certainties of W. R. Greg and the *Edinburgh Review* expressed in 'The Newspaper Press'. No longer a 'safety-valve in moderating discontent' (481); no longer dignified; the 'many-headed and unfettered Press' (481) has come out roaring, has adapted to, and in part engineered, the social and cultural changes that will take its readers into the new century. From the vantage point of 1890s culture, we take up the question of multivocality and gender in relation to the Victorian periodical press more generally. If the culture of the 1890s was 'Decadent' partly because of the way that it appeared to unsettle traditional gender boundaries, to what extent were the earlier journals also sites of instability and transformation? We examine how representations of gender are contested and reinscribed, and how the form of the periodical is particularly adaptive to these issues. Our discussion, therefore, considers the ways in which Decadence was predicated on cultural transformations in the relationship between gender and desire, and examines the tensions and ambiguities surrounding gender and sexual identity by referring to examples such as the *Yellow Book* where Ella D'arcy's co-editorship made publication more accessible to women writers of the period. This opportunity for expression was, however, limited, not only by the termination of the magazine, but by the social anxiety surrounding expressions of cultural difference as evidenced in the antagonism to the trope of the New Woman (*Punch*) and the reaction in the popular press to the trials of Oscar Wilde.

Despite its artificiality and its relative brevity as a cultural force, Decadence opens up questions of gender and representation which are crucial to the journalistic enterprise in the nineteenth century. The periodical, as a site of multiple discourses, always intersected by gender, is arguably the key cultural form of a dynamic, transformative age characterised by the proliferation and dissemination of knowledges. Once more it is instructive to turn to Eliza Lynn Linton – specifically, her article on the 'Girl of the Period', published in the *Saturday Review* of 14 March 1868 – for a sense both of the embeddedness of periodical literature in 'the period' and of the dialogism which characterises it. The original article itself demonstrates how the dominant ideology is both reproduced and contested, as the 'Girl of the Period' is compared with English girls of former times, who 'were content to be what God and nature had made them': 'Of late years we have changed the pattern, and have given to the world a race of women as entirely unlike the old insular ideal as if we had created another nation altogether' (339). We earlier quoted Margaret Beetham's observation that one of the roles of the magazine is to provide 'patterns, narratives and models of the self' to enable the female reader to become the woman she is. Linton's 'Girl of the Period' article not only attempted to reinstate an earlier pattern of angelic girlhood, as an alternative paradigm for the modern young woman to the despised figure of the *demi-mondaine*, but itself spawned a number of new models that troubled such conventional gender stereotyping.

The article, which was reproduced as a pamphlet that sold 40,000 copies for one printer alone and was reprinted for the American market in the *Saturday Review*, according to Merle Bevington in *The Saturday Review, 1855–1868* (110), sparked a huge controversy. Many of the responses took the form of reviews and comments in other periodicals, and many (those in *Punch, Judy* and *Tomahawk*, for example) were playful, comic or satirical in tone. But the article also elicited more serious responses from the feminist *Victoria Magazine* in pieces such as 'The Latest Crusade', for instance, and from thoughtful critics such as Henry James, who reviewed the American edition of reprinted articles from the *Saturday Review, Modern Women and What is Said of Them.* James himself provides a nice illustration, as Clair Hughes has deftly argued in 'Daisy Miller: Whose Girl of the Period?', of how journalism is imbricated in broader cultural practices, and of the discursive intertextual negotiations and dialogues that take place between genres. Some ten years after he had reviewed Linton's (then still anonymous) article, James published his controversial novella, *Daisy Miller*, which itself became the subject of debate on both sides of the Atlantic, because of its unconventional eponymous heroine. Eliza Lynn Linton wrote to James, as Hughes notes, coyly suggesting a kinship between her 'Girl' and Daisy – a misplaced notion that James was quick to squash (113–21).

Connections between the periodical and contemporary fiction were, of course, particularly well established. Not only were novels serialised and reviewed in journals, but journalists appeared in fiction of the period, most famously in George Gissing's *New Grub Street* (1891). However, Linton's article had a much broader cultural influence, generating a spate of other phenomena designated 'of the period', including customised 'girl of the period' fashion items and a Christmas burlesque. More interestingly still, for our purposes, among its many offshoots was an almanac (*The Girl of the Period Almanack* (1869 and 1870)) and a magazine (*The Girl of the Period Miscellany* (1869)).[6] The lively satirical *Almanack*, edited aptly enough by 'Miss Echo', features a variety of smoking, drinking, immodestly attired young hoydens engaged in a range of athletic, fast and unfeminine pursuits who serve to point up, by implication, how properly conducted, 'natural' young women should disport themselves. The *Miscellany*, which claims to have been established because of the immense success of the *Almanack*, offers a similarly satirical survey of the phenomenon for which the catch-phrase 'girl of the period' was coined.

Both Linton's contemporaries and recent commentators on her article note the limitations of her diametrical view of woman. Helsinger *et al.*, for example, observe that '[b]y establishing as woman's alternatives the melodramatic extremes of angel and demi-mondaine, Linton simply omits (or lumps with the demi-mondaines) that increasing number of respectable women who reject both angel and whore roles and want to extend woman's sphere without forsaking true womanhood' (1: 112). Indeed, it seems important finally to ask more generally to what extent the vast body of periodical literature that mediates Victorian gender ideology really largely conforms to a narrow range of stereotypes. However, if Linton's own construction of the 'girl of the period' is conventionally stereotyped, we only have to turn from her article to its after-texts to see much more complex gender formations at work. The very form of the *Girl of the Period Miscellany* resists the singularity of the concept. The first page of the first number of the journal is illustrated by a picture of eleven women around a table, over the title 'In the Editorial Sanctum', and the leading editorial wittily describes the different women who wrote for the *Almanack* now jostling for a place in the *Miscellany*. It is a female version of the more familiar glimpse behind the scenes into the masculine editorial sanctum that we find, for example in 'Nights at the Round Table' in the *Train*, in which the male contributors, 'discovered carousing' in a 'snuggery', engage in competitive banter about their work for the journal (59–64). The *Girl of the Period Miscellany* is un-equivocally portrayed as a collaborative venture (though marked by rivalry and still firmly under 'Miss Echo's' editorship), and the 'girl of the period' is represented as a multiform being. She is a girl who plays and a girl who works; she is 'the croquet girl', 'the nautical girl', 'the hunting girl', 'the archery girl'; she is 'the ballet girl', 'the lady's maid', 'the refreshment-bar girl', 'the sewing-machine girl' (Plate 1); she engages in private theatricals,

Plate 1. 'Girls Who Work', *Girl of the Period Miscellany* 1 (1869): 17.

and works in a house of business; she is an artist's model and an art student, a 'medical girl' and a 'fast-smoking girl', a factory girl and a governess. The advertisements suggest she is both a modern woman (who might be targeted for a product such as 'Wyatt's Golden Hair Wash for producing that Brilliant Fairness of the Hair so greatly admired') and a domestic angel (in the market for wedding trousseaux, baby outfits and layettes).

In short, when the magazine asks frankly 'What is the Girl of the Period For?', the answer is very much more complicated than Linton herself allowed. In these 'alarming' times, we are told, when there is an 'Enormous Female Surplus' (alluding to W. R. Greg's infamous article 'Why Are Women Redundant' (1862)), and when men such as John Stuart Mill have begun 'the work of Defeminization':

The Girl of the Period . . . is a natural outgrowth of the circumstances. She is an involuntary Protest. She is the masculine Giggle of the Hour. She is the Irony of the Situation. And perhaps we may discover, if we look closely, that she is not such a mere weed as she has been made out to be. (5–7)

And in the following issue, addressing 'The Irony of the Situation' in greater depth, a further question, 'What *is* the Girl of the Period' is answered in a way that firmly protests against the homogeneity implied by Linton's stereotyping:

Of course, to begin with, the period has a good many girls. Girls are everywhere. You cannot go into society, you cannot go to church, you cannot visit the theatre, you cannot walk the streets, without meeting girls. These girls are all girls of the period, because they exist at the present hour. Yet, though there is a family likeness running through nearly all this immense army of girls, they are by no means all of them Girls of the Period in the high typical sense which the phrase has acquired since it first found publicity. (33–4)

Linton's 'Girl of the Period' does not, for this writer, encapsulate 'the new feminine movements' that have emerged in the context of the new and faster pace of modern life. Indeed:

the Girl of the Period, taken in her grosser aspect – taken as she was sketched by a contemporary some time ago, is the helot or buffoon of these new feminine movements. She is the loud, brutal . . . the loud, coarse guffaw which arises out of the social wilderness at the idea of masculinizing woman. She says audaciously, 'Look at me; for I am the *reductio ad absurdum* of your theories.' You will never defeminize us, you will only get a form of womanhood in which the worst part of us will caricature the worst part of yourselves. (34)

By contrast with this hostile caricature of the modern girl, a 'better Girl of the Period' is invoked, one who:

unconsciously, smiles at both the helots and the revolters. She is not the buffoonery, but . . . the irony of the situation. There is a touch of exaggeration about her dress, but it is only a touch; there is an aroma of impudence – call it daring – about her manners; but it is a whiff, and no more . . . She receives, without knowing it, impressions from a thousand quarters, and, without knowing it, assimilates, registers, and reflects them all. She is not the masculinized guffaw, but she is the delicately-masculinized giggle of the hour. (34)

The article concludes with the advice that 'Miss Echo intends that the laugh and the discipline shall go round in the most impartial manner, till the whole table is in a roar of mirth, in which an undertone of peccavi shall nevertheless be distinctly audible' (34). This final laugh of the Medusa is evidence enough that, despite the best efforts of controversialists such as Eliza Lynn Linton, gender, like the periodical press itself, refuses determination; that Victorian attempts to construct a coherent and overarching gender discourse were contested in different ways and from different subject positions; and that the miscellaneous nature of the periodical and of periodicalism enabled that ironic laugh to echo into the next century and beyond.

CHAPTER ONE

The writing subject

'No one but a man could have written like this', declares the anonymous author of an article entitled 'The Reviewer of the Period' in *Tinsley's Magazine* in 1868, just one of a barrage of outraged journalistic responses to Eliza Lynn Linton's then still anonymous fulminations against the 'Girl of the Period' in the *Saturday Review* (618).[1] The writer of another anonymous article, 'The Women of the Day', on the notoriously misogynistic *Saturday* series, this time in *Saint Pauls*, guesses that its author is a young curate, determining that 'the articles, if not masculine, are certainly not feminine' (305). Identifying himself as a man, who wishes 'to treat the subject from a purely masculine standpoint' (312), he further complicates the gender politics surrounding the 'girl of the period' article and the series to which it belongs by his comments on the *Saturday Review*'s house style and readership. It is a paper, he avers, 'in which all things, human and divine, are treated . . . from the point of view of the clever college don, who belongs to a West-end club, spends his long vacation on the Continent, and is the accepted authority of his common-room' (303). Yet it is one 'which numbers among its readers an unusually large proportion of the female sex'. Moreover, adds this defender of 'The Women of the Day', '[i]ts politics, if I may venture to say so, are of an eminently feminine order; its cleverness is just of the kind which women think very clever; and its satire is of a calibre which women can understand and appreciate' (304). Articles such as these suggest how very complex was the gendering of journalistic discourse in the mid-nineteenth century. Moreover, they invite specific comparisons between the girl of the periodical and the reviewer of the period. The author of the article 'The Reviewer of the Period' poses the rhetorical question: 'Are English girls, as a class, to be stigmatised as next door to hetairæ because a few of their number . . . choose to dress immodestly and to talk slang?' observing '[a]s fairly might we accuse all reviewers of being intemperately and inconsiderately abusive because the *Saturday* indulges in such Billingsgate' (619). Raising as it does questions relating to the sex of the journalist, the autonomy and integrity of the writer's style and ethical position, and the gender of periodical discourse, the controversy surrounding Linton's 'Girl of the Period' demonstrates both the pervasiveness and the instability of the gender ideologies that inform and are reproduced by the periodical press.

The common practice of publishing articles anonymously, rather than over the signatures of individual contributors – a practice still widespread in the 1860s, but increasingly under attack – focusses such questions in particularly intriguing ways. On the one hand, anonymity enabled women to enter the profession of writing without having to reveal their identity and expose themselves to criticism for engaging in public discourse. On the other, it often forced them to write, if not necessarily in the style of 'the clever college don', favoured by the *Saturday Review*, then at best from the 'purely masculine standpoint' endorsed by the contributor to *Saint Pauls*. The 1860s was a decade in which both journalistic anonymity and the 'Woman Question' were the subjects of heated debate in the press, and yet they are topics which appear not to have been explicitly connected in the public imagination. Articles on female authorship and female authors, though, including features on female journalists, both generic and named, can be found in periodicals throughout the century, and a surprising number of women did write under their own names.

In this chapter we will address the question of the gendered writing subject in relation to both anonymity and signature, paying particular attention to the special dilemmas of the female journalist, whether performing masculinity or femininity; or, indeed, in different contexts, both. In so doing, we do not mean to suggest, of course, that it was only female writers who had to negotiate problematic questions of gender identity. Although Mary Ann Doane expressed the view some two decades ago in 'Film and the Masquerade: Theorising the Female Spectator' that 'sexual mobility would seem to be a distinguishing feature of femininity in its cultural construction' while 'the male is locked into sexual identity' (81), recent work on Victorian masculinities, through close analysis of the diverse and unstable formations of the masculine subject, has revealed it to be no less mobile a category than the feminine. Nevertheless, the work of feminist theorists on the feminine masquerade, equally with that of queer theorists on gender performativity,[2] seems particularly resonant in relation to the professional theatricalities and artifices that female journalists were obliged to perform in the Victorian period because of their still marginal status in the writing profession. Postmodern theories of gender as contingent and enacted may therefore be understood to inform and frame our discussion, though we are ever mindful of the very real constraints upon the historical Victorian woman's opportunities and capacity for liberatory self-transformation. As Kali Israel astutely observes in her study of Emilia Dilke, *Names and Stories: Emilia Dilke and Victorian Culture*, 'unequal access to resources, material and historical differences of position, privilege and experience, and powerful structures of prestige and exclusion, are not magicked away by masquerade'; and we 'would be wishfully misguided if, in attempting to locate temporary resistances, we neglect overarching institutional and discursive powers' (196).

I

Eliza Lynn Linton herself, the first woman to be paid a regular salary on a major newspaper, rather spectacularly demonstrates both the possibilities of and the constraints upon gender performativity for the Victorian female journalist. In perhaps her most extreme exercise in literary transvestism, the *Autobiography of Christopher Kirkland* (1885), she writes her own life reversing not only her own sex but also that of many of her characters 'for their better disguise' as quoted in George Layard's 'Preface' to *Mrs. Lynn Linton: Her Life, Letters, and Opinions*. Recounting 'Christopher's' entry into professional journalism, on the basis of her own experiences at the offices of the *Morning Chronicle*, she describes the exchange between the editor and the young aspirant:

'So! you are the little boy who has written that queer book [she had published a historical romance, *Azeth the Egyptian*, in the previous year, 1847] and want to be one of the press gang, are you?' he said half-smiling . . .
'Yes, I am the man,' I said.
'Man, you call yourself? I call you a whipper-snapper . . . I say though, youngster, you never wrote all that rubbish yourself! Some of your elder brothers helped you. You never scratched all those queer classics and mythology into your own numbskull without help. At your age it is impossible.' (266–7)

The editor, based on John Douglas Cook, sends Christopher/Eliza off to write a leader on a Blue Book, telling him/her to '"Keep to the text; write with strength; don't talk nonsense, and do your work like a man"' (269). Having passed the sex test, the protagonist is duly assigned a position; we are told, 'I filled the office of handy-man about the paper' (270–1).

This episode, and the style in which it is recounted, inevitably recall other accounts of Victorian women's attempts to enter the professional world of writing, such as Charlotte Brontë's letter to Wordsworth over the signature C. T., extracted in Elizabeth Gaskell's *Life of Charlotte Brontë*, with what Gaskell describes as its 'touch of assumed smartness', in imitation of 'the flippancy which was likely to exist in her brother's style of conversation' (202). Linton's overt simulation of a masculine subject position and style likewise recalls Harriet Martineau's response to a proposal by the editor of the *Edinburgh Review* in 1858 to write an article on the repatriation of black African slave-labourers to Liberia. 'I'm your man', she confidently informed its editor, Henry Reeve. In ' "I'm your Man": Harriet Martineau and the *Edinburgh Review*', Valerie Sanders recounts that when Martineau later submitted her article on 'Female Industry', she wrote to him 'I do hope you will like it, & that you will think I have succeeded in making it look like a man's writing' (36, 44). Another woman who recognised the value of assuming a masculine authorial persona was George Eliot. Before she adopted her pseudonym, while still writing anonymously for the press, she performed some convoluted sexual displacements in her articles for the *Westminster Review*, which she had secretly edited in the early 1850s. Thus, even as she argues for a proper recognition of women's intellectual and cultural talents, in her article 'Woman in France: Madame de Sablé' (1854), she positions herself as a male reader of the periodical press rather than as a female journalist, in her metatextual excursion on the growing power of the press:

As the old coach-roads have sunk into disuse through the creation of railways, so journalism tends more and more to divert information from the channel of conversation into the channel of the Press: no one is satisfied with a more circumscribed audience than that very indeterminate abstraction 'the public', and men find a vent for their opinions not in talk but in 'copy'. We read the *Athenæum* askance at the tea-table, and take notes from the *Philosophical Journal* at a soirée; we invite our friends that we may thrust a book into their hands, and presuppose an exclusive desire in the 'ladies' to discuss their own matters, 'that we may crackle the *Times*' at our ease. (15–16)

Undoubtedly the custom of anonymous publication in the press made such trans-sex discursive identifications possible for women trying to establish a foothold in the profession, as well as for women such as Eliot and Martineau whose reputations were such that they no longer needed to resort to such subterfuge. Indeed, it also enabled male contributors to write for magazines, such as the *Lady's Magazine* and, later, *Woman*, that were supposedly by, as well as for, women.[3] Yet the gendered context of such opportunistic acts of ventriloquism differed markedly between men and women. The wit and bravado of women's performance of a masculine voice often concealed the considerable personal and professional costs of being a woman in a man's world. Linton wrote of *Christopher Kirkland* to a female friend, 'It was an outpour no one hears me make by word of mouth, a confession of sorrow, suffering, trial, and determination not to be beaten, which few suspect as the underlying truth of my life' (Layard, 'Preface').

Leaving aside such knotty questions as the 'underlying truth' of a life, to consider instead the institutional and discursive parameters within which female journalists wrote, it is instructive to examine how even the terms of the anonymity debate itself were markedly gendered. In 'Salesmen, Sportsmen, Mentors: Anonymity and Mid-Victorian Theories of Journalism', Dallas Liddle identifies the three main positions that were taken in the debate:

Supporters of journalism's traditional anonymity rallied in defense of a paternalistic, mentoring model of discourse in which the writer, speaking the values of the larger society and invested with corporate authority, takes the role of instructor and guide to the reader. Some advocates of the new signature system responded that periodical publishing was, in economic fact, a marketplace governed by relationships between buyers and sellers of ideas, all of whom were unitary economic actors. Anonymity was inimical to the free and fair working of this market, since it hid information (the author's identity and qualifications) relevant to the value of an intellectual product, and gave editors and writers an incentive to produce inferior work. A second school of signature advocates sought higher moral ground and argued that the arena of public discourse, like the playing fields of Eton and Rugby, was a place to test and strengthen moral character, and that the adoption of signature would foster responsibility and forthright manliness among journalists. (33)

Liddle's focus is on male culture, and he does not allude to the implications for women's journalism of his analysis of the terms of the anonymity debate. But it reminds us how closely constructions of masculinity and constructions of femininity articulate with each other, for it is clear that none of these exemplary figures for the journalist – neither the paternalistic mentor, nor the trader in the literary marketplace, nor the sportsman on the playing fields of culture – offers a role that a woman could comfortably fill. It is only in the domestic sphere that women assume authority and offer mentoring advice in their own person or over a female signature, in the women's pages of general periodicals or in women's magazines. Furthermore, women are characterised as consumers and commodities, but ideologically excluded from participation as traders in the business economy. Christian Isobel Johnstone's anonymous article on 'Women of Business', in *Tait's Edinburgh Magazine*, begins:

Plate 2. 'The House of Business Young Lady', *Girl of the Period Miscellany* 1 (1869): 43.

We adore the sex! It is to be hoped that readers of our gallant miscellany have been made fully conscious that we neglect no occasion of ministering to the triumphs of the petticoat! Harriet Martineau, the sublime, – Mrs. Norton, the beautiful, – Mesdames Hemans, Hall, Gore, Austen, Fry, Somerville, Marcet, – have received in turn sufficient honours at our hands, sufficient homage at our knees! but for the lives of us, we cannot help abhorring what is called a capital Woman of Business! . . . It is the woman who goes out of her way to buy and sell, and plot and counterplot, whom we utterly abominate. (596)

The fact that the author of this piece was a woman assuming a collective male voice, only reinforces the inapplicability of the journalist-as-writer-in-the-marketplace argument to women. We need look no further than the pages of the *Girl of the Period Miscellany*, at a rather risqué apology for the 'House of Business Young Lady', at work in a showroom (Plate 2), to see the limits of women's role in business even as it was envisaged in this unconventional publication (43). And indeed no further than the *Girl of the Period Almanack* and an article entitled 'July. – The Amazon Athletic Club', for a sense of the perceived absurdity of their antics on a playing field (Plate 3).

Plate 3. 'July. – The Amazon Athletic Club', *Girl of the Period Almanack for 1869*.

One of the major questions about which the anonymity debate revolves is whether the journalist's voice should be individualised, original and identifiable, or speak the collective wisdom, in the flattened style of the journal. Originality seems to have been a particularly elusive quality for Victorian women to aspire to, and the field of writing was no exception, as an interesting article, 'Female Authorship', in *Fraser's Magazine* makes abundantly clear. It takes the form of a conversation between two women, one of whom is a writer (young, beautiful, happily married with children, rather than an ink-stained, bluestocking spinster), who is asked by her older friend about the trials of female authorship. One difficulty upon which she remarks is that she is constantly being advised to imitate the work of more successful writers: ' "Now our good friends would never think of telling Dr. Chalmers that he would do well to imitate the style of the *Pickwick Papers*, nor probably would they tell Wordsworth that if he wrote in the style of Horace Smith, his work would be more generally read . . . But they will not let us, little stars, possess our small talents in peace" ' (462). Yet at the same time as she is discouraged from developing her individual voice, and urged to copy the styles of other writers, she is criticised for her lack of originality, even for plagiarising from other writers, as she explains:

One person reads a poem of mine, and says, with a peculiarly knowing look, 'murmuring sound,' – is not that too much like Milton?
    'Not distant far from thence a murmuring sound.'
Nay, I assure you I scarcely exaggerate – and doubtless from that day my friend considers me a plagiarist, and declares he has 'found me out.' But they will not always give me credit for borrowing my ideas from so high a source; sometimes it is a passage in Mr. Brown's or Mrs. Tomkins's last work, that some unlucky expression of mine resembles, and which I am consequently thought to have borrowed, unconsciously, of course, as I am delicately told. (462)

When it comes to female authors, it seems, weighty matters such as the status of the individual in journalistic culture, the value placed upon individual writers with individual belief systems and individual styles, which were such key issues in the anonymity debate, are reduced to gossip and innuendo about a woman's capacity for original thought.

    That women all too often faced profound challenges in their pursuit of a career as a writer is made very clear in a number of mid-century periodical articles on female authorship. An 1864 article on 'Literary Women' in the *London Review*, for example, appears at first to be sympathetic to those 'clever women' who cannot understand 'why men in general entertain a strong objection to feminine authorship', and indeed rehearses what some of the more cynical explanations for their objection might be. However, it then goes on to offer the true reasons why 'literature is not a profession to which English gentlemen are pleased to see their sisters and their daughters turn'. With breathtaking circularity, the author explains that a broad and comprehensive experience of the world is necessary for a great writer, and that therefore no woman can qualify without first 'undergoing a defeminizing process' (328). We are told:

A literary education is the work of a long time; and women who write the best almost always display their want of its discipline sooner or later. Literary genius means among other things the power of bringing sympathy and passion under the stern control of artistic law. Without this self-control, passion itself becomes weak or luxuriant; and sympathy degenerates into weakness. There is no other training that gives it except the laborious study and appreciation of classical models; and this training is almost out of the reach of women. (328)

To be a great writer requires a classical education; this is unavailable to women; ergo, women can't be great writers; or if they do somehow acquire the necessary education, they must pay the price of their womanhood. In either case that problematical category, the female writer, is disqualified and disavowed.

But while articles such as these offered all too many disincentives for women to aspire to 'literary genius', and while others like 'On The Employment of Females' warned against 'the unrequited toil, the hopes, the fears, the utter blank of heart, that attend every aspirant to literary fame, whose abilities are mediocre, or whose patronymic is untitled' (305), the female author and her work did have a presence in Victorian journalism, as the subject of articles and reviews, throughout the century. After all, as Robert Williams in 'Female Character' declared in 1833 in *Fraser's*, 'No age has been so fruitful in female genius as the present. From all ranks of society women have come forth, and have distinguished themselves in almost every department of literature' (599). Such acclamation of women's intellectual breadth and capacity was, however, rare. More typically, reviews of publications by women, particularly in the early part of the period, were heavily prescriptive in delineating what it was appropriate for a woman to write. William Hazlitt, for example, anonymously reviewing Lady Morgan's *Life and Times of Salvator Rosa*, disapproves of her 'pretension' in taking on such a subject, declaring contemptuously:

Women write well, only when they write naturally: And therefore we could dispense with their inditing prize-essays or solving academic questions; – and should be far better pleased with Lady Morgan if she would condescend to a more ordinary style, and not insist continually on displaying the diplomatist in petticoats, and strutting the little Gibbon of her age! (318)

Felicia Hemans is greeted more approvingly in the *Edinburgh Review*, but the reader is again treated to a view of what woman writers can and cannot do. In particular, we are told in Francis Jeffrey's review of her *Records of Woman* and *The Forest Sanctuary*:

They cannot, we think, represent naturally the fierce and sullen passions of men – nor their coarser vices – nor even scenes of actual business or contention – and the mixed motives, and strong and faulty characters, by which affairs of the moment are usually conducted on the great theatre of the world . . . Perhaps they are also incapable of long moral or political investigations . . . They are generally too impatient to get at the ultimate results, to go well through with such discussions. (32)

A later review by Thomas Macaulay, of Lucy Aikin's *Life of Joseph Addison*, is critical of the author for not being sufficiently 'acquainted with her subject', and for being unreliable in her judgement of his achievements: 'It is proper . . . to remark, that Miss Aikin has committed the error, very pardonable in a lady, of overrating Addison's classical attainments' (197). Again, she has ventured beyond her proper literary sphere.

The review of Lucy Aikin's biography begins with a general discussion of whether a female author under review may rightfully plead 'the immunities of sex'. In the opening sentence, we are informed that '[s]ome reviewers are of opinion that a lady who dares to publish a book renounces by that act the franchises appertaining to her sex, and can claim no exemption from the utmost rigour of critical procedure', but that the present reviewer dissents from that view. This foregrounds one of the besetting problems for female writers in the period; the tendency on the part of reviewers, if not to disparage, then to patronise their womanly efforts. *Fraser's* demonstrates both tendencies respectively in the portraits of Harriet Martineau and Caroline Norton in William Maginn's 'Gallery of ILLUSTRIOUS Literary Characters'. The condescending tone of the encomium to the latter in 1831 gives a fair idea of how female authors were often viewed at this juncture:

Fair Mrs. Norton! Beautiful Bhouddist, as Balaam Bulwer baptises you, whom can we better choose for a beginning of our illustrious literary portraits, when diverging from the inferior sex, our pencil dares to portray the angels of the craft? Passionately enamoured, as we avowedly are, of L.E.L. – soul-struck by the wonders of Mrs. Hemans's muse – in no slight degree smitten by Mary Anne Browne – venerating such relics of antiquity as Lady Morgan or Miss Edgeworth – pitying, (which is akin to loving,) the misfortunes of Mrs. Heber or Miss — we yet must make Mrs. Norton the leader of the female band. She writes long poems – she is a sprig of nobility – and she is the granddaughter of that right honourable gentleman whose picture is suspended above her head . . . We display her as the modest matron making tea in the morning for the comfort and convenience of her husband. (222–3)

Within a few years the world was to see another side to the Honourable Mrs Norton, but for now her success in the eyes of this writer seems to owe more to her beauty and womanliness, not to mention her pedigree, than to her literary talent. By contrast, the portrait of Harriet Martineau later in the series (1833)[4] is a spiteful attack upon 'the fair philosopher' whom, we are told, no man is likely to seduce from 'the doctrines of no-population'; it is 'a wonder that such [pro-Malthusian] themes should occupy the pen of any lady, old or young, without exciting a disgust nearly approaching to horror' (Maginn, 'Gallery', 576).

II

There is plenty of evidence to be found in the pages of the press at mid-century to support George Eliot's acerbic comments in the *Westminster Review* on the critical reception of 'lady novelists', and its damaging effects on women's writing. While, for instance, the reviewer (probably William

Maginn) of Mrs S. C. Hall's *Sketches of Irish Character* in *Fraser's* of 1831 gushes 'We have a most stupendous regard for Mrs. S. C. Hall; and, as we do not remember ever to have beheld the beauty of her benevolent countenance, our readers will readily conceive that the lady owes the enjoyment of our grace and favour to her merits as a writer, and to our diligence as perusers!' ('Sketches of Irish Character', 100), the reviewer of Harriet Martineau's *Cousin Marshall* (again probably Maginn) writing in the same journal the following year declares '"What a frightful delusion is this, called, by its admirers, Political Economy, which can lead a young lady to put forth a book like this!" – a book written by a woman against the poor – a book written by a young woman against marriage!' ('On National Economy', 403), Eliot in 'Silly Novels by Lady Novelists' caustically observes how:

By a peculiar thermometric adjustment, when a woman's talent is at zero, journalistic approbation is at the boiling pitch; when she attains mediocrity, it is already at no more than summer heat; and if ever she reaches excellence, critical enthusiasm drops to the freezing point. Harriet Martineau, Currer Bell, and Mrs Gaskell have been treated as cavalierly as if they had been men. (161)

Dismissive of genuinely talented women writers, the patronising reviewer, 'in the choicest phraseology of puffery', according to Eliot, 'tell[s] one lady novelist after another that they "hail" her productions "with delight"' (161).

Eliot's own parodic 'phraseology of puffery' here interestingly anticipates Althusser's account in 'Ideology and Ideological State Apparatuses' of the mechanism by which ideology works to interpellate or 'hail' the individual as a subject:

Ideology 'acts' or 'functions' in such a way that it 'recruits' subjects among the individuals . . . or 'transforms' the individuals into subjects . . . by that very precise operation which I have called interpellation or hailing, and which can be imagined along the lines of the most commonplace everyday police (or other) hailing: 'Hey, you there!' . . . the hailed individual will turn round. By this mere one-hundred-and-eighty-degree physical conversion he becomes a subject. Why? Because he has recognized that the hail was 'really' addressed to him. (163)

This precisely describes how the patriarchal press interpellates the woman writer, according to Eliot's account. She points out the irony that it is only by 'recognising' themselves as acceptably 'silly' lady novelists that female authors gain the approbation of the reviewer. Fully cognisant of the formidable cultural power of the press, Eliot takes the opportunity of her own anonymous critical article in the *Westminster Review* to formulate a different paradigm for female authorship, one which serves as a blueprint for the novelist she will become.

As this example suggests, the periodical press was not so much the oppressive organ of a dominant ideology as a crucial site of ideological struggle, of those 'uneven developments' which Mary Poovey has so effectively analysed. While reviewers of a certain cast continued to 'hail' the productions of lady novelists 'with delight', others gave increasingly respectful critical consideration not only to 'feminine' writers, such as Jane Austen, who, according to Harriet Childe-Pemberton in 'Women of Intellect. Jane Austen', 'furnishes an instance of high literary talent with the most genuine womanliness' (378), but also to 'unfeminine' writers, including those sanctioned by Eliot, and indeed Eliot herself. And so, by contrast with the portrait of Harriet Martineau drawn for the *Fraser's* 'Gallery', William Howitt's view in the *People's* 'Portrait Gallery' of 1846 is that 'Harriet Martineau presents one of the finest examples of a masculine intellect in a female form which have distinguished the present age', and she is but one of a number of intellectual women who 'are setting a stirring example to their sisters to doubt the wise saws which the mouths of the mankind of all ages have uttered in patronising grandiloquism over the womankind, – "pretty creatures and clever – to a certain extent" ' (143). Howitt himself has no time for such '[s]weet courtesy! beautiful condescension!' '[B]ut is one or the other needed?' he asks. 'Just listen to a little fact' (143). Even if they seemed unable to ignore the sex of the author altogether (so exercised were they by the question whether it was a womanly soul or a masculine intellect that she harboured in her female form), male reviewers who allowed themselves to forget their chivalrous manners wrote in a more balanced way about women's literary work. In the case of a man such as William Howitt, marriage to a successful author and prolific journalist, Mary Howitt, may have helped him to view the business of women's writing as no more peculiar than men's. George Henry Lewes was notably less inclined to worry in public about those 'women [who] have made an invasion of our legitimate domain' ('A Gentle Hint', 189) after setting up house with Mary Ann Evans. Female authors are treated more matter-of-factly still in a periodical whose very name sanctions the association of women and journalism. An anonymous review of 'The Hon. Mrs. Caroline Norton' in *Eliza Cook's Journal* in 1853–4 declares 'Female authorship is now so common a thing, that the woman who has written a book is no longer regarded as a *lusus naturæ*. A woman who writes is not now considered "a blue," for the tint of female stocking has become all but cerulean' (39).

Caroline Norton, Mary Howitt, George Eliot and Harriet Martineau, as well as other successful authors such as Margaret Oliphant, first established themselves as professional writers and in many cases continued to support their literary work as novelists or poets, through their writing for the periodical press. Journalism offered hitherto unavailable opportunities not only for prominent literary figures such as these but also for women of more modest writerly ambition. An article entitled 'What Will You Write for the Magazine?' published in *Eliza Cook's Journal* in 1851 comically recounts the experiences of a supposed friend and correspondent of Eliza, asked by her to produce '"an essay," "a poem," at least a little tale, or if it was only an advertisement – a comic advertisement, anything would be acceptable to a magazine in its birth' (351). Utterly bereft of a subject and of all inspiration, the woman friend finishes by writing an advertisement: 'TO LET, with immediate possession, for a short time, the tenement lately occupied by the Advertiser's brains, they having gone for the season to enjoy the delight of wool-gathering' (352). Her husband is unimpressed, coolly remarking ' "Ah! it does not do for wives to turn authoresses! here have you, my dear, spent the whole evening to no profit – while little Johnny has contrived to set his pinafore on fire, and burned"'. As she rushes to the nursery, the would-be author 'secretly registered a vow to abjure for the future the Grey Goose Quill' (353).

Likely enough this piece – the submissive and self-deprecatory stance of which is, of course, nicely overridden by the evident fact that it was published – was a complete fabrication, perhaps even written by Eliza Cook herself, who continued to ply her own grey goose quill for some years to come and wrote proudly under her own name. A poet and journal editor, Cook was a woman who never seemed short of a topic to write about, and for whom the periodical press was a perfect vehicle. And she was not alone. Christian Isobel Johnstone, like Cook, both edited a journal, *Tait's Edinburgh Magazine*, and reviewed for it, with a special interest in bringing the work of new women writers to the reading public. According to Michael Hyde and Walter Houghton in the *Wellesley Index*, not only did she write over 400 articles between 1832 and 1846, but under her editorship the magazine employed an unusually high proportion of female contributors, including Harriet Martineau, Catherine Gore, Eliza Lynn Linton, Mary Russell Mitford, Amelia Opie and Mary Howitt (IV: 479). Marysa Demoor's *Their Fair Share* reveals just how important the role of the editor was in determining the gender demographics of a journal. Through her painstaking work on the *Athenaeum*'s 'marked file', she has discovered that, although it had a surprisingly large number of female contributors even in its first decades (including Geraldine Jewsbury who, according to Monica Frykstedt in *Geraldine Jewsbury's 'Athenaeum' Reviews*, published a staggering 2,300 book reviews in its pages in the 1850s and 1860s (15)), the final three decades of the century saw a considerable increase in the number of reviews by women, a fact which Demoor attributes to the changes which took place under the proprietorship of Sir Charles Wentworth Dilke.[5] She also observes a broadening out of the topics on which women were commissioned to write, although even in early to mid-Victorian journals, when women were typically assigned topics that were coded feminine, some notable female reviewers were given the opportunity to take on prominent male writers of the day. Some of the most memorable reviews of Ruskin's work, for example, are by women – George Eliot, Elizabeth Rigby, Emilia Dilke – while Lady Morgan's notorious reviews of Carlyle's *French Revolution*, *Chartism*, and *Past and Present* are only the best known of her notices of major cultural texts to be published in the *Athenaeum*.[6]

The reason why a study such as Demoor's is so valuable is that the identity of a great number of contributors to the Victorian periodical press is still unknown. As she notes, even prolific reviewers such as Geraldine Jewsbury 'do not figure prominently' in the principal resource available to modern scholars, the *Wellesley Index to Victorian Periodicals 1824–1900*, crucial though that is as a research tool. At mid-century, most women published anonymously, as was standard, and even where an article is said to be 'by a woman', such as an article of 1856 in the *Train*, with the title 'A Word or Two about Women', authored by One of the Sex' (181–5), or later, in 1880, in *Time*, 'Woman's Rights. By a Weak-minded Female' (114–18), the claim is not necessarily to be believed. But throughout the period some authors, women as well as men, were given a by-line when it was felt that their regular association with a journal would boost readership. Thus, as Margaret Beetham points out, in the 1830s and 1840s Mrs Hofland and Camilla Toulmin wrote signed pieces for the *Lady's Magazine and Museum of Belle Lettres*, and the names of prominent contributors were advertised on the cover (*A Magazine of Her Own?*, 43). And by the last decades of the century, when the practice of anonymity had been eroded, journals and in particular women's magazines are full of signed articles by women: Annie S. Swan and Lady Jeune, for example, writing for *Woman at Home*, Charlotte O'Conor Eccles in *Windsor Magazine*, Isabella Tod in *Leisure Hour*.

By the 1890s magazines for girls and young women were actively promoting journalism as a profession.[7] The *Girl's Own Paper* in 1890, for example, carried a signed article on 'Young Women as Journalists' in which it is considered to be 'the most natural thing in the world' for young women to seek a career in journalism. Its readers are warned of the hardships entailed in being a reporter, but are informed that '[a] great deal of the most effective work on our newspapers has been done by women; and, could it be told, the public would today be surprised to learn how much of the total is still done by them' (306). As part of a series in 1896 on 'How Women May Earn a Living', *Woman's Life* offers helpful practical advice to women on short story writing, and how to submit their work to a magazine (85–6). And in 1899, an article in the *Young Woman* undertakes to explain 'What it Means to be a Lady Journalist', beginning by pointing out that 'there are few professions which are more exacting':

Because my lady sees Miss Reporter at the dance, and the bazaar, and the afternoon garden party; at every fashionable function, and at half the theatres . . . my lady imagines that Miss Reporter's life is a bed of roses, which brings her into touch with everything that is beautiful, and makes no demand upon her which it is not a pleasure to fulfil. My lady's mistake is natural, but it is a mistake nevertheless, and as an increasing number of girls look with envious eye on the lady journalist every day, it is well that there should be a good understanding of what it means to be a lady journalist. (93)

Having disabused the reader of the idea that the job is an easy one, the anonymous writer makes it clear that, far from requiring shorthand skills alone, it demands a capacity for original and creative thought, particularly from female journalists. In an interesting reversal of the conventional wisdom about the gender of originality, we are told, 'Women are certainly not employed in journalism to do merely mechanical work of that kind. As a rule, they are engaged to do original work, which men could not do so well, or which they could not do, perhaps, at all' (93). Emily Crawford in an 1893 article in *Review of Reviews* on 'Women as Journalists' makes a similar point when she argues that women write well and have 'in a greater degree than men the faculty of throwing life into what emanates from their pens' (quoted in Demoor, *Their Fair Share*, 17).

   In 1898, Arnold Bennett published *Journalism for Women: A Practical Guide*, in which he advises would-be journalists to establish a base in London, to get themselves a reader's ticket to the British Museum, and to branch out into subjects that are not conventionally thought of as feminine. He also suggests which journals are most likely to accept their work, directing them to the high quality middlebrow general magazines. His was one of several guides for female journalists published around the end of the century. Frances Low wrote a series of articles in the *Girl's Realm* in 1903, which were collected in 1904 into a volume with the title *Press Work for Women: A Textbook for the Young Woman Journalist*, which was also intended to function as a practical manual for would-be journalists. Although somewhat disparaging of female journalism, after the manner of George

Eliot's critique of silly novels by lady novelists, it takes its subject seriously, and insists on the development of a proper professionalism among women wishing to enter upon a career in journalism. The case was put for women journalists in the mainstream press too. G. B. Stuart, for example, reports in the *Athenaeum*, for which she was a regular writer, on the paper she gave on 'Women in English Journalism' at the first international press congress in 1894: 'Miss Stuart's paper, after dealing with the specific qualifications which women possess for journalism, touched on their increasing number and power during the last thirty years, and maintained that they had created, not usurped their present position' (quoted in Demoor, *Their Fair Share*, 18).

By the 1890s, then, the female journalist had well and truly come out.[8] She had a professional association, in the form of the Society of Women Journalists, founded in 1894 by Joseph S. Wood, editor of the *Gentlewoman*, and she had a platform by virtue of her assured place in the pages of the periodical press. The eight-page 'Portrait Gallery of Contributors to the *Girl's Own Paper*' issued with the 1,000th number of the journal in 1899 (between 320–1) demonstrates how far journalism had moved from the anonymity debates of the 1860s. It was, by then, common practice to print a separate list of contributors as well as identifying the authors of each article in the index, and it is interesting to see how many are women, not only in women's and girls' magazines but in publications for men and boys, such as the illustrated monthly magazine, the *Young Man* (although the topics on which they wrote were notably gendered in journals like the *Boy's Own Paper*). Female journalists, such as Annie S. Swan, were featured and interviewed, much as celebrities and football players are in magazines today, and their views sought on the suitability of their profession for women. Arthur Lawrence's 'A Chat with Mrs. Sarah A. Tooley' in *Young Woman* on the topic of 'Interviewing as Women's Work', elicits the story of how she entered her career, which seems to have been genetically ordained: 'Any physiognomist', observes the writer of his subject, 'who noted the keen blue eyes and fine forehead, would have known that all Mrs. Tooley's predilections were for literature' (441). Interestingly, though, even as they focus so directly on the individual identity of the writer (we are told that 'the position occupied by Mrs. Sarah A. Tooley is well-nigh unique' (441)) such articles also draw attention to the continuing anonymity of a lot of journalistic labour. Here, the writer, while signing his own name below the article, points out that 'lady journalists do a good deal of interviewing work', but notes that '[a] great deal of such work is done anonymously' (441). Similarly, in an interview in *Woman's Life* titled

'Mrs Humphry ("Madge," of "Truth")', a woman described as '[o]ne of the most energetic and successful women journalists of the day', we are reminded of the anonymity conferred by the use of a pseudonym by her anecdote about a social function at which 'a lady was introduced to Mrs. Humphry's sister as "Miss — , 'Madge,' of 'Truth,' you know." "Oh no," was the prompt reply, "my sister is 'Madge' of 'Truth' "' (301).

The incident recalls Eliza Lynn Linton's story of twice being introduced to the writer of 'The Girl of the Period': 'The first time he was a clergyman who had boldly told my friends that he had written the paper; the second, she was a lady of rank well known in London society' (quoted in Layard, *Mrs. Lynn Linton*, 145). Yet though it may have been as hard to establish the truth of 'Madge' of 'Truth's' identity as it had been to discover the author of 'The Girl of the Period', by the 1890s the idea of women making a career in journalism was considerably more acceptable than it had been thirty years previously. Women writers were altogether more visible in mainstream periodicals as well as in specialist women's magazines. As Mrs Humphry, 'Madge', herself comments in her interview for *Woman's Life*:

The scope of women's work in the journalistic world is much greater now. When I first became a journalist only a few papers published ladies' letters, and these dealt principally with domestic servants, the management of babies, and similar subjects. Now women go in for golf, bicycling, and other games; in fact, the athletic girl is a new development, and as woman's world is widened, so is the field for women writers. (301)

As if to underscore her point, an advertisement for 'Cyclinia', a herbal preparation for the complexion 'specially for Cyclists', is printed alongside her article (302).

III

Like the female journalist herself, the athletic girl who had been a mere laughing matter in the 1860s is starting to be taken seriously in the 1890s, and the same might be said of the feminist, even though the niche audience of most women's magazines remained the woman with domestic responsibilities such as servants and babies to manage. These constructions of femininity are sometimes strategically connected in interesting ways, when a more adventurous woman's work is packaged in such a way as to appeal to women confined to the domestic sphere. Thus, interviews with women writers are frequently presented in the form of 'A Friendly Chat with the Girls', as in the series 'Between Ourselves' in the *Young Woman*, which has as its logo a sketch of a group of women having a cosy chat.[9] Connections between the writing woman and the new athletic woman are sometimes suggested by the illustrations, as in the picture of the author with her bicycle which accompanies the Baroness von Zedlitz's 1896 article in *Woman's Life*, 'Chat with Madame Sarah Grand' (501). As part of the same series, 'Chats with Well Known Women', the Baroness interviews the explorer and writer Mary Kingsley, bringing that most intrepid of travellers into the domestic drawing room for a fireside chat (431–2). In a similar fashion, articles designed to help women manage their finances are smuggled in among less weighty domestic material. Some women journalists seem to have moved from the one category to the other with ease. Charlotte O'Conor Eccles, for example, in one issue advises readers of the *Windsor Magazine* 'How Women Can Easily Make Provision for their Old Age' (315–18), while in another she writes on the topic 'Are Pretty Women Unpopular?' (737–41).

As 'Madge's' comments on the widening of the field for women writers suggest, though, while the range of new feminine types had indeed expanded in the course of the century, types they nevertheless remained. Athletic girls and the other 'new women' to be found in the pages of the late nineteenth-century periodical press were as stereotypically and exaggeratedly depicted as the domestic angels, girls of the period, and blue-stockings of an earlier era. Indeed, if the periodical press may be said to have provided a theatre for cross-gender performativity, equally it may be seen as providing a stage for the performance of femininity. In this context, Joan Rivière's concept of the masquerade of femininity is suggestive. In her foundational essay 'Womanliness as a Masquerade', Rivière analyses the strategic adoption of a mask of femininity by the intellectual woman who, having assumed the position of the subject of discourse rather than its object, then tries to compensate for her appropriation of masculinity by excessively performing femininity. As she explains it, 'Womanliness therefore could be assumed and worn as a mask, both to hide the possession of masculinity and to avert the reprisals expected if she was found to possess it – much as a thief will turn out his pockets and ask to be searched to prove that he has not the stolen goods' (213).

It is arguable that some female writers for the Victorian periodical press assumed and wore a mask of womanliness for the very reasons Rivière proposes, to compensate for their theft of the masculine subject position and thereby avoid reprisals. The mask took different forms. Most notable are those women, such as Isabella Beeton and Sarah Stickney Ellis, and the countless lesser-known writers for the domestic culture industry, who flaunted the persona of the domestic angel in contradistinction to their actual identities as professional writers. But no less excessive are the self-professed authorial athletic girls and modern girls, for whom the 'girl of the period' established a prototype. Even the feminist may be said to have publicly performed feminism in the newly established women's presses, exaggeratedly enacting her positionality as a woman.

Mary Ann Doane in 'Film and the Masquerade: Theorising the Female Spectator' argues that modern theories of the masquerade, based on the view that gender identity is arbitrary and contingent, see such evidently artificial enactments of femininity as subversive acts of resistance to patriarchal positioning (81). But can we reasonably attribute the politics of postmodern gender performativity to the Victorian writing subject? Or are these women writers rather to be seen as interpellated subjects, performing the femininity that ideology has prescribed for them, just as others performed masculinity under the mask of anonymity? While both theories of masquerade and of interpellation do help us to understand how Victorian women tried to negotiate the material conditions within which they worked as professional writers for the press, neither entirely captures the historical specificity of their problematic subjectivity and their uses of sexual style. It is in the context of the material form of the Victorian periodical that such theories may most usefully be invoked. For it was the fundamentally heterogeneous form of the Victorian periodical, its multiple and mostly anonymous authorship, its imperative of diversity, that provided a very particular space, both fluid and dynamic, in which women could negotiate a writing identity or writing identities. The periodical's very refusal of a single authorial voice, the calculated diversity of genres and modes both within the cover and between journals, encouraged experimentation, creating a medium of interpellation but also a cultural space in which interpellation might be resisted, a place in which gender was made and remade.

Anne McClintock maintains in *Imperial Leather: Race, Gender and Sexuality in the Colonial Context* that 'no social category exists in privileged isolation; each comes into being in social relation to other categories, if in uneven and contradictory ways', and gender came into existence 'in and through relation to' other categories, such as class and race. Furthermore, she points out, 'power is seldom adjudicated evenly' (9). Women writing at the end of the century still constituted only a small and relatively powerless proportion of what was a decidedly male profession; though more prominent and more accepted than their mid-century sisters, they encountered similar disincentives, experienced similar disappointments and frustrations, and resorted to similar tactics, which sometimes involved invoking their superior class position and using their connections. A number of hostile reviewers in the course of the period comment on the proportion of published female writers who are titled, while the editor of the *Cornhill* complains in his pages about an acquaintance who had been prevailed upon by a scheming woman to use his influence to get her translation of a tale by the Archbishop of Cambray into print, and had tried to take advantage of their friendship to foist her upon him – without success. When we examine the fine texture of stories about women's experiences of seeking to publish their work in the periodical press, what is most notable is the complexity of their response to the system that confronts them, the combination of powerlessness and feisty resourcefulness in their dealings with the world they inhabit, but also the particular social dynamics of that world.

One example must suffice to illustrate McClintock's argument that gender, sexuality, class and nation are 'articulated categories' within that social world (4). Having begun this chapter with the story of Eliza Lynn Linton's approach to a periodical editor, we conclude with the Irish writer and illustrator Edith Somerville's account, in a letter to her collaborator Violet Martin of a discouraging visit to Oscar Wilde, then editor of the *Woman's World*, in 1888, before the former had achieved fame or the latter notoriety (in *The Selected Letters of Somerville and Ross* edited by Gifford Lewis). After hawking her work around the editorial offices of the illustrateds, she writes:

H. and I went down to Oscar yesterday (he was out on Monday) sent him a letter and we were marched in. He is a great fat oily beast. He pretended the most enormous interest – by Egerton's advice I said I was the Bart's niece as Oscar knows him well – but it was all of no avail. Neither Carbery, Vernissage (with pictures and I wouldn't give it without,) nor possibly Atelier des Dames would he have. He languidly took the sonnets and is to return them by post. He talked great rot that 'French subjects should be drawn by French artists' – I was near telling him that, as Dr. Johnson said – 'who drives fat oxen must himself be fat'. He assumed deep interest in the 'Miss Martins', asked if they were all married: I said 'mostly all'. He was kind enough to say that Edith was pretty and nice – and bulged his long fat red cheeks into an affectionate grin at the thought of her. He then showed me a book of very indifferent French sketches – was foully civil, and so goodbye. I then took Carbery to *Cassells Family Mag.* Office. A dear little intelligent vulgarian in charge – such a relief. (67–8)

The encounter of this impoverished member of the Irish aristocracy with first the Irish expatriate Wilde, to whom she introduces herself as 'the Bart's niece', and then the unnamed 'intelligent vulgarian' nicely captures the national and class dynamics of which McClintock writes, as first Somerville is patronised by Wilde, and then the 'dear little' *Cassells* editor is patronised by her. But of course the gender dynamics are also intriguing. As the male editor of a women's magazine, Wilde occupies an ambiguously gendered position professionally. Although he was not at this point, as far as we know, disadvantaged professionally by his sexuality, still some years away from public exposure, he was presumably obliged to perform masculinity, to engage in his own form of gender masquerade. Later, of course, he was to theorise his belief in 'the truth of masks'.

It is interesting how prominent a theme dissimulation is in Somerville's short account of their meeting. He is, self-evidently to his visitor, playing a part. 'Foully civil', he 'pretended the most enormous interest' in her, and 'assumed deep interest in the "Miss Martins" ', his forced smile as insincere as his compliments. And yet it appears that, despite the artificiality of his own demeanour, and despite the aesthetic of the mask that he was to develop in his critical essays, the excuse he gives her for not accepting her French subjects is that they lack integrity, an integrity that can only be conferred, it seems, by the artist/writer being what he or she appears to be: ' "French subjects should be drawn by French artists"'. Somerville's silent retort, ' "who drives fat oxen must himself be fat" ', underscores the irony of this master of the performative adopting such an uncompromisingly essentialist position. Wilde's professed concern with the authenticity of the subject only has the effect of confirming the truth of masquerade. Indeed, the whole episode reminds us that it was not only women who were obliged to perform or to subvert masculinity in pursuit of a professional identity.

Edith Somerville's account of her attempt to interest the respective editors of the *Woman's World* and *Cassell's* in her work provides an amusing and illuminating vignette of one Victorian woman's attempt to publish in the periodical press. As it turned out, being the niece of a Baronet did not help in her case. Her next letter reports resignedly, '*Cassells*' [sic] has returned West Carbery. Oscar cleaves silently to the sonnets, and has doubtless – in a poetic frenzy – used them to light the gas' (Lewis, *Selected Letters*, 71).

Wilde himself, a writer for the periodical press, of course, as well as an editor, was consistently sceptical about journalism, and critical of its power as, not the so-called 'fourth estate', but 'the only estate. It has eaten up the other three'. 'We are dominated by Journalism', 'a really remarkable power', he complains in 'The Soul of Man Under Socialism', which appeared in the *Fortnightly Review* in 1891 (1,094–5). And yet he is clear that the power of modern journalism, which, he claims in an earlier essay 'The Critic as Artist' (1890), 'justifies its own existence by the great Darwinian principle of the survival of the vulgarest', is conferred by the reading public in the country which 'invented and established Public Opinion' (1,055):

It was a fatal day when the public discovered that the pen is mightier than the paving-stone, and can be made as offensive as the brickbat. They at once sought for the journalist, found him, developed him, and made him their industrious and well-paid servant. (1,094)

The truth of Wilde's perception of the significance of the press, and its tendency to pander to the worst prejudices of the reading public, was to be revealed all too painfully within a few years, but even at this point he knew where the real power lay: not with the editor of a journal, who could choose to accept or reject, or indeed light the gas with the unsolicited submissions of would-be writers; and not with the journalists themselves, 'because the unhealthy conditions under which their occupation is carried on oblige them to supply the public with what the public wants, and to compete with other journalists in making that supply as full and satisfying to the gross popular appetite as possible' (1,095). The true power of the press resides, at the end of the Victorian period as at its beginning, in its readers.

CHAPTER TWO

The gendered reader

There is 'one great leading principle', argues Fitzjames Stephen in an article titled 'Journalism' in the *Cornhill Magazine* in 1862, 'which underlies all the rest, and which affects, and, indeed, may be almost said to determine, the character of every separate branch of journalism'. This is the fact that 'a newspaper is beyond everything else a commercial undertaking'. Since 'the paper cannot be sold, unless the public are disposed to buy it', 'unless it does for the public something which the public likes it does nothing at all'. For this reason, Stephen concludes, 'Whatever may be the tone and bearing of journalists, they are in reality the servants of the public, and the course which they take is, and always will be, ultimately determined by the public' (Stephen, 'Journalism', 53). Such acknowledgement of the economic and consequently the cultural power of the reading public is rarely so bluntly expressed, but an underlying recognition of the determining role of the reader in the shaping of the periodical press is everywhere apparent in its pages. In editorials, articles, illustrations, letters' pages and advertisements, the readers of periodicals, considered *en masse* as 'the public', as differentiated groups, and as individuals, are constructed and conscripted, are cajoled, flattered and chastised. They are also invariably gendered. '[T]he public', we are informed in 'Periodicals' in 1849, 'goes to bed with a periodical in her hand, and falls asleep with it beneath her pillow' (182), a generic image of the reading public for periodical literature which manages to suggest both the voraciousness of the female reader and her leisured status. J. A. Heraud's 'Oliver Yorke's Epistle to the Reading Public' of 1832 similarly feminises the reader of periodical literature, figuring her this time as a seductive and fickle mistress:

> Sweet Public! O, you're a delicious creature!
>   'Pon honour, now, we couldn't live without you;
> You're so delectable in form and feature,
>   And such a fascination breathes about you. (2)

An illustration depicting 'Reading of the Period' (Plate 4), published in the Religious Tract Society's *Leisure Hour* in 1870, which foregrounds two young women at a railway bookstall, avidly scanning an array of 'Novels of the Period', with titles such as 'Bigamy', 'Incest', 'Suicide' and 'Murder', while the men in the other half of the picture space study the *Sporting World*, is principally intended to illustrate the text from the *Times* quoted below it: 'That crew of demireps, forgers, bigamists, pretty murderesses, and the ladies of equivocal reputation whom the British Paterfamilias admits so complacently into his drawing-room, provided they are wrapped up in the pages of fiction'. But it incidentally shows how reading preferences and practices were gendered in the period, and reveals something of the anxieties that surrounded the idea of the female reader, as well as suggesting the role assumed by the periodical press in protecting, directing, circumscribing and policing women's reading.

This chapter turns, then, to the question of the gendered reader of the Victorian periodical press, encompassing both the broadly conceived 'reading public' that was the object of so much journalistic attention and the particular reader who turned the pages, wrote letters to the editor and entered competitions. It speculates, where possible, about the identity of so-called 'real' readers,[1] and examines the myriad ways in which their participation is sought, attending particularly to the question of how the implied reader is constructed in gendered terms in the periodical text, how he or she is written into, discursively 'wrapped up' in, the pages of journalism.

I

It is explicitly modern journalism to which Stephen in 1862 and Wilde in 1891 address themselves in their respective discussions of the readerships served by the press and the dynamics of cultural power. Like many other writers in the last half of the nineteenth century, they associate journalism fundamentally with modernity, seeing it as the key cultural medium of modern life. In 'The Painter of Modern Life' (1863) Baudelaire, for example, takes the magazine fashion-plate as his instance of the art form that most effectively registers the nuances of modernity, by which he means 'the ephemeral, the fugitive, the contingent' (13), and as his representative of the modern artist or 'man of the world' (6) proposes Constantin Guys (1802–92), a graphic artist who was for some years at mid-century on the staff of the *Illustrated London News*. We recognise in this definition of modernity and its media the terms employed by Walter Bagehot in 1855,

READING OF THE PERIOD.

"That crew of demireps, forgers, bigamists, pretty murderesses, and the ladies of equivocal reputation whom the British Paterfamilias admits so complacently into his drawing-room, provided they are wrapped up in the pages of fiction."—*Times.*

Plate 4. 'Reading of the Period', *Leisure Hour* 19 (1870): 201.

when, in the first volume of the *National Review* (which he founded and edited), he compares modern journalism with that of an earlier generation, the 'first Edinburgh Reviewers' of his title. Bagehot identifies 'the talk of the man of the world' as 'the very model of our modern writing', and comments on the 'casual character of modern literature', of which he notes 'everything about it is temporary and fragmentary . . . The race has made up its mind to be fugitive, as well as minute' (Bagehot, 'First Edinburgh Reviewers', I: 310–12). Furthermore, again it is, according to Bagehot, the modern reader who determines the ephemeral and dispersed nature of modern writing, for 'the writer of the modern world must write what the world will indulgently and pleasantly peruse' (312).

Reflecting on the place of periodical literature in modern experience, Bagehot nominates 'the merchant in the railway' (311) as the type of the modern reader of magazines and reviews, thereby identifying a new kind of 'common' reader, also in and of 'the world', one who is definitively connected with commerce and with the modern technologies of production, distribution and travel. His linking of the steam-driven press and railway and what another journalist, E. Noble in 'Readers and Writers' called the '"fast" living' (34) of the modern citizen was to become a cliché in the many discussions of new reading habits to be found in the periodical press over the next decades (see Kelly Mays, 'The Disease of Reading and Victorian Periodicals', 169–70). Indeed, a year after Bagehot's article appeared, in 1856, a new journal called the *Train* was launched which included in the first of its five numbers 'The Song of the Train' which played on their metaphorical connection:

> The steam is up and away we go!
> On a road that's bright and new;
> Old coach proprietors, heavy and slow,
> Our course with anguish view.
>
> (59)

The modern reader, for whom, as Bagehot wrote in an article in the *Fortnightly Review* of 1871, '[a] quicker mode of travelling has come in, a hastier mode of reading' than in the days of the old mail coaches and the Quarterly Reviews (Bagehot, 'First Edinburgh Reviewers', II: 376), is decidedly a consumer; 'People', we are told, 'take their literature in morsels, as they take sandwiches on a journey' (I: 310). He is also, as we noted earlier of Bagehot's designation of the modern writer as a 'man of the world', of the masculine gender.

How does such a formulation of journalism as the quintessential literary form for modern life apply in the case of the woman reader? While images of women buying reading material at the station and reading on trains had a certain currency in later decades, at mid-century, when Bagehot aired his definition of modern journalism, middle-class women remained ideologically positioned in the home. Mrs Ellis's 'woman of right feeling' in *The Women of England* was taught to ask herself each morning 'Is any one about to set off on a journey; I must see that the early meal is spread, or prepare it with my own hands' (33), together, presumably, with the sandwiches that will be consumed along with the magazine purchased from the railway bookstall. It was not so much life in the fast lane as the demands of her domestic day that determined the middle-class woman's choice of reading matter that was 'temporary and fragmentary'. Writing in the early 1850s, before she went to the Crimea, Florence Nightingale movingly evokes the fractured existence of women like herself in *Cassandra*: 'I have a different aim every half-hour, without comprehensiveness, connexion, consistency' (26). She is preoccupied by the disjointed nature of middle-class women's lives, seeing their piecemeal day as typifying the fractured condition of modern civilisation, and she protests against 'the maxim of doing things at "odd moments"': 'When people give this advice, it sounds as if they said, "Don't take any regular meals. But be very careful of your spare moments for eating. Be always ready to run into the kitchen and snatch a slice of bread and butter at odd times. But never sit down to your dinner, you can't you know"' (71). Here, in a text where food, appetite and starvation are pervasively powerful tropes signifying women's intellectual desires and deprivations, the notion of literature 'in morsels' is associated not with the benign image of 'sandwiches on a journey' but with hunger, eating disorders and malnutrition. 'We know what can be done at odd times', writes Nightingale, 'a little worsted work, acquiring a language, copying something, putting the room to rights, mending a hole in your glove' (71). She might have added 'reading a review or the women's page of a magazine'. At any rate, what can be achieved by a woman in the 'odd moments' permitted her by prescriptive writers on domestic manners such as Sarah Ellis and Isabella Beeton, who advised women never to embark on an activity that could not readily be interrupted, is clear to Nightingale: 'Nothing requiring original thought: nothing, it is evident, which requires a form, a completeness, a beginning and an end, a whole, which cannot be left off "at any time" without injury to it' (72). The miscellaneous and mediated content and fragmentary form of the periodical review and the magazine would seem specifically designed for the purpose.

Such examples disclose the gender of the discourse of modernity, and complicate the image of the modern reader that formulations like Bagehot's suggest. The pace of modern life demands, as he contended, a periodical literature that provides topical news, information and cultural capital in manageable 'bytes'. This is the masculine readership Fitzjames Stephen has in mind when he writes of the 'busy classes' in 'Journalism', for whom the leading article forms the greater part of their reading:

In our days, men live like bees in a hive. They are constantly occupied in ingenious efforts to produce small results, in which for the most part they succeed. This leaves men very little time to use their minds upon any other subjects than those which their daily round of duties presents, and accordingly they are forced to live upon intellectual mince-meat. Their food must be chopped up small before they eat it; and it must be so prepared as at once to tempt the appetite, and assist the digestion. (53–4)[2]

Yet for Nightingale, such invalid food does not nourish but rather starves the woman trapped at home. She harnesses images of the modern press in her rhetorical plea for intellectual sustenance:

If we have no food for the body, how we do cry out, how all the world hears of it, how all the newspapers talk of it, with a paragraph headed in great capital letters, death from starvation! But suppose we were to put a paragraph in the 'Times', Death of Thought from Starvation, or Death of Moral Activity from Starvation, how people would stare, how they would laugh and wonder! (220; see also 70)

In Nightingale's experience, women of the higher classes lived under such a regime of social manners and triviality that they could only snatch odd moments for such personal pleasures as reading. Yet for more misogynistic commentators, a scatter-brained preference for shallow and inconsequential snippets, an inability to concentrate on anything of weight and substance, was fundamental to female pathology, and was infecting and emasculating modern culture, as exemplified by the huge expansion and regrettable intellectual decline of periodical literature, with disastrous effects on the reading habits of the nation. Kelly Mays argues that 'The feminization of the reading public was in one sense quite literal. Women readers were not only numerous, but also were understood to be desultory readers *par excellence*', citing a series of essayists who represented the female reader as fatally deflected from the properly serious task of reading by gossip, knitting, children and other domestic distractions which they allowed to disrupt and mangle even the most coherent of texts. And yet, she notes, 'Within descriptions of the reading problem there was a continual slippage between criticisms of women readers per se and of the feminine quality of mind they exemplified', and a palpable fear that 'this "feeble and indecisive" order of mind was being produced more generally, becoming as typical of men as of women, as these indiscriminate, "desultory and omnivorous reading" practices themselves became the habit of all' (178–9).

The fragmentary form of the periodical lent itself as readily to rhetorical association with the woman at home, then, as it did to the merchant on the train, only for different reasons. The two figures were not, of course, unconnected. The middle-class merchant on the train aspired to support a leisured wife at home, the signifier of his success and status, and she required suitable reading for a lady of leisure. As Kathryn Shevelow argues in *Woman and Print Culture: The Construction of Femininity in the Early Periodical*, the entrenchment of the middle-class gender economy around the distinction between the man who worked and the woman who stayed at home meant that leisure, which had always been a marker of class, 'became also a marker of gender' (55). Margaret Beetham has shown how the woman's magazine played a significant role in the gendering of the concept of leisure, produced for female leisure time, and also producing leisure, in the form of embroidery patterns, craft activities (such as making wax flowers), and of course reading (*A Magazine of Her Own?*, 30–1). However, leisure was by no means confined to wealthy women of a certain class; rather, it was a complex discourse in a period which, even amidst the quickening pace of modern life, afforded more leisure time to the multitude than had ever before been enjoyed, and paradoxically enough it too, equally with modernity, is associated with the flourishing of the periodical as a literary form. 'It is because reading has become the leisure relaxation of so many among us' that the demand for monthly periodicals 'has increased with such rapidity' ('Trollope and *St. Pauls*', 2), writes Anthony Trollope in 1867, defending his launch of a new journal, *Saint Pauls*, at a time when the consumption of literature was being condemned as excessive, characterised as 'overfeeding', 'devouring' and 'mental gluttony' (quoted in Mays, 'Disease of Reading', 173).

Baudrillard observes in *The Consumer Society: Myths and Structures* that in the modern consumer society time is a commodity like any other. Leisure time is accorded a distinct status from work time, and it must be spent appropriately. Leisure is obligatory, 'the *duty* of the citizen' (Baudrillard, *Consumer Society*, 80). The declared fact that 'in the present day leisure hours are becoming more frequent, and will probably become still more so' provides the *raison d'être* for the magazine the *Leisure Hour*, which takes time in its first number to position itself and the leisured readers it addresses in 'A Word with Our Readers': not 'idlers', but those who have done a good day's work and now enjoy an hour of well-deserved leisure; not exclusively 'the sons of genius or wealth', but also 'the working man'; indeed, 'the thoughtful of every class', 'peer and peasant', 'master and man' (8–10). Its implied reader is male, even when the subject under discussion is female employment and female leisure. One 'grave fact bearing on the employment of women', we are told in 'Female Employment. II. Educated Workwomen', 'is the excess of luxury – an excess which makes the household expenses so far beyond what they used to be in the olden times':

A man, with all the will in the world, cannot now maintain the female members of his family in a style commensurate with what he considers his own or their position in society. It has even been hinted that he finds his better half at times a burthen almost too heavy for his purse to bear, with her immeasurable yards of silk, velvet, lace, and embroidery. (54)

It is not to this pampered woman of leisure that the *Leisure Hour* addresses itself, but to her poor, hard-working, put-upon husband.

Some periodicals are more gender inclusive in their readerly address, and plainly regard their constituency as including both the leisured reader and the reader in a hurry, 'desirous of brevity' (Bagehot 'First Edinburgh Reviewers', 1: 311). Eliza Cook offers in her opening editorial, 'A Word to My Readers', 'a plain feast, where the viands will be all of my own choosing, and some of my own dressing' to a readership constructed in a homely metaphor as 'a host of friends at my board' (1), and yet the first article in the first number of her journal, on 'Cheap Reading' describes the 'present era' as one of 'intellectual congestion and physical distress', in which 'the fever of the mind absorbs almost the pangs of hunger; the craving desire for knowledge keeps pace with the ravenous demand for bodily sustenance', and invokes the modern consumer as the man on a train: '"Wolverton! Wolverton! Stop here five minutes, gentlemen!" There is a general rush; the living load issues from those ponderous vehicles, and scarcely one returns without some cheap publication' (2). In such publications, we are told, 'men's acts . . . speak, the world is stereotyped, and facts constitute the food given by these gigantic granaries of intelligence to nourish reflection, as they concentrate to the focus of a glance, the virtues which sustain, the crimes which shock whole empires' (2). Yet both forms – the 'cheap publications' aimed at the 'hungry' traveller on the train, and the journal like *Eliza Cook's*, also cheap but catering to the well-nourished family by the fireside or the guests around the table – are viewed favourably as contributing to the common goal of conducting 'all classes' along 'the royal road of reading',[3] which is seen as a means of transformative personal empowerment (3).

The *Leisure Hour's* address to readers had declared 'let there be no inter-mingling of work and play' (8); however, work and play, instruction and amusement, typified the mixed reading experience offered by most Victorian periodicals, whose miscellaneous format enabled items designed to pleasurably engage the reader to coexist alongside articles of a more serious bent. The boundaries between work and leisure, although enshrined in the text, were unstable for the woman at home who, even if she had a moment to relax, found herself reading about household management and domestic affairs in magazines designated for her leisure hours, home being constructed by publications such as the *Englishwoman's Domestic Magazine* as 'a contradictory site of work and leisure' (Beetham, *A Magazine of Her Own?*, 68). They were similarly unstable for the working-class reader, who was encouraged both by the periodicals that sought the patronage of work-ing people and those written for a socially superior readership to use any available leisure hours in self-improvement. Richard Altick comments on the number and diversity of self-culture publications produced in the 1850s, observing in *Writers, Readers, and Occasions* that 'All periodicals, down to the cheapest and crudest, paid at least lip-service to the age's ideal of democ-ratized learning' (170). Women readers and working and lower middle-class readers occupied distinct categories in the Victorian debates about popu-lar reading habits; nevertheless their constituencies obviously overlapped (as Kate Flint observes in *The Woman Reader 1837–1914*, 'the working-class woman was doubly "other"' (135)), and similar questions were at stake regarding the benefits and the dangers of the expansion of the reading audience in relation to both the gender and the class of the new readership. Altick's work in the 1950s on the huge explosion in the size and range of the reading public that took place during Victoria's reign, whilst not notably attentive to gender, does point to the fact that by the final decade of the century female readers wielded considerable power over what was produced for popular consumption, and acknowledges (though does not pursue) the more general point that the democratization of reading involved women of all classes: 'No analysis of contemporary literary taste and taboo can over-look the numerous and assertive presence of women as wives, mothers, and guardians of morality and decorum' (Altick, *Writers, Readers, and Occasions*, 217).

II

Altick's groundbreaking social history of the mass reading public in nineteenth-century England, whilst acknowledging the difficulty of reconstructing the actual English common reader of his title, assembles a great deal of valuable statistical information about the circulation figures of periodicals and newspapers at key moments in the century, analyses public debate on the expansion of the reading public, and describes the economic, social and material conditions of that cultural explosion, and it inaugurated a series of further important studies of Victorian readers.[4] Whilst their approaches to the subject vary considerably, what is never in doubt is that there was a veritable explosion in the size and the social, economic, intellectual and cultural range of the British reading public. This was due to a number of factors: the unprecedented increase in literacy rates resulting from the broadening provision of state education; the removal of stamp and paper duties (in 1855 and 1861 respectively) and the introduction of rotary presses and, later in the century, typesetting machines, which lowered the cost yet improved the quality of periodicals; improved mechanisms for national distribution; new forms of domestic lighting, by gas and later for the wealthier classes by the incandescent electric lamp, which made reading more comfortable. Altick notes that 'Obviously the greatest increase in periodical-buying occurred among the lower-middle class and the working class', adding that '[i]n the same year that the *London Journal* sold close to half a million copies an issue, *Punch*, addressed to an upper- and middle-class audience, circulated 40,000 and the *Athenaeum* only 7,200' (Altick, *English Common Reader*, 358). But the escalation of reading in Britain was, and was perceived to be, a universal phenomenon. An article of 1849, one of many on this extraordinarily precipitous development of a mass reading culture, proclaims, 'A great revolution there has been, from nobody's reading anything, to every body's reading all things' ('Periodicals', 182).

This revolution in the reading habits of the nation meant a massive increase in the reading market for periodicals, and new audiences from all classes of society which the proprietors and editors of new journals were keen to capture and conscript, often making use of a similar rhetoric of direct readerly address to that deployed by Victorian novelists. As Garrett Stewart observes, 'The act of literary reading is not just a cultural disposition, part of an economy of leisure or an ideology of edification. It is also a locally positioned enterprise of reception within a socially inflected network of intertextual signals, a reception marked, precoded, co-optive' (6). Writing of the 'reading-in-progress that makes . . . a given Victorian novel happen as text' as part of his discussion of 'readers in the making', Stewart cites Henry James's retrospective comment on the Victorian achievement of George Eliot: 'In every novel the work is divided between the writer and the reader; but the writer makes the reader very much as he makes his characters' (6). One may see a similar process at work in periodical literature, which is perhaps not surprising given the prominent place of fiction and the significant participation of novelists in periodical publication. They themselves were very conscious of the connections between their respective activities as novelists and as journalists or editors, and of their relationship with their readers. As he prepared to launch the monthly *Cornhill Magazine* in 1859, Thackeray wrote to Anthony Trollope: 'One of our chief objects in this magazine is the getting out of novel spinning, and back into the world. Don't understand me to disparage our craft, especially your wares. I often say I am like the pastry-cook, and don't care for tarts, but prefer bread and cheese; but the public love the tarts (luckily for us), and we must bake and sell them' (quoted in Altick, *Writers, Readers, and Occasions*, 163). And bake and sell them he did, 'an astounding total, considering its price [a shilling], of 120,000 copies' for the first number (Altick, *English Common Reader*, 359). Trollope himself later acknowledges the demands of the newly expanded literary marketplace in 1867 in the 'Introduction' to the first number of his own journal, *Saint Pauls*, in which he addresses himself to his 'wished-for readers'. As the editor of a new magazine, he declares, he hopes to meet the needs of 'those increasing thousands of readers whom the progress of education is producing', further explaining that 'The SAINT PAULS MAGAZINE is not started because another special publication is needed to satisfy the requirements of the reading world, but because the requirements of the reading world demand that there shall be many such publications to satisfy its needs' (1). This is Baudrillard's '*dialectic of penury*' (67) *avant la lettre*. What modern consumers seek is not so much a particular commodity, 'another special publication [that] is needed', as difference. Their desire for difference is, as Trollope intimates, insatiable.

Trollope's emphasis here is on the imperative of reader choice in the modern literary marketplace, and it is fascinating to examine how different journals cater to the ever-increasing range of interest groups and specialised readerships. The intended readership of a periodical may often be gleaned from its title. *Saint Pauls* itself, while not explicitly naming its 'wished-for readers' within its title, may be said to gesture towards a readership that is establishment and metropolitan, but other journals address their intended audience more directly and particularly, identifying themselves in their choice of name as existing to serve the interests of a clearly defined niche market. Furthermore, the general style and content of the journal will typically reinforce the implied readership suggested by the title. Hence, the

Boy's Own Paper has a masthead, illustrations, articles and columns clearly designed to appeal to boys,[5] with a strong emphasis on manly and patriotic adventure stories, the imperialist ethos, sport, pets, collecting and health (how to deal with boils being one of the most frequently asked questions). Gender supersedes class in the magazine's own account of itself. We are told in '"Boy's Own" Artists at the Royal Academy' that '[t]he most casual glance at the current volume will abundantly illustrate what we have thus been able to accomplish for boys at no greater charge than one penny per week, thus bringing our richly freighted pages within the reach of all classes, and uniting in a happy bond of brotherhood rich and poor alike' (697). Notwithstanding such claims, the paper appears to address that class of boy who is at Eton, en route to Oxbridge, and destined to become a bishop, a judge or a colonial administrator. Its stories are often highly class-bound, as in the case of one in which the author of 'Amateur Sewersman' tells how he became a sewerman for a day, and announces 'It is a repulsive way of earning a living' (818), in a way not calculated to appeal to sons of these and other manual labourers.

The 'home reader', the construction of whom will be described more fully in Chapter 4, is similarly addressed through a number of channels. In the case of the *Family Economist*, as we will later discuss, the implied readership is suggested not only by the title, but by the verbal, visual and graphic detail of the title page (Plate 5). Brian Maidment observes in 'Domestic Ideology and its Industrial Enemies: The Title Page of *The Family Economist* 1848–50' that 'the low price of the magazine, the unequivocal address to "the industrious classes", the vignette of the tidy cottage interior, the improving mottoes which form the typographical border, and the Christianized, patriotic invocation of the verses all suggest a periodical explicitly directed to a respectable, ambitious, but socially deferential artisan readership' (27). And *The Home Circle*, as its crowded frontispiece conveys (Plate 6), with its busy representation of every conceivable stage in family life – the babe in arms, the schoolboy, the courting couple, the blushing bride, the paterfamilias carving the Sunday joint, the mother presiding over her tea-table, the old couple by the fireside – claims to address itself to everyone in that domestic circle, from 'the Heads of the Household – the Parents' to 'the young branches of the parent stem' (8).

What such examples suggest is that even those periodicals that aim to appeal to a fairly broad audience, and include matter of general interest, nevertheless carefully address themselves to particular groups within that wider intended readership. They typically carve up their pages into sections directed at specific sub-categories of readers, and determinedly

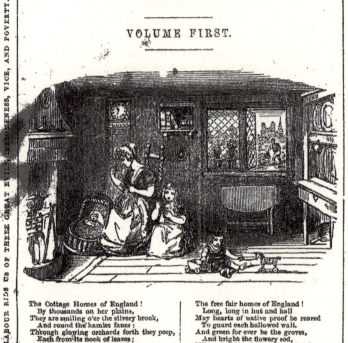

BEGIN WELL IF YOU MEAN TO END WELL.

THE
FAMILY ECONOMIST;

A Penny Monthly Magazine,

DEVOTED TO THE MORAL, PHYSICAL, AND DOMESTIC IMPROVEMENT
OF THE INDUSTRIOUS CLASSES.

VOLUME FIRST.

LABOUR RIDS US OF THREE GREAT EVILS—IRKSOMENESS, VICE, AND POVERTY.

A GOOD TEMPER IS ONE OF THE PRINCIPAL INGREDIENTS OF HAPPINESS.

The Cottage Homes of England!
By thousands on her plains,
They are smiling o'er the silvery brook,
And round the hamlet fanes:
Through glowing orchards forth they peep,
Each from its nook of leaves;
And fearless there the lowly sleep,
As the bird beneath their eaves.

The free fair homes of England!
Long, long in hut and hall
May hearts of native proof be reared
To guard each hallowed wall.
And green for ever be the groves,
And bright the flowery sod,
Where first the child's glad spirit loves
Its country and its God.

LONDON:
GROOMBRIDGE & SONS, PATERNOSTER ROW.
AND SOLD BY ALL BOOKSELLERS.
1848.

EDUCATION IS A SECOND NATURE.

Plate 5. Title Page, *Family Economist* 1 (1848).

Plate 6. Title Page, *Home Circle* 1 (1849).

inscribe difference. Thus *Chambers' Edinburgh Journal*, that rather uncompromisingly earnest publication, launched in 1832 as one of the first cheap family periodicals, and principally directed at the intelligent artisan seeking self-improvement, nevertheless represents itself in 'The Editor's Address to His Readers' as offering appropriate matter for 'readers in all grades of society' and as accessible to '*every man in the British Dominions*'. It then goes on to categorise that broadly designated readership, referring to what it has in store for 'the poor man', for 'those men who reflect deeply on the constitution of man', for 'Artizans', for 'the Naturalist', for 'the ladies and gentlemen of "the old school"', for 'the ladies of the "new school"' and all 'fair young country-women in their teens', and for 'boys' (1–2). In each case, William Chambers specifies what this particular sub-section of readers likes to read; in the case of boys, it explains not only what they like to read but also how to make them readers. *Eliza Cook's Journal* is similarly all-embracing, seeing the power of the press as lying in the fact that, as 'Notices of New Works: The Fourth Estate' declares, 'The newspaper has a voice for everybody' (381), and in Cook's 'To My Readers' it is similarly classificatory. Designating itself as 'family reading' (65), it has its 'Mother's Page' and its 'Lesson for Little Ones', but it also runs feature articles on subjects such as 'The Working Man' and 'Antagonism of Classes', as well as on a large range of women's interest topics, from 'Home Power' to 'The Legal Wrongs of Women'. Later journals with different agendas than the early Victorian self-improvement periodicals similarly try to cover all bases by appealing to both general and specific markets. The conservative Christian magazine the *Quiver*, for example, in 'To the Readers of "The Quiver"' ecumenically promotes a 'broad and catholic, and at the same time earnest and evangelical, religion' (832), and trusts that the journal will be acceptable not only to heads of families, but also to the children and servants. But lest it should lose focus because of the breadth of its reach, it targets particular categories within this wider readership, and offers specialised columns, such as 'A Sermon to the Little Ones', 'Words for Women', a regular feature on 'Woman's Sphere', and Edward Garrett's series 'The Family Council', which covers topics such as 'The Education of the Daughters of the House', 'The Boys' Start in Life' and 'The Welfare of Young Men'.

It will be apparent even from this small sample that, alongside the special interest journals directed at niche markets, there were many periodicals that, building on the format of the miscellany, aimed to appeal to a miscellaneous range of readers with very different spheres of interest. It will also be apparent that the key determinants of difference in the construction of periodical readership, as in other arenas, were gender and class, and that these were, to invoke McClintock again, 'articulated categories' (4). Increasing numbers of journals were, of course, specifically directed at women, although the word 'woman' itself is generally not used early in the period, unless with the qualifier 'English' or in the context of what Florence Nightingale wryly refers to as '"woman's mission" (with a great M)' (214), because, as the editors of *Nineteenth-Century Media and the Construction of Identities* point out, 'the word "woman" retained its derogatory class identity as something other than a "lady" until late in the period, when it was finally embraced by the "new woman"' (Brake *et al.*, *Nineteenth-Century Media*, 5). The titles of the early *Lady's Magazine*, the *Englishwoman's Domestic Magazine* and the *Servants' Magazine* differentiate overtly between class categories in designating their readerships, while those of feminist journals, such as the *English Woman's Journal*, and late nineteenth-century magazines, such as *Woman* and *Woman's World*, suggest that they aim not only at a wider and more inclusive female market, but also at the modern 'new' woman. Female readers were positioned in other ways too by journals such as the *Christian Lady's Magazine*, *Mothers in Council*, the *British Mother's Magazine*. Then there were those magazines which, though claiming to have something for everyone, catered more to women's interests and often specifically addressed themselves to 'the family reader', as female readers were euphemistically called. Thus although the *Home Circle*, as we have seen, embraces the entire family, in 'Woman: Her Position and Influence' it particularly celebrates 'woman', in the year of its launch in 1849, as a stabilizing force in this 'lurid period of revolutionary passion' (56), and often explicitly writes for a female readership. There is a similar gender emphasis in *Eliza Cook's Journal*, which abounds in articles for and about women, and everywhere offers advice and reassurance to its female readers from Cook's 'The "House of Lords" and the "House of Commons"': 'Don't be alarmed, gentle reader' (97); to her 'The Philosophy of Luggage': 'Let us here declare, for the private benefit of our lady friends . . .'; 'Never travel with a bandbox, ladies' (161, 162).

More often, though, women are constructed as the minority readership of journals which, although ostensibly non-gendered, are aimed particularly at men, and only a small portion of the paper is dedicated to their narrowly defined interests. This might take the form of a 'Ladies' Page', where subjects such as fashion, millinery, fancy-work and matrimony feature large. Within the bounds of the 'Ladies' Page', journals generally construct their female readers as belonging to, or aspiring to, a particular class. Thus Madame Elise, in the ladies' page of *Bow Bells*, a journal launched in 1862 that made a strong push for women readers by the inclusion of needlework and dress patterns, addresses herself explicitly to those 'Dear Young Ladies' who wish to better themselves by modelling themselves on women of fashion and nobility, and offers advice about appropriate strategies for self-improvement. The editor of *Tinsley's Magazine*, Edmund Yates, reassures his readers in the Preface to its first number in 1867 that 'the Magazine will never be without one special article for lady-readers' (iii), by which he appears to mean an article relating to fashion or personal ornament. Thirty years later, the editor of the *Windsor Magazine*, sounding in 'A Foreword' at this point in time decidedly dated, similarly takes pains to woo the woman reader, declaring that 'the WINDSOR MAGAZINE offers no monopoly to man'. He (or perhaps she) promises that 'The hearth, on its feminine side, will take a serious interest in educational questions, and especially in a project which deeply concerns the welfare of women'. But all bets are hedged by the undertaking to provide for the frivolous as well as the seriously inclined female reader. As well as engaging to cover such weighty topics as 'a Marriage Insurance scheme, the most important feature of which is the provision of dowries', it is noted that 'For women's lighter fancies, there is, we trust, excellent provision' (3).

Readers are inducted into the gender order, as they are taught to understand their class position, from an early age in the Victorian periodical. The Christian journal the *Children's Friend* often carries articles for girls and for boys on facing pages which convey very different messages to their young readers. Thus 'A Word to Little Girls' begins 'Who is lovely? It is the little girl who drops sweet words, kind remarks, and pleasant smiles as she passes along', and urges its reader to 'strive everywhere to diffuse around you sunshine and joy', for 'If you do this you will be sure to be beloved' (42). Meanwhile, on the opposite page, the piece for boys is entitled 'What Will You Do?' and is about their career choices (43). And in a later number of the journal, where the story for girls, 'She Took Out the "If"', tells of a little girl who 'was awakened to anxiety about her soul' as she listened to a Bible story at a meeting (182), 'A Boy's Sermon' on the facing page begins with Harry announcing 'I'll be a minister, and preach you a sermon' (183).

There is plenty of evidence to suggest that such social conditioning was ubiquitous in the Victorian periodical press. However, there are also counter-indications that trouble the notion that Victorian journalism illustrates an unproblematised middle-class gender ideology at work. The gender of the reader, for example, is not as fixed and stable as we might expect, even in the case of journals carrying unequivocally gendered titles. Boy readers entered the knitting and sewing competitions organised by the

Girl's Own Paper, for instance, and an article published in the journal in 1882, entitled 'Etiquette for our Brothers', begins with the announcement 'It is a source of much satisfaction to the Editor of THE GIRL'S OWN PAPER, and no less so to the members of his staff, to find that the magazine has proved acceptable to the brothers of our girls' (74). Capitalising on the fact that the journal has a male following, the author goes on to use the article as a medium for interpellating boys. The *Young Woman* also boasts of having a male readership and attracting male correspondents. Thus in the literary section of one correspondents' column, 'Answers to Correspondents' in 1896–7, we read the following replies:

YOUNG WOMAN'S BROTHER. – Thank you for the above information [identifying authors].
   YOUNG MAN NO. 2. – Please do not apologise for your kind communication. Having a number of male readers and male correspondents is a triumph of which I believe few other publications intended for poor weak women can boast. Here letters from male readers are of frequent occurrence; but we are trying our hardest not to be puffed up or vain-glorious in consequence. (118)

Conversely, the 'Correspondence' of the *Boy's Own Paper* regularly includes replies to letters from girls, such as Edith Tapsall, who writes for advice on feeding rats, and Clarice, who enquires about nursing as a profession for girls (592).

   Kate Flint has written about the surveys of female reading carried out in the latter decades of the Victorian period that aimed to classify and determine the reading practices of women and, particularly, girls (154–62). She argues that 'the concept of reading is brought into play as a marker of sexual differentiation, mirroring the assumptions of publishing itself' (154), but also notes that the authors of such surveys observe transgressive tendencies among the readers of whom they write: 'Charlotte M. Yonge went so far as to doubt that boys were in fact the major consumers of "boys'" books, believing them to be 'more read by mothers, sisters, and little boys longing to be at school, than by the boys themselves' (154–5). Indeed, the *Girl's Own Paper* responded to girls' demand for adventure stories by regendering their favourite hero, and running a series with the title 'Robina Crusoe, and her Lonely Island Home'.[6] Following his own survey, Edward G. Salmon drew up lists of what were, in his view, boys' and girls' authors in his 1886 article 'What Girls Read' for the *Nineteenth Century* (including Yonge herself on the girls' reading list), but he too concedes that girls enjoy reading boys' books, sometimes more than their own:

There are few girls who boast brothers who do not insist on reading every work of Ballantyne's or Kingston's or Henty's which may be brought into the house. *The Boy's Own Paper* is studied by thousands of girls. The explanation is that they can get in boys' books what they cannot get in the majority of their own – a stirring plot and lively movement. Probably nearly as many girls as boys have read *Robinson Crusoe*, *Tom Brown's Schooldays*, *Sandford and Merton*, and other long-lived "boys" stories. Nor is this liking for heroes rather than heroines to be deprecated. It ought to impart vigour and breadth to a girl's nature, and to give sisters a sympathetic knowledge of the scenes wherein their brothers live and work. One lady writes to me: When I was younger, I always preferred Jules Verne and Ballantyne, and *Little Women* and *Good Wives*, to any other books, except those of Charles Lever'. (524)

With boys reading the *Girl's Own Paper* and girls reading the *Boy's Own Paper*, deconstructing the very binaries that such magazines apparently work so hard to reinforce, we are reminded that whilst periodicals invariably had an ideological agenda, they were also commercial undertakings that were obliged to turn a profit. It might be said, in fact, that the instabilities of a journal's gender politics, and particularly of its readerly address, are closely bound up with broader questions of its form and its cultural identity, and that these are by their very nature evolving and 'unevenly developing' as a matter of economic necessity. Although it is sometimes convenient to classify the large mass of periodicals into categories, it is fair to say that very often journals did not have a fixed identity, partly because of their miscellaneous authorship, but also because they were always responding to market pressures, and therefore always in a state of change. In the case of the early issues of a journal, when neither its identity nor its readership has been fixed, the interaction between the text and its readers is, of course, especially critical, as Andrew King has demonstrated in his fine-grained study, 'A Paradigm of Reading the Victorian Penny Weekly: Education of the Gaze and the *London Journal* '.

Particularly in their first few years of production, periodicals are typically feeling out their market, experimenting with their style and offerings, their format and their contents, in an endeavour to pull in readers, and sometimes we may see quite notable changes of direction. The upwardly mobile *Dublin Penny Journal*, for example, shifts its target market to a very different socio-economic group when it presents itself in the form of a collected volume. We are told in the 'Preface' to its first volume that 'having completed a year in its more humble form, as a Weekly Publication suited to the pockets of the poorer classes of society, [it] now appears before the public in the more matured and imposing shape of a Volume, not unworthy, it is to be hoped, of the library of the scholar and the gentleman' (iii). In a bid to attract and retain readers in a highly competitive market, editors and proprietors often had to decide either to go up-market or to make their journals cheaper. Samuel Beeton, for instance, chose the former option for the *Englishwoman's Domestic Magazine* when in 1860 he brought out a new series in a larger format, raising the price of standard issues to sixpence, in response to competition from both newly established journals directed specifically to women and what Patricia Anderson in *The Printed Image and Transformation of Popular Culture 1790–1860* calls the 'second generation of illustrated penny miscellanies' launched in the 1840s and 1850s (84), which were by this point making particular efforts to appeal to female readers. As Margaret Beetham points out, such positioning and repositioning of a periodical's readers, though market driven, 'is something more than market targeting: it affects the contents, the price, the style and the tone in which readers are addressed' (*A Magazine of Her Own?*, 12).

Inevitably such instabilities in the implied readership of a journal are often intersected by gender and class, as in the case of the journal *Lads of the Village*, which transformed itself after only a year in production from a strictly one-gender magazine to one addressed to a broader readership. An 'Important Notice' in 1874 advises the reader that, as from 1 May, the *Lads of the Village* will be incorporated into the *Home Reader*, explaining that this is as a result of pressure from its readers:

In announcing this change, we may briefly state that we make it in deference to the expressed wish of a very large number of friends. We have frequently been urged to adopt a more general title, as THE LADS OF THE VILLAGE necessarily confined the publication to a special class; and, after mature deliberation, we have decided on taking the step, feeling sure, from the patronage hitherto accorded us, that success will be certain. While still maintaining every feature of importance that has characterised the LADS, and secured its popularity, we shall be a welcome guest to old and young alike. (223)

That this change of direction, broadening and lifting the target readership, is driven by economic considerations is made quite clear:

Under the new title we shall appeal to a wide-spread constituency; in fact, we shall cater for the million, and endeavour to make the Journal interesting, entertaining, instructive, and amusing. And in doing this, we hope to speedily treble and quadruple the circulation already enjoyed by THE LADS OF THE VILLAGE. (223)

The promised new gender balance is backed up by a preview of what the revamped journal will have to offer: 'a powerful, and deeply interesting serial story' with the title 'A Wingless Angel', clearly designed to appeal to women, and the dashing adventures of Peter Pickle, to cater for the surviving laddish element. Furthermore, we are told of '[a]nother novel and interesting feature that cannot fail to add to the attractiveness of the magazine:

CHIT CHAT
OR
TEA TIME GOSSIP.

Under this heading Fashions, and passing topics of the day, will be discussed in a pleasing and original form. This portion of the paper will be made specially interesting to ladies. Gentlemen are particularly requested not to read it, as they will be provided for:

IN THE SMOKING ROOM
Where ladies will not be admitted. (223)

Notwithstanding such arch reinscriptions of the gender binaries signified by the tea-table and the smoking room, as a consequence of the radical trans-sexing of its implied readership the ladies have been admitted to the all-male sanctuary previously offered by the *Lads*.

III

We recognise in the simulated intimacy and solicitousness of the periodical's address to its 'dear readers' the kind of orchestrated performance of personal relationships that for Baudrillard defines human relations in the modern consumer society. But it is difficult to ascertain how effective the promises, endearments and directives of editors were in enticing particular classes of reader to buy their journal. There is little hard evidence about the 'real' readers of the Victorian periodical press, at either end of the market, beyond the circulation statistics that have been gathered by scholars such as Altick and Alvar Ellegárd (which do, of course, give us a valuable broad picture of the reading public and of relative sales figures for different journals, and different kinds of journals). Taking the instance of one of the most popular early Victorian socially improving publications, *Chambers' Journal*, Altick asks 'Who bought these papers?' (not the same question, of course, as who read them). He quotes William Chambers's own idealistic and probably generous assessment of his readership, in his memoir and in the pages of the journal itself, but adds the qualification that 'while not necessarily untrue, it is subject to some discount' (Altick, *English Common Reader*, 336–7). Such partial accounts of the popularity of a periodical, by the proprietor, editor or some other interested party, may be supplemented by independent evidence, such as the testimony of working-class autobiographers, and Altick gives some examples that support Chambers's assessment of the extensive distribution and favourable reception of *Chambers' Journal* among its intended audience. We ourselves have come across references which give a sense of the reach of the journal's circulation, most notably the following vignette in 'Notes on a Residence in Van Diemen's Land' published in 1844 in *Simmonds's Colonial Magazine and Foreign Miscellany*, describing a group of 250 convicts sent to Maria Island:

One would have supposed that such a party of men would have had sent with them, wheelbarrows, spades, shovels, rakes, and pickaxes, so necessary and indispensable for the work they had to do; but no! these were all forgotten, and were not received until a month after; but they had a plentiful supply of *Chambers' Journal*, the *Penny Magazine*, and such like works; and instead of being engaged in useful labour, they were to be seen in groups, those who could not read listening to those who could, or looking about, sunning themselves. (170–3)

But, revealing as they are, such sources are by their very nature anecdotal and ad hoc, giving us a glimpse of a small sample of 'real' readers, but hardly a representative one.

As numerous critics since Altick have conceded, it is hard to find systematic and reliable evidence about the actual historical readers of nineteenth-century periodicals (Ellegárd, *Readership of the Periodical Press*; Klancher, *Making of English Reading Audiences*, 3; Beetham *Magazine of her own?*, 10–12; Warren 'Women in Conference', 122). The readers of the higher class of journalism remain as elusive to modern commentators as the anonymous 'Unknown Public' for penny literature of whom Wilkie Collins wrote in 1859 in the sensationalising and racialising tones of contemporary social investigators on the 'unknown country' of 'darkest England'.[7] Moreover, the empirical studies of nineteenth-century reading that dominated the scholarship of the 1950s to the 1970s, which asked questions such as who could read, who did read, and what did they read, have by and large been superseded by more textually focussed and theoretically framed critical studies that have replaced the 'empirical' reader with a 'textual' reader. Patrick Brantlinger in *The Reading Lesson* has drawn attention to the need to bridge the divide between the sociology of the common reader and the rhetorical analysis of how readers are produced and conscripted by texts because, as he argues, 'no sociology of readers can fathom exactly how actual readers responded to texts. Neither, however, can a strictly rhetorical approach get at real readers reading' (16). Furthermore, to neglect the 'real' reader is to privilege the ideological positioning of the reader by and in the text, and diminishes our sense of readerly agency, of how the person turning the pages might have resisted, or at least participated in, that positioning.

In the absence of a materialist history of women's reading, it is politically incumbent upon the feminist critic to try to recover what Judith Fetterley calls the 'resisting' reader in her title, *The Resisting Reader: A Feminist Approach to American Fiction*, or what Lynne Pearce has more recently proposed as the 'implicated' reader, in pursuit of a more interactive model of text–reader relations.[8]

But how do we locate that reader in the context of the Victorian periodical press? While it seems more likely that women would have read journals that catered to and constructed feminine taste (by, for example, making a practice of reviewing and serialising work by female authors, in the case of the more intellectual publications, and of including paper patterns and recipes in the case of the penny weeklies), than those that made no effort to appeal to women readers, we can only speculate about the female readership of mainstream journals. Presumably periodicals directed at women were commonly read by women, even if we doubt claims such as that of Samuel Beeton that he has 'sixty Thousand English-women-volunteers as a corps of trusty partisans' of the *Englishwoman's Domestic Magazine* (iii). But again we remain largely in the realm of speculation when it comes to detail, as were contemporary commentators. Even Salmon, in his article on 'What Girls Read', hesitates to put a figure on the popularity of the *Girl's Own Paper*, which was 'started in 1880' and, he reports, 'in 1884 was said to have attained "a circulation equalled by no other English illustrated magazine published in this country" ', adding the qualification 'Whether this is so, or not, however, it has undoubtedly met with a success of which editor and proprietors alike have equal reason to be proud' (520).

Nevertheless, Salmon writes with more conviction about the huge rate of participation in the magazine's prize competitions, noting of one that '4,956 girls took part in endeavouring to secure a prize for the best Biographical Table of famous women', that '[o]ne sack crammed full of these required five men to carry it upstairs' (this claim is footnoted with a reference), and that '[t]he tables came from all parts of the world', including from one lady who 'was so enthusiastic as to send the table across the seas enclosed as a letter at the cost of thirty shillings' (521). The specificity of Salmon's material examples, both singular and by the sackload, is notably possible only when the readers are also contributors, and for the modern commentator on the Victorian periodical reader it is similarly principally when she or he writes back to the journal, by entering a competition, submitting an article or entering into correspondence with the editor or an agony aunt, that the 'real' reader comes into view – and even then it is questionable how far that elusive figure corresponds to his or her textual construction. Is 'Tabitha Glum', of

Lansdowne, Bath, who writes to *Blackwood's* in 1844 on the subject of 'old maids' and their neglect in the current rage for books such as Mrs Ellis's on the social role and duties of wives and mothers, a female reader writing pseudonymously or a completely fictional fabrication ('A Bewailment from Bath', 199–201)? Is 'A. S. G.', who contributes 'A Boy's Account of the Coming-of-Age Dinner' held to celebrate twenty-one years of the *Boy's Own Paper* at the end of the century, really a 'boy' with a moustache ('oh yes! I've got one coming') with a schoolboy's appetite for the 'ripping' and 'rattling' good 'grub' laid on, or a journalist mimicking an imagined boy-reader's perspective and drumming up loyalty to the magazine (218)? The *Boy's Own Paper* draws a picture of its typical correspondents in a humorous illustrated item on 'some Boys who constantly write to the Editor' (Plate 7) which is perhaps based on its postbags but which conforms to the boy types to be found elsewhere in the journal and is more likely to be a product of the comic illustrator's fancy (128). The letters pages themselves, in both this and the *Girl's Own Paper*, construct readers who are fulsomely grateful to the magazine for its advice and its beneficial effect on their lives, such as 'Liaceloga', who writes to the *Girl's Own* column, 'A Dip into the Editor's Correspondence', 'the girls of England must be grateful to you for the amount of advice, instruction, and amusement which you provide for them' (582). Writing, as required, under a pen-name, they occupy an indeterminate position as 'real' readers and writers.

Discussing the ubiquitous 'Answers to Correspondents' sections of mid-century 'family' papers such as the *Family Herald* and the *London Journal*, Altick comments that he 'suspects that many of the queries, especially the ones which today would be addressed to reference librarians, were concocted in the editorial office', but he adds that 'to the extent to which the questions were genuine', such columns 'provide an instructive panorama of the humble Victorian reader's everyday perplexities, above all in connection with flirtation, courtship, and marriage' (*English Common Reader*, 360–1). Research undertaken more recently by Lynne Warren on the publication of names and addresses of readers participating in the late nineteenth-century magazine *Woman*'s weekly competitions suggests that they at least are genuine and that the magazine's claim to be read by middle- and upper-class women is accurate. As Warren herself notes, since this information relates to only a small sample of the journal's readership, it 'must be treated with caution'; it does, though, bring us closer to an idea of the woman who 'actually paid her penny and read the magazine' (122).

In her pursuit of the 'real' reader of *Woman*, Warren goes on to examine the magazine's correspondence pages as a textual site for the negotiation of

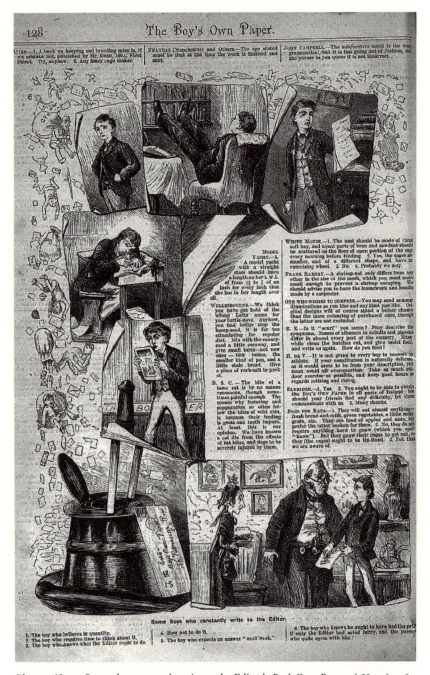

Plate 7. 'Some Boys who constantly write to the Editor', *Boy's Own Paper* 3 (1880–1): 128.

reader identity, often involving strategic interventions by both reader and editor in the struggle for control over that identity, especially in relation to gender (123). Her interesting article suggests ways in which the figure of the 'real' reader, as agent and maker of her own meanings, may be sought in the correspondence columns of other Victorian journals. An earlier journal for women, the *Englishwoman's Domestic Magazine*, offers a particularly rich example of how female readers make their voices heard in a periodical with a notably autocratic male editor and publisher, Samuel Beeton. The 'Answers to Correspondents' page and 'The Englishwoman's Conversazione' feature, always placed at the back of each number as its last items, reflect the many-faceted ideal of female culture promoted elsewhere in the magazine, and regularly include correspondence on such topics as fashion, needlework, recipes, household and gardening tips, etiquette and courtship. In the former, it is only the answers, not the readers' actual queries, that are printed, crammed onto the page in very small type, while the 'Conversazione' is more expansive, and typically includes the other side of the dialogue, though often mediated by the editor. The impression given is that a vast number of subscribers, forming an engaged and vociferous reading community, write letters to the journal. Every few issues contains a notice to the effect of the following: 'We answer our correspondents as soon as we can, but the great mass of correspondence prevents us answering month by month' ('Answers to Correspondents', 5 (1862): 191). The editor confides 'Our experience of letter-writing and letter-receiving is something that could not be contained in two volumes of this Magazine' ('The Englishwoman's Conversazione', 5 (1862): 192). While Beeton is quick to exploit any opportunity to advertise the popularity and loyal readership of his magazine, there are several indications that these pages are generated by genuine readers. Although on some occasions the editor appears to parody a typical postbag ('We are at home, John, remember, whoever calls, A, E, I, O, U or even W and Y . . . Mrs. Smith with her anxieties about Selina's "coming out" . . . Mrs. Brown in difficulties with her servants . . . INDUSTRIOUS, who seeks our advice in an important matter . . . the CONSTANT READER – unique selection of name, is it not?' ('The Englishwoman's Conversazione', 8 (1863–4): 192), other items, such as the lists of 'manuscripts respectfully declined' that appear in these pages in most issues, the recording of contributions received, and the acknowledgement of moneys donated for charitable causes, have the ring of authenticity. The correspondence and 'Conversazione' pages construct a sense of a community of readers, who are invited to enter into dialogue with other readers (as their letters often do) and with the magazine itself, in the person of the editor.

Beeton's own mode, in these pages as in his editorial prefaces, whether he is being avuncular, chivalrous, coyly flirtatious or spiteful, is generally patronising to his female readers. He is in turn hyperbolic, mock-serious, arch and sarcastic, positioning his patrons as vain, weak, fearful and ignorant creatures. His response to 'J. Purr', is typical of many: 'Our correspondent, not a young lady, we think, is in a terrible fright about our going to war with France, or France going to war with us'. For Miss Purr, the 'most terrible of all questions' in the event of war would be how she would get hold of the latest Paris fashions, but he is able to reassure her and all readers that 'the force of fashion alone, we believe, and the immense interests connected with the ENGLISHWOMAN'S DOMESTIC MAGAZINE, would keep this nation from a war with France' ('The Englishwoman's Conversazione', 1 (1860): 48).

However, if the correspondence pages provide a further forum in the journal for the production and consolidation of bourgeois gender ideology, they are also a site for its contestation. There are a striking number of answers to questions about work and education for women. Often the response itself is flippant, as in the case of 'Poor Puss' (related, perhaps to Miss Purr?) who has 'nothing to do':

Shall we send you Florence Nightingale's address, or Mrs George Dawson's, or Lady Shaftesbury's? or perhaps Miss Burdett Coutts would accept off-hand the services of one who 'yearns for some congenial employment for mind and hand.' You are anxious not to 'dissipate your energies,' and you are right, very right, in that desire. Whether on lover, husband, friend, or society (as gentle guide i' the midst) concentrate all your affection; then the sweet breath of gratitude will carry your name down the stream of futurity far in proportion to your labours – when they are sagaciously chosen – being intensified. Lay your case before Harriet Martineau, Westmoreland, and she will advise you what to do, if anybody can. ('The Englishwoman's Conversazione', 4 (1861–2): 48)

But we are at least afforded a glimpse of a 'puss' who seems to have shared the yearnings of the young Nightingale (herself often represented icono-graphically in the press as a bird). Furthermore, in almost every number of the journal the editor responds to the queries and unsolicited manuscripts of would-be writers, and fields questions about whether there are oppor-tunities for its readers to work for the magazine itself. He writes back to E. DAVIES, for example, 'We are overdone with MSS., or we should be happy to look at yours. You must believe us when we say we are sorry it is not possible to oblige our numerous applicants for employment' ('Answers to Correspondents', 4 (1861–2): 191).[9] Sometimes he forgets his chivalrous manner, and snaps at or ridicules the hapless authors who send in their work. Thus to M. D. M., who writes for advice about writing and publishing, he replies impatiently 'M. D. M., and those who are like unto thee, have mercy on us and the rest of thy fellow-creatures' ('The Englishwoman's Conversazione', 4 (1861–2): 284). But even so, M. D. M. and those who are like her establish themselves as a presence in the journal.

Through their selection and editing of their readers' letters and their chivalrous rejection or rude dismissal of more substantial unsolicited submissions, Beeton, and other editors of other magazines, enacted a kind of cultural superiority and power that Bagehot, Fitzjames Stephen and later Wilde believed they did not in reality possess over the readers whose servants they were. Furthermore, the readers whom we glimpse in their extracted phrases, like M. D. M., who had the temerity to ask for 'directions how to write a tale, corrected, and fit for publication', and 'by what monthly or weekly serial it would be most likely to be accepted', refuse to be positioned as passive readers, rather constructing themselves as active contributors to the journal's economy, as writers. This suggests the possibility of other kinds of readerly resistance to the journal's construction of them, and parallels other categorical instabilities sanctioned by periodicals – is the reviewer, for instance, a writer or a reader? Alongside the high-handed rejections and requests that readers who do not have the benefit of a personal introduction by someone on the staff desist from submitting unsolicited manuscripts, we find in other numbers of the *Englishwoman's Domestic Magazine* the promise that 'Any articles submitted shall have our best consideration', as well as expressions of gratitude to individual readers whose work has been accepted ('The Englishwoman's Conversazione' 4 (1861–2): 96; 7 (1863): 144). This reminds us that readers of the Victorian periodical press frequently acted as unpaid contributors, not only of needlework patterns and recipes, conundrums and instructions for wax flower-making, but also of articles and reviews.

In *Feminism and the Politics of Reading*, Lynne Pearce identifies 'a need to move away from the polarization of texts and readers as "active" and "passive" within a narrowly hermeneutic model of text–reader relations, and to recognize instead an alternative model of reading, which . . . characterizes the text–reader relationship as non-instrumental and implicated' (14). The relationship between the periodical press and its readers in the nineteenth century furnishes a suggestive *historical* literary field for the examination of such a model. For it is a model that not only offers a suitable methodology for reading the Victorian periodical reader, but also, in its emphasis on the interactive relationship between text and audience, seems particularly appropriate for a press that increasingly saw itself as a medium of cultural exchange in which the reader was genuinely and fundamentally implicated. As the century entered its final decade, a new journal was founded by W. T. Stead, dedicated, states the 'Programme', to mediating the media at a time when '[t]here are already more periodicals than any one can find time to read' (14). In 'A Word to Those Who Are Willing to Help', it offered a considerably more significant place than the marginal position afforded by the letters page at the back of the magazine:

The success of the REVIEW OF REVIEWS will depend chiefly on the extent to which the readers, or a certain proportion of them, cooperate with the Editor. The last thing which I desire is to be a mere man in a pulpit droning a monotonous monologue in the ears of his hearers. The secret power in all journalism, daily, weekly, or monthly, is the establishment of close touch between the Editor and his readers, and the creation in the minds of the latter of a consciousness that their cooperation is essential to the success of the former . . .

I want to make this REVIEW a medium of intercommunication throughout the whole English-speaking world . . . I need the eyes, the ears, and the brains of all my readers to help me in my task. I want their suggestions how to improve the REVIEW, I want their ideas as to how to secure its universal circulation, and I want their practical help in securing subscribers . . .

What I want is to get into more or less personal direct communication with a picked body of men or women, if they are earnest enough, who will not hesitate to work for the REVIEW and the ideals which it upholds as zealously as hundreds and thousands are working for the ideals of churches and the shibboleths of parties. I want to get to know in every community in the whole English-speaking world, the name and address of the thoroughgoing individual who can be relied upon not to spare himself or herself in working with me on the lines of this REVIEW for the well-being of English-speaking folk all round the world. (53)

Three decades on from Beeton, Stead's gender-inclusivity, and his generally democratic approach, strike a quite different note, as does his open recognition of the crucial role of readers (and not only their subscription fees) in the economy of the periodical as a 'medium of intercommunication'. But notwithstanding his view that readers make a fundamental and tangible contribution to the success of a journal dedicated to a process of pre-reading, sifting and providing a guide to the 'mighty maze of modern periodical literature', it is for Stead in the relationship with them forged by the editor that the real key to that success is to be found.

CHAPTER THREE

Editorship and gender

Editors of the periodical press in the age of Victoria were constrained by
the economic need to make their journals desirable – had indeed to seduce
and to retain a readership, and were always aware, or should have been,
that their periodicals were a commodity on the market to be consumed.
As Fitzjames Stephen remarks in 'Journalism' for the *Cornhill Magazine* in
1862:

> unless it complies with the conditions of commercial success it can exercise no
> sort of influence, and give no currency to the opinions which it expresses. This
> principle ultimately determines the character of all periodical literature. (53)

In the 1830s, as we have seen, reading was the grand new skill, providing
a ready market and yet simultaneously promoted and discountenanced by
the press strictly along class lines. The *Magazine of Domestic Economy*, for
instance, in 1836, subscribes in 'On the Establishment of a Reading Society,
or Book Club' to the idea of local reading societies or book clubs, while
carefully demarcating the eligible participants as individuals 'whose minds
are sufficiently cultivated to desire the enjoyment of select reading' (134).
The author asks:

> How are the persons to whom we allude to secure the leisurely reading of the last
> new periodical, – of the well-written novel, everywhere praised, – of the biography
> of the statesman, or the warrior, abounding in important information for every
> man, – or the narrative of a voyage of discovery, the first reading of which is the
> next best thing to the first sight of the terra incognita? (134)

Self-promotion is revealed in two ways here, by the listing of the periodical
first and by the intimation that periodical reviews will inform (the right)
readers what titles are 'well-written' and which contain 'important information'. However, as Patrick Brantlinger discusses in *The Reading Lesson*,
the reaction to Chartism and the Chartist press reveals to what extent national literacy was no longer an upper-class monopoly and for that reason

77

had become an upper-class threat, demonstrated no more tellingly than in Carlyle's ill-informed outburst against a people he dismissed as capable only of expressing themselves through 'hieroglyphic picture writing' (93–5). Other periodicals did aim at a lower socio-economic readership, their editorial policies framed around the belief that literacy would resolve the nation's political and social problems rather than add to them. Later in this chapter we will demonstrate how this shift works by comparing the *Edinburgh Review* and *Eliza Cook's Journal*, the former offering reviews of the material described in the foregoing quotation, the latter designed for the new and eager readers of the artisan class.

The voice of the editor is, however, almost always inflected with a sense of superiority over the reader, adopting a tone of natural ascendancy. This is true across the entire range of journals, from the influential quarterlies to the penny weeklies. What is more, the assumption of unquestioned editorial authority is particularly noticeable, whether the readership is male or female, whether the editor is female or male. It is more obvious, however, in periodicals addressed to the working classes or children, and indeed with regard to these two categories functions similarly for both.[1]

The question in considering the issue of editorship and gender is how to manage the press's diversity, reflected even in the very names of individual journals – *Tit-Bits*, *Bentley's Miscellany* – yet at the same time how to locate some kind of homogeneity to enable a focussed discussion of editorship and gender issues. In addition there is the need both to be empirical, that is to keep the periodical material always in sight, and to locate a way of reading that offers access to Victorian editing practices generally.[2] Margaret Beetham, in 'Towards a Theory of the Periodical as a Publishing Genre', maintains that an 'editor or proprietor will try to enforce a certain consistency of style and position' and that editors are involved in 'processes of negotiation between authors, proprietors and readers' (25) and this is irrespective of gender. With these issues in mind we decided to take a journal's house style, Beetham's 'certain consistency of style', and then consider whether that 'house style' constitutes a dominant discourse with which to explicate editing, editorial policy and editorial practice, in what nevertheless remains both an ephemeral and a heterogeneous medium.

If we accept one of the many meanings of 'discourse' as including the formal treatment of a subject, then examining the house style of any one journal will answer as a means of exploring the roles of editors and editing. Every journal, be it quarterly, monthly or weekly, had its formal house style, which becomes its dominant discourse. Such a discourse is the journal's delimited 'field of objects' (using Sara Mills's terms in *Discourse*) and in a nineteenth-century context, periodicals and their proprietors and editors might be described in Foucauldian terms as agents of knowledge, and, depending on the periodical's politics, the dominant discourse, the house style, reveals both what it chooses to promulgate and what it excludes. Inevitably then, house style will involve a narrowing of the field of vision in precisely the same way that Foucault understood discourse generally as causing such restrictions of vision (Mills, *Discourse*, 51).

Each journal's individual house style puts in place what it tries to construct as a set of standards which it tries to represent as normal and which most nearly represent how that journal wishes to present itself to the public. At a very literal level then, a periodical's house style is indeed its formally constructed voice, its dominant discourse, and that same style inflects every topic the periodical addresses. As the author of 'Editing' for the *Contemporary Review* insists, 'an editor who has planned to maintain a given tone and colour in his periodical is, of course, entitled to see that no contributor breaks up the unity of effect which he desires' (519). But at the same time, because each periodical had an individual voice, articulating a specific discourse, there are going to be variations which can only be addressed by noting the kinds of variations, as represented by individual periodical titles.

Gender intersects the discourse of house style generally and the particular house styles of individual periodicals either reaffirm the prevailing text of gender ideology (that is the separation of men into active, public lives and women into passive, private lives) – despite the way in which women's and men's actual lives were clearly changing – or alternatively subvert and challenge the status quo. The periodicals commonly believed they had the potential to be ahead of the times and the potential to make a difference in the political and social lives of their readers. This is best demonstrated in an empirical way, and again we will, later in the chapter, explore these issues more fully by focussing on the house styles of the *Edinburgh Review* and *Eliza Cook's Journal*.

The *Contemporary Review* continued to address issues of editorial power perhaps most famously in two 1886 articles by the noted editor W. T. Stead, 'Government by Journalism' and 'The Future of Journalism'. Stead is forthright about the power of journalism, and the editor in particular, when in 'Government by Journalism' he describes the editorial pen as 'a sceptre of power' (661). Stead recognises the vital nature of the relationship between editor and reader, claiming that an editor 'must keep touch with his readers' (655), readers who renew an editor's 'mandate' each time they buy a newspaper or journal (655). However, journalists wield 'absolute authority' and 'decide what their readers shall know' (662). While Stead attempts to describe this power as altruistic, as sound citizenship, his confident claim that 'the editorial *we* is among many millions the only authoritative utterance' (667) still has the power to strike a chord of dismay.

In 'The Future of Journalism' Stead proposes that those same readers form a network across the country, supplying editors with opinions and views from their particular districts. Those readers will be 'voluntary unpaid associates', rewarded with free copies of the particular journal they work for. Stead's vision of this impossibly Utopian, altruistic role for readers he sees as the ultimate form of government:

By this co-operation between a newspaper and selected readers, it will be possible to focus the information and experience latent among our people as it has never been done before, and to take an immense stride towards the realization of the conscious government of all by all, in the light of the wisdom of the best informed. (675)

What qualities must such an editor have? According to Stead, such an editor must be 'a real man, who has convictions, and capacity to give them utterance in conversation as well as in print' (668). In this brave new world of print journalism the only women included in the master plan are among wealthy men and women who might devote money 'to found a newspaper for the service, for the education, and for the guidance of the people' (671). Later we will discuss the 1840s journalism of William and Mary Howitt. Their stated aims can barely be differentiated from these of Stead despite the four decades which lie between the two editorial 'mandates', to use Stead's term. This similarity of tone reveals how editing operates as a power dynamic no matter what the forum.

In 1877, like Stead, the author of 'Editing' in the *Contemporary Review* claims that in 'order to be really abreast of the time, you must sometimes go boldly before it' (518). If this were so, gender ideology across a broad range of periodicals would not so constantly and even rigorously reaffirm separate texts of femininity and masculinity so consistently throughout the century. Bold, but not too bold seems to be the order of the day. The author of 'Editing' sees this restraint as a form of politeness, the 'respect due to what is called public opinion' (518). Gendered ideological restraints, for instance, are characterised in the rhetoric of Harrison Ainsworth's 'Preliminary Address' in the first volume of *Ainsworth's Magazine* (1842–54) by his declaration that as his magazine will be the 'visitant of families', many subjects will be forbidden which 'fitted for illustration in a separate form, can have no place on this "more removed ground" ' (iv). Ainsworth thus declares his field of action to be removed ground, limited and restrained by the presence not only of 'Mothers' but of 'Daughters' too. Content is thus intersected by gender ideology here. In this case, the gendered divide is not created or contested, but merely re-affirmed.

Individual male and female editors and reviewers also subverted such discursive practices as the use of the pronoun 'we' and the anonymity of the author, to reshape gender issues or re-present them in alternative modes, or ignore them outright. There are thus two kinds of gendered practice to be considered in editing as revealed by house style: that which works assiduously to maintain the separate spheres ideology and that which equally assiduously attempts to breach it.

Some gendered editorial practice was clearly dictated by the polemics of any one journal in question. When Bessie Parkes and her friends first thought of taking over the *Waverley Journal*, Parkes had written to Barbara Leigh Smith (later Bodichon) a statement of purpose to which they remained steadfast as Jane Rendall records in ' "A Moral Engine"? Feminism, Liberalism and the *English Woman's Journal*':

This journal endeavours to collect all facts relative to the important question of Remunerative Employment for Women, and reports upon all legal questions affecting their welfare. It also devotes especial attention to the great movement of social reform, and partakes of the character of a domestic Magazine, containing Literary Reviews, Fiction, Poetry, and Scientific Papers of a popular character. (115–16)

Sheila R. Herstein in 'The *English Woman's Journal* and the Langham Place Circle: a Feminist Forum and Its Women Editors' has shown that as editor and proprietor of the subsequent *English Woman's Journal* (1858–66), Parkes and Bodichon had to make a choice between addressing the issues which had caused them to start their own journal in the first place or seeking popularity and high circulation figures at any cost (69). In the retrospective 'Review of the Last Six Years' of the first editor, Bessie Parkes wrote:

a subject cannot be at once popular and unpopular, rich and poor, clothed in purple and fine linen, and undergoing incessant fear of a social martyrdom. If it had been wished to start a brilliant and successful magazine, some eminent publisher should have been secured and persuaded to undertake active pecuniary interest and risk; all the best known female writers should have been engaged, "regardless of expense;" *and then* – good-bye to the advocacy of any subject which would have entailed a breath of ridicule; good-bye to any thorough expression of opinion; good-bye to the humble and ceaseless struggle of all these years. (219)

Parkes firmly believed that in choosing 'advocacy', the women of Langham Place had remained true to their 'purpose and plan' (219) despite the fact that financial failure was the inevitable outcome. For them the discourse was primarily a political one. Similarly, and earlier, the editors of *Howitt's Journal* (1847–8), the husband and wife team William and Mary Howitt, also saw their role as one of advocacy for a class they termed 'the million' in their 'Address to their Friends and Readers' (1). Advocacy then becomes the dominant discourse of both the *English Woman's Journal* and *Howitt's Journal*, yet at the same time a range of beliefs and ideas embraced by both sets of editors acted as discursive constraints, an issue we will explore further in the next chapter.

Brian Maidment in 'Magazines of Popular Progress and the Artisans' points out that in 'magazines of popular progress', such as *Howitt's Journal*, *Tait's Edinburgh Magazine* and *Eliza Cook's Journal*, women were editors and contributors 'in ways quite unparalleled elsewhere in the period'. He adds that Eliza Cook, Mary Howitt and Christian Isobel Johnstone had 'central roles in formulating and disseminating the ideas of popular progress' and determines that their presence in relation to journals like these, which were aimed in part at an artisan readership, needs further explanation (93). As far as Johnstone is concerned, Michael W. Hyde records in 'The Role of "Our Scottish Readers" in the History of *Tait's Edinburgh Magazine*' that she was aware of the reading public as 'the only patron and paymaster' (136) and was personally popular with women readers (139). Hyde adds that her business partner, William Tait, although aiming the journal at 'industrious operatives' recognised that 'the bulk of *Tait's* readership would inevitably come from liberal but respectable, middle classes in Scotland and Britain' (138–9). Certainly all three women came from backgrounds that allowed greater flexibility in what a woman might or might not do and Johnstone, in particular, was a key element in *Tait's* respectable circulation figures as George Troup, a later editor, confirms (Hyde and Houghton, '*Tait's Edinburgh Magazine*', IV: 479).

The real anomaly regarding house style is, as we have already intimated, that it is both a discourse and a set of discursive constraints, so that it shapes and restrains, much as women's clothing of the period shaped and restrained their bodies. Moreover, there remains a list of outside constraints which affects the construction of house style, such as libel laws and prevailing ideologies (gender is, of course, the particular one to be considered here, but class also intersects this, as does religion). Stephen Elwell, in ' Editors and Social Change: A Case Study of *Once a Week* (1859–80)', indicates that all the editors of this particular periodical represented traditional middle-class gentility. 'Their economic and social roots were at least two or three generations deep. . . . In short, they were not typical'. Elwell contends that their middle-class identity meant they were not in touch with the mainstream, which accounts for the periodical's eventual failure (32).

One of the most common metaphors used of the periodical press and journalism in the nineteenth century was a military one. The recurrence of this metaphor suggests it is used as a trope to express ideas (and anxieties) about authority, particularly editorial authority, and to a lesser extent, hier-archy, and to assert some kind of control in the most aggressive metaphorical language. Thus any one periodical title has attached to it a team or an army, the owner or proprietor of which is the government, the editor a general, or commander-in-chief, and the writers, the troops. The metaphor chimes in very precisely with some of the features we have been discussing.

As observed in the Introduction, G. H. Lewes infamously uses the mil-itary metaphor in a diatribe against the entrance of women into literature generally, in an article published in 1847 in *Fraser's Magazine*. Lewes's con-cern here is with competition from women for publication within the periodicals, that is competition among journalists themselves, the female section of which he dismisses, not directly, but by association, as 'ill-trained troops'.[3] Half a century later Arnold Bennett in *Journalism for Women. A Practical Guide* (1898) is still voicing the same complaint, that women 'are not expected to suffer the same discipline, nor are they judged by the same standards. In Fleet Street femininity is an absolution, not an accident' (10). These two examples, so separated by time, signal to what extent mainstream journalism conformed to gender ideology.

Not surprisingly, given the extent of the competition, the periodical press must have been viewed as a field of battle, and not just of the sexes. The battle was for supremacy, for the highest readership, for a reputation for quality, for the hearts, minds and purses of its consumers. And the use of a military metaphor to express these issues was not restricted to men. Bessie Parkes, writing to Barbara Bodichon of the quarrels which had beset the Langham Place group, tells her the 'battle is won if the soldiers reckon their lives in the question. Our little band of faulty, stormy, clever warm hearted women are to me just representative of the dangers of the whole movement and I'll never desert them or it' (quoted in Rendall, 'A Moral Engine', 134). Clearly Parkes saw herself and Bodichon in terms of a military hierarchy and her declaration that she will never desert her 'little band' (and the diminutive is no accident) is internalised paternalism. Bodichon supplied the money for the venture and Parkes is as a general reporting back to government of small insurrections among the troops, who are, however, basically loyal.

Inevitably the successful periodicals were those with the most able editors, well practised, professional, practical, a leader who, in John Stuart Mill's words, cited by Ann P. and John M. Robson in 'Private and Public Goals: John Stuart Mill and the *London and Westminster*', is 'a general-in-chief' who rallies 'the scattered hosts around him' (236). As our examples show, the military metaphor appears to have been more prevalent in those periodicals which took a particular political stance. Less politicised periodicals, the *Cornhill Magazine* for instance, preferred markedly less aggressive metaphoric language with which to express a sense of editorial practice. The *Cornhill*'s first editor, William Makepeace Thackeray, employs the image of a voyage, embracing his readers as 'fellow-travellers' (128) in 'Roundabout Papers. – No. I'. Nevertheless a sea-voyage aboard ship still produces a very particular hierarchical authority indicated by references to 'passengers' and 'the Captain' which differentiate very specifically between the two. Thus the *Cornhill*'s first number is launched with these final words from Thackeray:

So have I seen my friends Captain Lang and Captain Comstock press their guests to partake of the fare on that memorable "First day out," when there is no man, I think, who sits down but asks a blessing on his voyage, and the good ship dips over the bar, and bounds away into the blue water. (128)

In 'Roundabout Papers. – No. IX', Thackeray returns to the metaphoric figure of the voyage, to extend it with a slightly more aggressive tone and possibly a more personal one. Here writers are equated with galley-slaves 'doomed to tug the oar and wear the chain' (759), suggesting that Thackeray's task as editor has become a burdensome one. However, he quickly rebukes himself by asking 'what man has not his oar to pull?' (759). He designates himself as the 'captain of a great ship' and adds as explanation of editorial principle:

I have not sought to direct or control the opinions of our passengers, though privately I might differ from them; my duty being, as I conceived, to permit free speech at our table, taking care only that the speaker was a gentleman of honour and character. (760)

Ironically, despite styling himself 'Captain', and his support of free speech, Thackeray's decision to end Ruskin's series of essays with the November 1860 number, later published as 'Unto this Last', was dictated by the magazine's readers. Ruskin recalls in the 'Preface' to *Munera Pulveris* (1872)

Thackeray explaining that the 'outcry against them became too strong for any editor to endure' (*Works*, XVII: 143). Oscar Maurer Jr in 'Froude and *Fraser's Magazine*, 1860–1874' notes the outcry had included the cancellation of subscriptions (223). As Christian Johnstone had said nearly thirty years earlier, the reading public is 'patron and paymaster' (quoted in Hyde, 'The Role of our "Scottish Readers" ', 136).

In 'Roundabout Papers. – No. IX' Thackeray also reveals his very specific gendered view of both the contributors to, and the readership of, the *Cornhill*. While the word 'passengers' is, we think, now doing double duty, representing both contributors and readership, it does not represent both men and women, as the word 'gentleman' shows. Judith L. Fisher notes in her study, 'Thackeray as Editor and Author: The Adventures of Philip and the Inauguration of the *Cornhill Magazine*', that liberalism 'identified the "natural leaders" in politics with the moral and socially defined "gentleman". Such leaders should educate the masses who were gaining more and more power' (7–8). And, while new periodicals entering the field are 'adventurers', a comparatively loaded term, Thackeray declares there is room on 'the wide ocean' for everyone, announcing that the 'old days of enmity and exclusiveness are long over' (760). Thackeray's shift in metaphoric language, therefore, reveals a significant shift in editing and marketing strategies for the periodical press from those of his predecessors. Moreover, his magnanimity creates a particular kind of identity for the *Cornhill*, an identity which extends out into the community. For all this, Thackeray's magnanimity did not extend to women as his association with the consistently misogynistic *Punch* would indicate.

Thackeray's regular editorial column, 'Roundabout Papers', which typically included such titles as 'On Two Children in Black', 'On Screens in Dining-Rooms', 'On a Joke once Heard from the Late Thomas Hood', was said to contain these following elements writes Barbara Quinn Schmidt in 'In the Shadow of Thackeray: Leslie Stephen as the Editor of the *Cornhill Magazine*': '. . . charm, warmth, sentimentality, nostalgia, natural discursiveness, compactness, gentle humour, authorial pronouncement, autobiographical confession, wit, sustained harmonic tone, topicality, felicity of detail and allusion' (78). A list such as this suggests the complexity of the discourse we are describing, except that these elements might all be summed up as being part of an editor's tone, voice or authority. Lynne Warren's study of the correspondence columns of *Woman*, under the editorial control of Arnold Bennett and Fitzroy Gardner from 1890–1900, contends that editorial comment allows the editor to 'shut down' the range of possible meanings in a periodical's discourse 'by showing the reader how to interpret them' (124). The authority in an editor's personal column always has this effect which must surely be more profound when the editor has a public reputation as is the case with Thackeray. The editor mediates information to the readership and the content of that information, as Roger Fowler points out in *Language in the News. Discourse and Ideology in the Press*, is not facts about the world but ideas. These ideas can then be presented using any or all of those multifarious facets of Thackeray's editorship. Other terms to express the concept 'ideas', says Fowler, include 'beliefs, values, theories, propositions, ideology' (1), and whatever 'is said or written about the world is articulated from a particular ideological position' (10). Thackeray, like many a showcase editor used to launch a new periodical and attract a readership, remained as the *Cornhill*'s editor for only a relatively short period (1860–2). Such famous editors were often replaced by less notable but no less remarkable people who proved much more efficient. Journals appear to survive under the editorship of the latter for significantly lengthy periods. The case of Thackeray, as with other periodicals we have explored, seems to suggest that once a journal is established, its survival is far more contingent upon an efficient maintenance of its established house style, than on the presence of a particular 'name' as editor.

The particular ideological position of some journals is revealed in their very title. The politics of *Woman at Home* produces no surprises except for the fact that so late in the century this journal, and others like it, is so very conservative. Annie S. Swan is still, in, for example, 'Life and Work at Home', arguing for home as 'the nursery of souls' (62), an argument well over a century old by 1894. The titles of the great majority of periodicals, however, give little away unless they are aimed at specific activities, *Photographic News*, for instance, or the *Cycle Magazine*. Periodicals which take the name of the proprietor or the publisher are by far in the majority and are less easily categorised. Thus in the first instance, it is usually the contents, the kinds of articles, stories, poems and so on, which will signal to any prospective reader a journal's editorial position, but a surer indicator is the tone and content of the prefatory statement. The prefatory statement becomes the primary means of establishing any journal's ideological position regarding any number of issues: politics, class, gender and so on.

Of the periodicals we have surveyed, few do not offer an editorial statement some months into publication (usually for the first volume) variously labelled 'Preface', 'Introduction' or 'To our Readers', and occasionally something more imaginative, William Maginn's 'Our Confession of Faith' (1830) for *Fraser's Magazine*, for instance. The prefatory statement, with few exceptions, describes the kind of periodical this is, exclaims at its early success, promises to maintain a high standard and implies the kind of audience it aims to reach, although the tone in which all of these factors are described varies considerably. Audience or readership is almost invariably class-determined and the targeted readership is either written down to or fulsomely appealed to, depending on who is being addressed. In this procedure, the editor at the same time almost inadvertently produces a thumbnail sketch of editorial policy. The *Family Economist* (1848–60), in 'A Few Words to our Readers', describes its readership as 'those whose means are scanty, whose resources are few, and who stand in need of useful knowledge' (217) and signals 'useful knowledge' and the education of the working class as the basis of editorial policy, and thus the chief substance of its contents.

Journals were either monthly or quarterly, and some of the latter became famous as long-running and influential publications dominating the reviewing side of the periodical press for decades, and occasionally for over a century. The *Edinburgh Review* which began in 1802 announces in its 'Advertisement' that as a journal of review it will be highly selective and will consider only 'works that either have attained or deserve, a certain portion of celebrity' (iii). This policy determined several key factors. It dictated that the *Edinburgh* would be issued only quarterly, enabling 'a greater variety for selection', and, 'for the full discussion of important subjects', allowed some articles to be of 'greater length' (iv). The *British and Foreign Review*, launched in 1835, presents itself in Christopher Bird's 'Introduction' as escaping the 'partial and limited' domestic scene of existing publications implying, without naming them, such journals as the *Edinburgh Review*:

There remains, therefore, a chasm to be filled up, by a journal that shall embrace an ampler field of operation, collect the gleanings of literary research, and bring into one store-house the dispersed grains of science, as fast as they are brought to maturity by the intellectual industry of Europe. (5)

The editors of such journals use phrases like 'English men' and 'our public men' with impunity, and when such terms as 'the British public', or 'every individual' or the 'English reader' occur, they remain gendered male; men speaking to men about issues which dictate the content of these particular journals and in which only men are involved: politics, commerce, science, history, polite literature. Nevertheless we would assume that they knew they had female readers, and that the reading public generally knew that they also used female writers. For instance, when the *Westminster Review* came under the management of John Chapman, the 'Prospectus' announced the periodical to be 'under the direction of new editors'. It is now generally accepted that one of these editors, Marian Evans (later novelist George Eliot), actually wrote the 'Prospectus' which notably declares that they will accept independent contributions in the form of articles 'to facilitate the expression of opinion by men of high mental power and culture' (iv). The *Westminster* also declared itself to be radical in supporting very particular reforms such as extension of the suffrage and national education.

However, gender is the key factor, with class and religion, used by other editors actually to signal content and editorial policy. Misogyny and anti-feminism are two obvious gender factors in the nineteenth century. Early in the century an homogenous term like 'readers' is designated male as we have shown. In the 1840s Harrison Ainsworth, as already noted, writes women into the readership of *Ainsworth's Magazine* but sees their presence as a limitation so that some subjects (he specifies 'politics and scandal') will have to be 'consistently' excluded (iii, iv). Similarly, although not in the same exclusionary sense, William and Mary Howitt, as editors of *Howitt's Journal*, announce in their 'Address' that 'it shall be our anxious care that not a word or a sentiment shall appear in this Journal which the most refined individual may not read aloud in the family circle' (2).

By the 1860s, however, Anthony Trollope as the editor of *Saint Pauls* declares in his 'Introduction' that 'We will be political if we are anything' and later reaffirms this declaration to include both sexes: 'He and his friends who will work with him intend to be political, – thinking that of all the studies to which men and women can attach themselves, that of politics is the first and the finest' (3, 4). Trollope's apparent inclusivity is interesting here, perhaps the more so because of the contrast with some of his anti-feminist novels from the same period, and with women-only journals from later in the century which are still trying to maintain the separate spheres philosophy against all the odds. *Woman at Home* and the *Windsor Magazine* are two specific examples. Today, of course, we would think of this philosophy as a political ideology, an ideology which Trollope would have embraced, whereas for Trollope, politics means the activities of the British House of Commons. As John Sutherland so rightly reminds us in 'Trollope and *St. Paul's* [sic] 1866–70', *Saint Pauls* 'was to be a magazine for gentlemen, written and conducted by gentlemen' (118).

In some of the periodicals we surveyed, the prefatory statements employ metaphoric language in which the appearance of the new journal is gendered in some way, as noted in our Introduction. In *Fraser's*, for instance, the awkwardness of self-introduction is addressed in the comic tone of the whole, Maginn's shifts from likening the journal to a 'blushing maiden' to suggesting that in reality it more closely resembles the 'lumbering and

floundering gestures of a young squire from the country' and that the
modern prospectus tends, like Lady Macbeth, to 'protest too much' ('Our
"Confession of Faith"', 1, 2). *Fraser's*, as it turned out, was to survive, and
John Skelton, reviewing its first fifty years in 'Our Past and Our Future',
recalls Maginn's opening article, contending that while it contains many
things 'of little importance now' it is nevertheless written with 'dash and
brightness' (1). Skelton draws his reader's attention to the Maclise cartoon
for the first number of 1835 showing the editor addressing his staff and
writes that he 'cannot imagine a more brilliant staff, or a more catholic and
genial one' (1). In the staider 1870s, however, Skelton also declares that in
its early style the magazine suffers from an 'excess of robust animal vitality.
It is not merely strong, but uproarious. It smacks . . . of the humours of
the tavern or the wine-room. . . . The time has passed for all this; and men
are more moderate, on the whole more subtle, in their literary humours'
(9–10). In looking ahead to *Fraser's* future, however, it is gendered strictly
male: sparkling, writes Skelton, with 'manly and humorous thought' and
encouraging 'all that is aspiring and high-minded and free with a manly and
ordered freedom' (10). Above all, he hopes that *Fraser's* will interpret to the
English mind, 'Scottish and Irish national sentiment' and 'the many social
and political features of our Colonies' because English ignorance 'reflects
injuriously on our national history' (12). These latter are issues which our
next two chapters address in more detail but we note here the way in which
the passage of time can modify house style to some extent and in some
cases.

The *Literary World*, in more prosaic mode than the élan of *Fraser's* early
numbers, hopes in its 'Advertisement' that its readers find 'pleasure' and
'profit', those 'agreeable handmaids to improvement' (i). But sixty years
on, the *Windsor Magazine. An Illustrated Monthly for Men and Women* in
'A Foreword' is perhaps the most extraordinary in this regard because the
language is no longer only a joke or a cliché as we noted in the Introduction.
Rather it posits entrenched ideological positions that betray its editorial
policy as deeply anti-feminist and profoundly class-bound:

There are some periodicals, no doubt, which bounce into popularity by the power
of mere flourish, just as a girl whose charms are of a somewhat bold type makes a
masculine circle captive to an audacious freshness. We are old-fashioned enough to
regard that kind of success with a distrustful eye. When the first flush of conquest
is over, it does not wear well. The audacity remains, but the freshness goes off.
Far more likely to endure is the less obtrusive beauty which steals into the manly
heart by a postern gate, while its rival is flaunting a transient triumph on the
battlements. (1)[4]

What our brief survey of prefatory statements consistently reveals, however, is that in many cases women were not specifically written out of editorial policies but rather were more often written in, especially as the century progressed. Even if that writing in was seen as limiting the topics and the language, editorial policy as a discourse more frequently catered for women than otherwise and many journals seemed to pride themselves on consulting the wants of both sexes. Whether the periodical was aimed at working-class readers to promote self-education, or at the more leisured classes who sought merely to be amused, there was a consciousness that women as a readership were a too-present force to be safely ignored, even if the time-worn platitudes could still dominate the discourse. The *Welcome Guest* implicitly recognising in its 'Preface' no class or gender divide, has received letters of praise from both 'the sterner and the softer sex', and as proudly boasts that theirs is 'a staff of gentlemen of experience and standing in periodical journalism' and that their plain speaking is not offensive as confirmed by the 'vast jury of our fair countrywomen' (iv). In its very title the *Welcome Guest* signals the concern of the age, that the style and tone of periodicals should be domesticated, able to be taken anywhere, house-trained. House style is indeed both enabling and yet, simultaneously and conversely, restricted by the moral codes and mores of the time.

To explore some of the foregoing issues more specifically, we turn now to consider that mandarin quarterly, the *Edinburgh Review*, and for comparison *Eliza Cook's Journal*. Like its Tory rival, the *Quarterly Review*, the Whig *Edinburgh Review* held its position as a major quarterly review periodical throughout the nineteenth century. Its dominance in the world of letters can be attributed more than anything else to its editorial style; its house style became a hallmark for consistency and a particular 'quality' that assumed male supremacy. The editors determined at the outset in their 'Advertisement' not merely to review new publications, but 'to confine their notice, in a great degree, to works that either have attained, or deserve, a certain portion of celebrity' (iii). Houghton quotes Francis Jeffrey, the first long-term editor (1803–29), as professing that the *Edinburgh* would 'go deeply into *the Principles* on which its judgments were to be rested; as well as to take large and Original views of all the important questions to which these works might relate' (1: 416). These 'large and original views', published anonymously, were provided, for the most part, by a small team of independent and highly qualified men upon whose work Jeffrey, nevertheless, imposed his editorial authority, cutting, altering, enhancing as he saw fit. Jeffrey's statement establishes a primary feature of the *Edinburgh*'s house style which for the readers of 1802 was an innovative and lively variation on all to which they had become accustomed. Houghton also points out that the *Edinburgh* offered new topics too such as political economy, and considerable space for 'practical and theoretical science' ranging from engineering to medicine (1: 417).

Jeffrey's long editorial reign (twenty-seven years) established not only a publishing style: title, format, print, article length, subject matter, but also a literary style which remained, for the most part, unchanged throughout the century, although as Joanne Shattock in *Politics and Reviewers* notes, Jeffrey's successor Macvey Napier 'favoured shorter articles' to restore variety (25). Eventually the journal shifted from nine to an average of eleven to thirteen articles (25). Nevertheless, it is quite extraordinary to see in 1812 a review titled 'Malcolm on India', and then in 1880 a review titled 'Lord Minto in India' in a journal with precisely the same title with which it began in 1802, and with almost an identical layout, down to the brief header titles provided for each article. As Louis James notes, consistency of format 'itself becomes a form of communication' ('Trouble with Betsy', 351).

For all its innovative style and independence of mind, the *Edinburgh* remained a highly conservative organ. Scanning its contents pages it is clear that politics and social reform were indeed issues about which the *Edinburgh* felt strongly. The *Edinburgh* was after all established in the period prior to Catholic emancipation, to the abolition of slavery, when oppressive game laws operated, when the people were subjected to a whole range of petty laws and harshly punished for infringement. Perhaps most importantly for any periodical libel was a punishable offence attracting imprisonment and an incentive to maintaining a moderate tone. Various reforms in the ensuing three decades changed the condition of Britain to a more liberal, more democratic one. Henry Brougham, who soon became part of the regular writing team, was an effective reformer, his 'indiscretion and rashness' (quoted in Houghton, *Wellesley Index*, 1: 418) nevertheless toned down by the *Edinburgh*'s innate conservatism. Arthur R. D. Elliott, who took over the editorship in 1895, in a centenary article celebrates the *Edinburgh*'s moderate stance, 'of resistance to obstructive Toryism on the one hand, and, if need be, to reckless Radicalism on the other' (quoted in 1: 421).

But there was more to the *Edinburgh*'s house style than its domestic politics, important as that is. Travel books, for instance, are regularly reviewed throughout the century and in considerable numbers. It is clear that editorial policy embraced from the outset and maintained a vision of an expanding British Empire and that empire's place within not just a European context, but a global context. Explorers, travellers, tourists, the memoirs and journals of British army and naval men, are all given consistent house room, sometimes to be praised, sometimes to be mocked. Perhaps the conservatism of the *Edinburgh Review* is most clearly expressed, however, in the strict gender divide not only maintained but reinforced as the century progressed. This divide can be seen in critiques of both men's and women's writing. For instance, in 'Hope on Household Furniture' Richard Jeffries expresses contempt for any man occupied with a topic so 'paltry and fantastical' and condemns Hope's lack of manliness, despising 'the study of those effeminate elegancies' and suggesting that it would be beneath the dignity of most men 'to be eminently skilled in the decoration of couches' (479). Hope's writing style is likened to 'a flashy shop-bill' and lambasted as 'exquisitely bombastic, pedantic, and trashy' (479). Gendered terms are employed to divide poor Mr Hope's publication from those of other men engaged on works of greater solemnity and import than his 'solemn foppery'.

The *Edinburgh*'s attitude to women's writing comes then as no surprise. Extraordinarily few women wrote *for* the *Edinburgh* in comparison with the practice of other periodicals of the same status, but women's publications at least were reviewed consistently, if not in any great number, especially those publications in which women are the memorialist handmaids to famous men, or families, a continuing practice until late in the century.[5] Nevertheless, women generally remain under-represented throughout the 1800s in the pages of the *Edinburgh*. This said, some Victorian women writers received regular reviews, Anna Jameson, for instance, and George Eliot, the latter still being referred to as 'he' in 1868 long after the secret of George Eliot's female identity was common knowledge. The critiques of women's writing are almost always gendered and were so from the outset. Thomas Brown, reviewing Amelia Opie's *Poems* (1802) in the first number, attacks her versification in strict gender terms clearly indicating that some kinds of poetry belong only to men:

The regular heroic couplet she has also *attempted*; but a line of ten syllables is too large for the grasp of her delicate fingers; and she spans her way along, with an awkward and feeble weariness, whenever she lays aside the smaller verse. (115)

This gendered position, that poetry is a masculine domain, remains entrenched throughout the century and not only in the *Edinburgh*. John Dennis, writing for *Fraser's* in 1882 and reviewing Margaret Oliphant's *The Literary History of England in the End of the Eighteenth and Beginning of the Nineteenth Century* (1882), assures his readers that Mrs Oliphant 'knows how to read and write, and there is a rapidity of movement in her history which carries the reader along smoothly and pleasantly. The stream is shallow, but it is clear' (509). He takes issue with most of her estimates of the various poets considered but praises her 'skilful workmanship' (519), the latter word relegating Oliphant, as a writer, to the second rank.

In 1849, in line with its declared interest in social reform, the *Edinburgh* accorded a lengthy review by W. R. Greg to Elizabeth Gaskell's *Mary Barton*, a work 'palpably . . . the production of a lady' but distinguished for its social agenda as the header for the review on page 403 indicates in announcing: 'Not to be regarded as a mere Novel'. Greg's review of Gaskell shifts significantly from the *Edinburgh*'s usual approach to women's writing. Gaskell is praised for not merely 'getting up' a topic and her 'earnest and benevolent purpose' is never in doubt ('Mary Barton', 403). Nevertheless Gaskell's innocent radicalism, signalled by Greg as a female failing, clearly alarms the *Edinburgh*'s basically conservative approach and the same arguments which were produced to condemn Frances Trollope's *Michael Armstrong* (1839) are rehearsed here:

Notwithstanding the good sense and good feeling with which it abounds, it is calculated, we fear, in many places, to mislead the minds and confirm and exasperate the prejudices, of the general public on the one hand, and of the factory operatives on the other. (403)

Greg does not determine Gaskell's choice of topic to be improper, in the way that Hope's study had been an unsuitable choice for a man, indeed it is considered carefully and equitably as a work of 'higher pretensions' and the review is distinguished for its criticisms of Gaskell's work which are not based on gender, but rather on 'artistic' errors and errors of 'fact' ('Mary Barton', 412). The contrast with the review which immediately follows it by C. S. M. Phillips of Agnes Strickland's *Lives of the Queens of England from the Norman Conquest*, is striking. Strickland is subjected to critical severity because she has ventured into what Phillips deems a male preserve – history. The review begins with the premise that women writers are 'illiberal' because of their 'imperfectly disciplined' temperaments (435). Phillips adds that ladies 'who assume masculine functions must learn to assume masculine gravity and impartiality' (436). This vaunted 'gravity and impartiality' would have been considered integral to the *Edinburgh*'s house style. In conclusion Phillips declares he has not invoked the superior authority of Macaulay against Strickland because 'we had no need of such a champion for the attainment of our immediate object; and have preferred winning our little battle with our own forces' (462). Thus his review ends by his invoking once again a military metaphor, although the war against women need only be a 'little battle'.

We remarked earlier that George Eliot received consistent reviews from the *Edinburgh* and we wanted to end this discussion by considering an anonymous review of *Daniel Deronda* in 1876 in which Eliot is recognised for her 'gravity and impartiality' even if they are not the words employed. However, the tone of this review is uneasy, moving back and forth between praise and an uneasy negativity. Eliot's fame is initially attributed to 'that better part of the public which forms the taste of the world'. Forty years earlier, as we show at the start of this chapter, the author of the article on Reading Societies in the *Magazine of Domestic Economy* expresses precisely this sentiment. Thus the connection between class and reading taste has, for the *Edinburgh* at least, barely shifted. However, Eliot is 'respected by the public', 'frankly endorsed or received with acclamations by that broader mass of readers who form the final tribunal' and, in a hierarchy gendered strictly masculine, has 'outstripped even those who hold the highest place . . . Bulwer Lytton . . . Thackeray . . . Dickens' (442). Her work indeed attracts 'the keener intelligences among the crowd' (443). What is particularly noticeable here, however, is a declining register that implicitly condemns popular taste in the terms used of Eliot's readership: the 'public', the 'broader mass of readers', the 'crowd', developing an uncertainty that such widely held favourable opinion is worth anything.

The reviewer also suggests that 'the very critics who helped to make it have grown timid before this universal fame' (442), indeed that the intensity of the applause for Eliot has 'alarmed and silenced us' (442). The reviewer is amused to see newspaper critics attempting to modify the enthusiasm for Eliot without committing themselves, concerned not to lose favour with the public. Yet this same critic is caught in the same bind, attempting to modify, without directly attacking, the object of a perverse antipathy. It is decided that 'spurious enthusiasm' and 'false applause' are injurious both to Eliot and to 'public taste', and that Eliot has had the misfortune to become fashionable. The ambivalence is directly a product of ideology; Eliot offended in so many ways, personally by living openly with George Henry Lewes; spiritually by publicly disavowing Christianity in favour of humanism, offences that might be overlooked in a man, but certainly not in a woman. She endured, as her journals show, ostracism for many years, and then against all expectation, succeeded in winning fame and popularity anyway, in which the offences were cheerfully overlooked, even forgotten. She lived out a sexual revolution and overturned the mores of her day. For the *Edinburgh* reviewer at least, there is no accounting for public taste as he or she shifts from one position to the other, one moment questioning Eliot's position and the next conceding to popular opinion, declaring (but still expressed in the negative) that we 'are not sure that any woman writer, with a mind so broad, so large, so able to conduct a mental investigation to the end, so little apt to be seduced into digression, or moved into change of purpose, has ever been' (443–4).

As a contrast to the *Edinburgh Review*, we chose to consider *Eliza Cook's Journal* as representative of a range of periodicals of limited run, but targeting as specifically as the *Edinburgh*, their own reading audience along class and gender lines. At one time *Eliza Cook's* outsold Dickens's *Household Words* and Sally Mitchell argues in *The Fallen Angel. Chastity, Class and Women's Reading*, on the grounds of internal evidence, that its readers may have been 'like the editor, mature single women' (28). Cook's readership is far more likely to have included the artisan class and may not have been divided along gender lines nearly as rigidly as Mitchell suggests. While many contributions in Cook's *Journal* carry their authors' signatures, research has revealed that among the regular contributors was Samuel Smiles who had been editor of the *Leeds Times* and who wrote some of the more radical feminist leaders for Eliza Cook, as we will discuss later. Cook's magazine, like her poetry, had a wide general appeal. Like *Household Words*, it was not illustrated.

Eliza Cook is an exceptional figure at mid-century and yet was apparently accepted on her own terms, successfully publishing her volumes of poetry which ran to several editions and as successfully publishing the journal which appeared under her name for five years. The *Athenaeum* in reviewing 'Melaia, and other Poems' described her as 'a sort of L.E.L. for the working classes', her work calculated 'to please the not very select readers of a provincial newspaper' (914).[6] Notorious for adopting male-style dress and her curly hair cut short, Cook stepped back and forth across the gender divide with the notoriety apparently doing her no harm whatsoever. She was awarded a civil-list pension in 1863 and she continued to receive royalties from her early publications of poetry until her death in 1889 Joanne Shattock in *The Oxford Guide to British Women Writers* informs us (116). A late account in 'Our Portrait Gallery' in *Bow Bells* of 1865 expresses some anxiety that:

so much strength of intellect and powerful poetic imagination stamped her efforts, that she was considered to be a *masculine* writer . . . but . . . the energetic tone of her writings never trespassed beyond the tenderness, taste and sympathy of a high-souled woman. (18)

In Cook's prefatory statement 'A Word to My Readers' she addresses various issues that reveal a certain canniness in her approach. To begin with, she denies that by joining 'the universal march of periodicals' she is undertaking any form of 'literary gambling'. It seems to be important to Cook that she make her awareness of the precariousness of periodical publishing clear to her audience. Secondly, she addresses the political purpose of her journal, but expresses this in gendered terms:

> nor am I anxious to declare myself a mental Joan of Arc, bearing [a] special mission to save the people in their noble war against Ignorance and Wrong. I simply prepare a plain feast, where the viands will be all of my own choosing, and some of my own dressing, hoping that if what I provide be wholesome and relishing, I shall have a host of friends at my board, whose kind words and cheerful encouragement will keep me in a proud and honourable position at the head of the table. (1)

Like the military metaphor, that of 'food for thought', as previously discussed, was also popular in periodical prefaces, but Cook's use of it here is striking because of the various ways in which it functions. It declares her sex, it doubles on that declaration in recognising woman's role as that of nurturer, and it puns on her own name, but at the same time, it establishes a hierarchy (just as Thackeray's Captain of the ship at the Captain's table does), and it establishes a role which in this period would normally be considered male. Cook announces herself as head of the house with the phrases 'my board' and 'head of the table'. She feels able to take on this role because as a popular poet she has already brought her 'wares' successfully into the literary marketplace. House style in Cook's case is almost literally that. The tone and general tendency are always domestic. Cook does react against didacticism, however, in noting the tendency to talk down to 'the people':

> Let it not be imagined I am appointing myself any *particular* right to lead or teach 'the people.' Let it not be said that I am striving to become a moral 'Mrs. Trimmer'[7] to the million; rather let me confess that I have a distaste for the fashion so violently adopted of talking to 'the people,' as though they needed an army of self-sacrificing champions to do battle for them, and rescue them. (1)

Cook's refusal to engage with this kind of demeaning rhetoric might well account for her success with her designated readership. Nevertheless, as the articles and some of the short stories in her journal show, *Eliza Cook's Journal* had an editorial policy which she describes as aiding 'the gigantic struggle for intellectual elevation' to perfect 'social and political civilization' (1).

While never overtly feminist, *Eliza Cook's Journal* regularly addresses domestic issues which affect women, such as women and work, and regularly employs women as writers. Named contributors include Eliza Meteyard ('Silverpen'), who published serials and short stories regularly in *Eliza Cook's Journal* (and in several other periodicals as well) and supplied occasional articles such as 'Libraries for the People'. Julia Kavanagh and Anna Maria Sargeant are also named contributors. A mostly unnamed but prolific contributor was Samuel Smiles, formerly editor of the *Leeds Times*.[8] Work for women is perhaps less of an issue in a journal in part designed for the working class because it was far more commonplace for working-class women to work than for women of the middle class. Thus an article like Samuel Smiles's 'Industrial Schools for Young Women' is 'in favour of the education of the young women of the working classes' (81). Feminism comes into play in the statement which follows this, moderated as it is in the second part of the sentence with due acknowledgement of the current ideology of the day:

Women have strong claims upon the consideration of society; first, because they constitute one-half of the human race; and, secondly, because the moral well-being of the other half mainly depends upon them. (81)

A survey across 1849 to 1852 reveals a range of articles on, for and about women, the titles of which indicate a gradual shift in attitude and emphasis. 'Our Women Servants' to 'Home Power' to 'The Vocations of Women' to the 'Wrongs of Englishwomen' to 'Men and Women – Education of the Sexes' to 'Treatment of Women'. Five of these six articles are given precedence by being placed at the front of the particular numbers in which they appear under the journal's masthead. While none of these carries any signature in the journal, Samuel Smiles's name has been attributed to 'Home Power' and 'Men and Women – Education of the Sexes'. It is clear that others of these titles may have been written by Smiles as well, because similar ideas are repeated and even statements, for example, the two statements in the foregoing quotation are repeated in various other articles. Notably an argument, contrary to the common ideology of the day, develops across these articles which concludes, as Smiles states in 'Men and Women', that men need to be elevated 'to a position of equal moral and social advancement' with women 'so that the one portion of our race may not act as a drag and hindrance to the progress of the whole' (97). In other words, the cant of the day that women only need guard the morals of the home, and that women are a 'drag and hindrance' to progress is being challenged by what is obviously the editorial policy, the house style, of this journal.

Furthermore, the article 'Treatment of Women' outlines specifically how woman is disadvantaged in having 'no legal rights', in having no existence as a citizen, in being 'always a minor', in still taking rank 'in the eye of the law, among man's goods and chattels' (225). None of these articles reveals a specific style that might indicate the sex of the writer and in part this is because the 'woman' question could legitimately be written upon by women or men.

These articles dealing with the woman question are not the only ones, however. A decade before Thackeray produced his 'Roundabout Papers' for the *Cornhill Magazine*, Eliza Cook was publishing, at irregular intervals, a similar style of humorous, chatty column for her own journal with titles like 'A Word on Slang', 'Best Rooms', 'A Back Street', 'The "House of Lords", and the "House of Commons"' and 'A "Dashing" Wedding', all of which imply a writer who is out and about, and all of which are mildly comic in a common and recognisable style. Cook's occasional articles more often than not address the class divide – for instance, the middle classes are told not to ape the wealthy by maintaining a 'best room' which Cook describes as a 'domestic Iceland' ('Best Rooms', 74); or the wealthy but restless, even bored, audience at Her Majesty's theatre for the opera are compared to their disadvantage with 'the artizan class, with grimed shirt-sleeves turned up to the elbow . . . all quietly absorbed in a classical, dry play' at Sadler's Wells ('The "House of Lords"', 98).

Unlike Thackeray's, however, Cook's columns always employ the plural 'we', an editorial style most commonly associated with a male voice, despite bearing Eliza Cook's name under the individual column title, and despite some of them appearing as leaders under the banner of her journal. Moreover, the writing itself suggests a male rather than a female persona. It is interesting to observe that ten years on Thackeray may comfortably use the more personal 'I' form and a comparatively modern style, whereas Cook is adopting the older *Fraser's* style to enable a jocose form of writing with a moral or sting in its tail. In part the reason seems clear: that women should not be out and about in the first place, and that by writing comically they offend against the rigid decorum of the day; that is, being funny is, for a woman, inappropriate behaviour. Cook quite radically signals the restrictions on women by adopting the male persona while retaining her own feminine name. She also signals, perhaps incidentally, or even accidentally, her own sexuality. More importantly for this study, she critiques the dominant house style of periodicals like the *Edinburgh Review* by her ironic positioning of herself as both male and female. At mid-century came considerable debate about anonymous journalism, as we have already discussed.

Dallas Liddle suggests it was believed that 'signed journalism would trigger revolutionary change' (31–2). Cook's use of a house style endemic to that section of the periodical press most dominant and most popular in the century, her use of a corporate 'we', enables her to address particular class and political issues in the style most familiar to an 1850s readership while ironically signalling the possibilities of change.

CHAPTER FOUR

Gender and the 'Politics of Home'

The 'Politics of Home' addresses both the political public domain of national government and the political private domain of domestic government. How these might intersect or contradict, and the extent to which the periodicals play a part in those intersections and contradictions, will be the focus of this chapter. The press played a major role in the formation and propagation of ideologies of home constructed strictly along gender lines. Sentiment and sensationalism became staples of domestic journalism. Earlier we discussed W. T. Stead's essays for the *Contemporary Review* on the power and the future of journalism. In 'Government by Journalism' Stead readily recognises the inherent power of the press noting that for 'the purpose of moulding a constituency into his own way of thinking, the editor has every advantage on his side' (655). Stead is here conflating 'constituency' and 'readership'. What is more, Stead insists that sensationalism (and, we would add, sentiment) is a perfectly legitimate means by which to mould the 'constituency', which at one point he terms 'the British householder' (657). He offers a pseudo-scientific description of sensation as essential (hearing, seeing, feeling, thinking) (670), and while he condemns 'mere froth-whipping', nevertheless he speaks out for an 'indispensable' and a 'justifiable' sensationalism, 'to arrest the eye of the public and compel them to admit the necessity of action' (671). Stead justifies his position on sensationalist journalism because of its achievements within the public domain of home:

It was the sensationalism of the 'Bitter Cry of Outcast London', emphasized by a journalistic sounding-board, that led to the appointment of the Royal Commission on the Housing of the Poor. And it was sensationalism that passed the Criminal Law Amendment Act. (672)

Within the private domain, to achieve a sentimental vision of home, an idealisation turned into a domestic reality, seems to be a primary aim of many of the journals we surveyed. Female readers are assured that the accomplishment of this vision is to be managed by shrewd economy, attention to comfort and practical domestic administration. These specific issues are focussed on through the lenses of gender and class. For our purpose, it was found practical to consider a small number of journals on the understanding that they represent a very broad range indeed.

I

Rosemary Marangoly George in *The Politics of Home. Postcolonial Relocations and Twentieth-Century Fiction* writes that:

[c]onsiderations of the space marked "home" have for the most part been read as the terrain of conservative discourses. "Home" has been abandoned to its clichés. (3)

This domain,[1] the domestic space, because gendered female, became locked into a series of negative epithets (George's 'clichés') that diminished its relevance to the wider world: 'ordinary', 'everyday', 'common', 'simple', 'humble', the usual designations tied to class which are then transferred to that space: the space of Home. George argues that realist novels:

in English in the last hundred years have situated themselves in the gap between realities and the idealizations that have made "home" such an auratic term. As imagined in fiction, "home" is a desire that is fulfilled or denied in varying measure to the subjects (both the fictional characters and the readers) constructed by the narrative. (1–2)

When the *Magazine of Domestic Economy* issued its first number in 1836 the journal positioned itself very precisely in that particular space, both as regards its readership and its political focus, and in opposition to the mainstream journals with their focus on Tory or Whig or Radical politics, with the following epigraph:

We are born at home, we live at home, and we must die at home, so that the comfort and economy of home are of more deep, heart-felt, and personal interest to us, than the public affairs of all the nations in the world. (n.p.)

The shift signalled by the appearance of this journal away from matters to do with the nation is also class based, of a kind very conveniently illustrated by Felicia Hemans's poem 'The Homes of England' first published in 1828 in *Records of Woman: with other Poems*, and consistently reprinted in periodicals, for instance in *Youth's Instructer* and *Saturday Magazine*. Strictly hierarchical, the poem begins with the 'stately homes', moves to 'merry homes', to 'blessed homes', to 'cottage homes' and finally to the 'free fair homes', be they hut or hall. The poem can be read as both sentimental and unswervingly patriotic, positions the *Magazine of Domestic Economy* embraces. Its response to this sentiment is, however, coupled to the advocacy of a philosophy of domestic economy which will bring about Hemans's Utopian visions of 'gladsome looks of household love', and cottage homes 'smiling o'er the silvery brooks'.

This ideological evidence points to an actual readership that is 'comfortable' to use one of the *Magazine of Domestic Economy*'s own terms from its 'Preface', that is, for the most part middle middle class, despite the declaration in the 'Preface' that the proprietors would wish to 'render the work accessible to even the humblest families, by the lowness of its price' (iv). The articles on household management assume the presence of several servants and the ability to pay people to come in and do the monthly wash. Moreover, by 1842 this policy of accessibility to lower income readers has changed, the title is altered to the *Magazine of Domestic Economy, and Family Review* and the price is doubled as announced in an 'Address' in which the proprietors propose to remedy the lack of sufficient space for illustration and so on 'by increasing the size of our Magazine, and by making the price one shilling instead of sixpence' (iv). The magazine came to an end in 1844, the price rise making it uneconomic and the competition from so many other similar journals in that precise period no doubt also contributing to its demise.[2]

As Mary Poovey explains in *Making a Social Body*, the meaning of the term *economy* was originally linked exclusively to household management. In the eighteenth century the term came to be linked to *political* and so broadens to include the management of national resources (6). From there, Poovey adds, comes the development of Political Economy as a science responding in part to poverty and which by the 1820s becomes a call for poor-law reform 'demanded on evangelical, economic and political grounds' (10). The *Magazine of Domestic Economy*'s use of the term 'domestic economy' is carefully explained both in the 'Preface' and in the 'Introduction' to Volume One and is framed in opposition to the broader public ramifications embraced in the idea of either form of political economy. The 'Preface' posits this periodical's interpretation of 'domestic economy' as far broader than that of its competitors, claiming it is not simply about the economic spending of money but rather about two key topics: 'the user, and the things used' (iv). It is difficult to determine precisely how this is different, except for the focus on 'the user'. It seems obvious that this term is almost immediately synonymous with 'reader' and 'consumer', both key words within the economy of the periodical press itself.

While *Domestic Economy*'s discussion in both the 'Preface' and the 'Introduction' carefully employs non-gender-specific terms of its target readership, such as 'reader', 'human character', 'inmate', 'user' and 'friend', by the time we get to the 'Introduction' its sharper focus starts to tell a different story. Initially, the author of the 'Introduction' states that economy and its proper practice 'as applied to domestic affairs' will help to regulate 'our social existence' (i). This in turn enables the proprietors and conductors to assert that every topic, no matter how remote, connected to the 'welfare of society' can come within their scope (i). The 'Introduction' then offers a more complex list of topics and issues which future numbers will address, and this list bears an uncanny resemblance to the abundant articles and books of instruction addressed specifically to women. The magazine will thus also address the 'cultivation of the mind'; the 'formation of virtuous principles'; the 'preservation of health'; 'attention to the sick'; the 'restriction of expenses to income'; 'care and education of children' and the 'regulation of time' (i). These are all topics directly connected to the practical administration of home. Without overtly doing so, all of these topics are gendered female and will recur time after time in the mass publishing of conduct books and treatises on women throughout the century, their various messages reiterated and represented in periodical articles, short stories, poems, advice columns and reviews addressed to or written about women.

One of the *Magazine of Domestic Economy*'s first articles, however, 'Household Duties and Operations', is, in abrupt contrast to those prefatory pieces, very gender-specific indeed, even reader-specific because the topic will be important to 'the young housekeeper' and 'necessary for her guidance' (4). She must be the 'faithful steward' of her husband 'in the distribution of the income which it is his duty (as it will also be his pleasure) to provide' (4). It is too easy to take this periodical to task for its gendered assumptions that the young housekeeper will be happily married to a man who understands his duty. The magazine, in providing that parenthetical comment linking 'duty' and 'pleasure', reveals its consciousness of another reader who is implicitly reminded of his role within domestic economy. Brian Maidment argues, in another context, discussing two similar but different title-page vignettes from the *Family Economist* (1848–60) that 'the consolatory ideology of respectability is haunted here by fear of its implacable enemies' ('Domestic Ideology', 46). These 'enemies', as it turns out, are constituted in one contentious figure, the undutiful husband. The conclusion Maidment draws from his reading of the vignettes, we may also draw from our reading of 'Household Duties and Operations', 'that middle-class ideology is more fractured, more conscious of its own repressions and fantasies than might be expected' (46) even when the evidence is as marginal as a figure lurking in a doorway or a throwaway remark in parenthesis.

There is one other article, in volume 1 of the *Magazine of Domestic Economy*, we wish to consider in some detail: 'Woman in Domestic Life'. At the outset this article offers those truisms which will continue to be repeated in any number of periodicals in every decade of the nineteenth century: that woman is the 'most essential member of domestic society'; that the 'treatment which woman receives in society . . . is the best index of the degree of civilisation of that society'; that 'the manner in which woman conducts herself is the *index* of the moral state' of her society and that moral state 'is the foundation of all domestic happiness as well as of all prosperity and greatness, whether public or private' (65); and finally, 'it depends upon woman whether man shall enter upon the duties of life, as man, duly prepared both in capacity and in habits for the performance of them' (67). This range of woman's responsibilities is especially significant given the author's suggestion that woman's domestic actions impinge on the public domain because it is at this point that the argument simultaneously suggests women have a real power in the public domain and yet burdens them with the responsibility for male failure within that domain. The article then goes on to make a very specific claim for the function of the domestic within national life as a kind of patriotic effusion which belongs to the sentimentalising, even mythic discourse, earlier commented on as located most tellingly in Hemans's poem. The author writes:

home is the true place of happiness; that which alone can make compensation for all the troubles, and toils, and struggles, with which men of all classes must meet in public life, and business, and occupation of any description. We also endeavoured to show that England is in a peculiar and especial manner *the land of home* – that no men exert themselves either so strenuously or so successfully to promote the comforts of their homes . . . and therefore no men have such strong claims as Englishmen for a fair and adequate return for these their hearty, incessant, and generally speaking successful labour in promoting the welfare of their homes. This argument is not grounded upon any basis of fictitious sentiment. . . . It is grounded upon that foundation of strict equity and even-handed justice, without the constant observance of which there can be no domestic comfort, and by necessary consequence no national greatness. (66)

Perhaps the most disturbing element in this grand statement is the extent to which it actually *is* grounded upon 'fictitious sentiment', in other words on an ideology which women's economic and political powerlessness makes it impossible for them to realise while at the same time insisting on their responsibility for it. Later the article will insist, glibly, on the 'division of labour' as 'public and professional labour of man' and 'home and domestic labour of woman' (66) without any consciousness of the inherent contradiction in all this, of the implied operation and function of the domestic within the public domain that their own earlier statements have suggested.

In the second part of this article, the author once again insists that 'the happiness of domestic life, and the tone of national character, depend more upon woman than upon all other causes taken together' (129). More interesting still is the extent to which this attitude becomes a fixed ideological position espoused by both women and men, so fixed indeed that even Emily Shirreff, the first Mistress of Girton College, could state in 'College Education for Women' published in the *Contemporary Review* in 1870 that:

wide and honourable as we justly consider the field of social exertion, of profitable industry, of scientific research, greater – aye, and nationally more important – than all these is that responsibility for the welfare of each new generation that God has placed in the hands and bound upon the hearts of women. (66)

What is striking is the surviving connection made between the domestic and the national good. Moreover, it is arguments such as these that contribute to the construction of imperialist dichotomies like 'Home' as opposed to 'Colonial' and the use of a domestic paradigm in the ideological construction of such public domains is an issue addressed in Chapter 5. As George acknowledges, such binarisms are after all necessary because homes and nations 'are defined in the instances of confrontation' (4) and as Anne McClintock argues so convincingly in *Imperial Leather*, 'colonialism took shape around the Victorian invention of domesticity and the idea of the home' (36), to which we would add that this Victorian 'invention' owes its widespread dissemination chiefly to the periodical press.

In the decade following the first number of the *Magazine of Domestic Economy*, other periodicals proliferated. Brian Maidment names *Howitt's Journal*, the *People's Journal*, *Eliza Cook's Journal* and the *Family Economist* among others as seeking to offer 'a cultural, philosophical, literary, and possibly even a political and ideological alliance between progressive elements within bourgeois culture and intellectually ambitious sections of the artisan class' ('Domestic Ideology', 27). But, like the *Magazine of Domestic Economy*, there were other more conservative journals as well, and the one we wish to examine in detail here is the *Home Circle*, in part because it began in the same year as *Eliza Cook's Journal*, in 1849 and had an almost identical run, ceasing publication in 1853, but was different, to some degree, in style and content. It should be noted that such differences would vary considerably in degree and that these two journals also accepted contributions from the same authors; the poet W. C. Bennett and the author Percy B. St. John are just two instances. The *Home Circle* provided illustrations and, at a penny a number, was affordable. The *Home Circle* appears to promote a bourgeois culture that is not progressive but rather intent on preserving a dubious status quo, even a kind of stasis, expressed in the poem titled 'The Home Circle', in the first number, which incites 'Obedience still to / Domestic Controul [sic] –' and advocates of home 'beyond its dear region / Not seeking to roam' (8). However, the periodical also names its contributors who are listed according to sex, women in the first and left-hand column, men in the right.[3] These contributors, according to the 'Address', are chosen as writers 'from whom a purer stream of literature was known to flow' and, rather oddly, as writers 'who have worked long and laboriously at the expense of health and comfort', whose labour is a 'labour of love' (iii). These terms suggest a social mission, and are words used more often to describe the activity of women writers rather than that of men, and imply (without any firmer evidence) that the editing and writing of the *Home Circle* was controlled and managed predominantly by women.

The title page vignette (see Plate 6), produced for the first number of the *Home Circle*, is a complex steel engraving briefly discussed in Chapter 2. The lifestyle suggested by the vignette is a comfortable upper middle class one intimating not only plenty, but a certain luxury as well, and is strictly gendered. On the left-hand side moving downwards in a circular progression you see the advance of a young man from babyhood through to old age; on the right, the progress of a young woman. The young man is university educated, he courts, marries, has a family, works hard at his desk and reaches retirement with his spouse by his side. The young woman in the illustration, rather than university educated, is reading the *Home Circle*. She marries, and then at mid-life is shown presiding at the tea-table resplendent with large urn and good china. The illustration supports a comment Lori Anne Loeb makes in *Consuming Angels*, that by mid-century the perfect wife had been transformed into the perfect lady, with a 'life of leisure punctuated . . . by social occasions rather than family responsibilities' although Loeb goes on to argue that this stereotype actually distorts reality (20–1), just as we would argue the *Home Circle* vignette does. At the centre top of this illustration sit two women. On the left a grandmother dandles the baby who will become the young man; on the right a young mother hears her girl-child's prayer while another more restive toddler sprawls on her knee. Feminine rectitude, discipline and order within the home are the keynotes of the vignette. Nothing threatens this perfect circle. There are no 'natural enemies' within.[4]

At this point it could be assumed that the possibly female editorial team is strictly conventional and conservative. While women have been given some kind of precedence in the 'Contributors' listing, generally the 'Address' and the vignette maintain women strictly within a circumvented domestic space and apparently without agency. However, in the articles themselves this ideology begins to break down and in part this is because the actual readership at which this particular journal is aimed is upper middle class, rather than middle middle, lower middle or artisan. For instance, one of the earliest articles in the first number is titled 'To Fathers. The Duty of Provident Investments' and addresses the 'HUSBANDS AND FATHERS OF ENGLAND' as a specific class who are called upon to observe prudence and economy (9). The article uses very strong language, suggesting that 'improvidence . . . becomes a crime in the head of a family' (9). This insistence on a male duty to exercise and practise the 'principles of economy' (10) relocates responsibility in interesting comparison to the *Magazine of Domestic Economy*. No longer a parenthetical hint, the declaration of ultimate responsibility for the family's financial wellbeing is spelled out in capital letters.

The family's moral wellbeing remains the responsibility of women. In 'Woman: her Position and Influence', however, this basic ideology seems to take on a level of female political agency that is unusual. The article is set within a specific political time-frame, 'this lurid period of revolutionary passion' (56),[5] and maintains its focus throughout on woman as sole agent, in comparison to 'Woman in Domestic Life' who can only act through male agency. The *Home Circle* article specifically and unusually addresses women of all classes. The author claims that the home influence of English women has prevented 'bloody revolution in England', an influence 'produced by our *domestic*, and not by our *political* attachments' (56). The word 'domestic' is carefully separated from 'political' yet this article recognises female activity and the domestic domain as conforming to a science of government that today can now indeed be termed 'political' but in the nineteenth century can only be described as a 'peculiar kind of power', as the phrase is used in the following statement:

Woman, when she fairly takes the *peculiar kind of power* which she possesses – and possesses only, in the British Isles – when she sheds as she does in them, patience and endurance over the whole character of the people – when she is Mother, Helpmate, and Wife – when she thinks, and loves, and toils, and profits, for the good of the wide family – she sobers down the tone of society – she invests it with self-respect – she gives it stability, and disarms it of intemperance – and so is the creator of qualities which keep men upon their balance, and preserve them steady. (56; emphasis added)

This statement fails to limit female power to the individual household, rather the household *is* the state, 'the British Isles', *is* 'society' as a whole, and woman has both moral and religious power 'over the will of the nation' (56). The verbs are politically active – 'possesses', 'sobers', 'invests', 'disarms' – and all of them are connected to the pronoun 'she'.

In 'Magazines of Popular Progress and the Artisans', Brian Maidment, with reference to determining an implied reader and, in turn, a journal's generic affinity, concludes that some periodicals 'exist as forms of social discourse rather than as direct statements of social opinion' (85). He adds that there is a major difference between these two ideas and this becomes apparent in the *Home Circle* article because the analysis of tone, opinion and rhetoric, to use his terms, complicates the discourse significantly. To begin with, the article is dominated by the journalistic 'we', but the use of 'we' shifts focus. At one moment it is used as if speaking for the reader: for example, 'We have congratulated ourselves in England upon the moral abstinence of our own community' (56). At the next moment it is used on behalf of the journal: 'and now we are prepared to enunciate a belief that the Home Influences of English women have had more control over these commanding results' (56). However, at a crucial moment in the article, 'we' is abandoned altogether and replaced with a direct address to 'you':

You must infringe liberties, stir revenges, abolish socialities, and even break hearts, before you can get the Women of England to sanction strong rebellion. (56)

The 'you' addressed here is another reader altogether, separated from 'we' and 'us'. This reader is outside the group, a lone individual, a misanthrope, potential revolutionary and destroyer of British homes, isolated, but hopefully overwhelmed by the domestic defence constructed against him, a pronoun used advisedly because the article has banded all the women of England together regardless of class, from Queen Victoria to 'lower life', a group organised on nationalistic grounds only, but given surely at this rhetorical moment a political power based solely on the word 'home'. At the end of the article, the third person plural 'they' is used to misquote a truism, a cliché which the journal then overturns to produce what is finally a direct statement of social opinion:

They say that in England "every man's house is his castle" – but most surely every "woman's castle is her H O M E;" and we have the strongest faith in the direct influence of that fact upon the destinies of our country. (56)

The final article selected for consideration from the *Home Circle* is very different again. Published in 1849, this article is unequivocally a direct statement of social opinion. And it addresses indirectly the proposition that every woman's castle is her home. The article is signed 'Mrs. White', an excellent example of a journalist whose articles consistently appeared under her own name. Probably Caroline Alice White, she also contributed similarly styled pieces to other journals. There are two groups of (possible) readers White might be addressing. The first group, with whom she identifies, and which presumably constitutes the majority of her readers, is an upper middle class one for whom her article can be only self-congratulatory. Her position is one of surveillance. The second group, who is most commonly referred to by White as 'they', is of the artisan or working class, and is being rebuked. This second group is constructed as inferior, as 'other'. Sara Mills, in her article 'Gender and Colonial Space', argues that this term has become a 'rather abstract binary opposition' when used of racialization (126) but it nevertheless conveys succinctly the social and spatial divides that White's journal article so tellingly provides to the first superior level of readers whose mission, like that of any coloniser, is a civilising one and who obtain, in the article, as Mary Louise Pratt puts it in another context in 'Conventions of Representation', a 'relation of dominance' that is set up between 'seer and seen' (24–5). The second group is written up as 'actually in need of intervention from the outside' to use Pratt's terms again (25). White's article is titled 'A View of the Dwellings of the Working Classes, Taken from a Back Window'.

Victorian explorers aestheticise what they see, implicitly controlling unknown territory with their words, as a painting is controlled by its genre, its mode, for instance, the 'picturesque', and by its frame. This kind of aestheticisation, Pratt argues, gives 'social value' to an explorer's discoveries and where there is 'aesthetic deficiency' ('Conventions of Representation', 25) this can be used to suggest the dominance of superior over inferior. The metaphor of the painting allows what is seen to be framed, managed, controlled and rendered non-threatening. The relation between seer and seen in White's article uses the same kind of metaphor and while the issue is class rather than race, the outcomes, dominance and control, are the same. Rather than landscape, White is constructing domestic interiors, like those of the seventeenth-century Flemish or Dutch schools, sometimes termed 'naturalist', which writers like George Eliot were soon to invoke as part of their own realist aesthetic.

George Eliot's introductory pages to her review of cultural historian Wilhelm Riehl's *Die bürgerliche Gesellschaft* (1851) and *Land und Leute* (1853), 'The Natural History of German Life', are interesting to read alongside White's article. Eliot is critical of writing which fails to obliterate 'the vulgarity of exclusiveness'; which perverts sympathy for 'the life of our more heavily-laden fellow-men' (54); which teaches people to feel only for heroic artisans and sentimental peasants, rather than 'for the peasant in all his coarse apathy, and the artisan in all his suspicious selfishness' (55); and Eliot dismisses the 'tendency created by the splendid conquests of modern generalisation, to believe that all the social questions are merged in economical science' (55). Eliot is attempting to combat the idea of the stereotype, the peasant or artisan of cliché. As she notes, some images are 'habitually associated with abstract or collective terms' (51) when what she demands is 'concrete knowledge' or 'real characteristics' (52). And while Eliot probably never read White's piece, the lack of 'concrete knowledge' is precisely the problem with it, that White's idea of 'home' is as clichéd as those 'idyllic ploughmen', 'idyllic shepherds' and 'idyllic villagers' of which Eliot is so contemptuous; home has indeed been 'abandoned to its clichés' (George, *Politics of Home*, 3).

The windows in the buildings opposite to White's lodgings are viewed from an upper-storey bedroom and represent a series of individual 'homes'. Their condition reflects the condition of the people who live behind the panes, one casement she describes thus:

some [panes] are starred and *held* together with a daub of putty, like a piece of sticking-plaister [sic] some are full of seams and patches, and scarred like a drunkard's face; two are wholly out, and look as if it had two black eyes. There is a reckless, repulsive air about it, as conclusive of the owner's character as the oaths, and violence and frequent crashes that every few days alarm the neighbourhood. (White, 'View of the Dwellings', 217)

White's elevated position metaphorically represents both her social and her moral position and at the same time practically offers her an enabling vantage point from which to spy into and describe the individual homes presented to her view. The word 'view' which she uses in her title helps to suggest a certain detachment, as if a proscenium arch separates her from what she sees and possibly accounts for the degree of objectivity within her discourse.

Each window both frames, but its condition also predicates, what is seen, and thus White manages her discourse as a form of social realism that is spurious because she condemns what she sees in its failure to conform to a particular domestic standard. Indeed White directly connects 'morals and repair' (217), yet only late in the article does she admit that the external disrepair of the buildings might possibly be the responsibility of the landlords rather than the tenants (218).[6] And although White admits that the immediate area 'is locally what is called a quiet street and respectable neighbourhood' (217), which no doubt helps to explain her own presence in lodgings in that vicinity, yet she reveals that the area is used commercially because the various buildings overlook:

a stone-cutter's yard, with its smoke-grimed figures of mythological men and women, its funeral urns and mural monuments – its ceaseless movement of saw and chisel – and busy groups of dusty workmen, many of whom we have traced home through the passages, up the stairs, and across the lobbies of the tall, dingy, dirt-incrusted houses opposite. (217)

The dirt and grit from a stone-cutter's business would surely make any housewifery an almost impossible chore. She also later admits that there is some excuse for the appearance of 'the wretched homes and housewives' (218) because any water has to be carried up innumerable flights of stairs and all brought down again. The lodgings which White subjects to her gaze are clearly overcrowded with up to seven people to a room: '[e]ach separate cell of those brick and mortar hives swarm with inhabitants' (217). Yet she determines that 'there is an equality of degradation about this colony of needy toil, admitting only of the degrees of comparison, – bad, worse, worst' (217).

White's degrees of comparison are also applied roundly, and without compassion, to the women who live here: 'Close at hand sits Sloth, in a woman's form, sunning herself at a window . . . there is an abandonment of idleness about her, from her slip-shoes to her half-put-on cap and open gown – a soft, lymphatic laziness' (217). Of another household she writes that light 'is a great reformer of untidiness; it writes slut on dusty chairs and tables' (218). Another woman whose time 'seems wholly occupied in mending, washing, and cutting bread-and-butter . . . has . . . industry, but no method' (217). While Eliot argues in her article that all the social questions cannot be resolved with economical science, White states firmly:

It is a painful thought, that much, very much of the moral and physical pollution existing in the dwellings of the poor rests with women. Want of cleanliness and thrift are greater enemies to the well-being of a household than even the want of room and convenience. (218)

There is, however, one shining window that is an exception. White's gaze is so penetrating she can even see that the towel the young housewife gives her husband to wipe his brow 'if not smelling of lavender . . . is whole and clean' (219). Though they live high up in an attic room, their window 'has bright panes' (217) – all the better for Mrs White to gaze in – a 'white sun-blind, and a hanging garden of flower-pots upon the parapet' (217). This paragon is 'the only housewife, too, of the community whom we have seen methodically of an afternoon bring her little basket to the casement, and sit down to work' (219). The stereotype thus presented is then carefully re-framed within the window with a more elaborate rhetoric as 'the little shining one upon the roof with its musk and mignionette [sic], sun-blind, and singing lark, and the green curled tendrils and bright flowers of convolvulus framing it' (219). George Eliot's article, on the other hand, suggests that such idealised pictures are 'noxious', because they encourage 'the miserable fallacy that high morality and refined sentiment can grow out of harsh social relations, ignorance, and want' (55).

These two articles by Caroline White and George Eliot, so opposed, so diverse, demonstrate the broad range of thinking at mid-century on social questions. As Sheila Rosenberg summarises it in 'The "wicked *Westminster*": John Chapman, His Contributors and Promises Fulfilled', the *Westminster* challenged 'orthodox views on Church and society' and was committed to 'free and fearless inquiry' (244), and as Laurel Brake makes clear in 'The *Westminster* and Gender at Mid-Century', it 'regularly scrutinised' questions of gender (248). Between 1855 and 1857, writes Brake, the *Westminster* treated gender 'as a calculated part of its radical campaign, with gender arising in a range of settings – literature, divorce, property, fashion, education' (254). All of these 'settings' belong to the politics of home.

The *Home Circle*, as its title so readily suggests, seems committed to preserving the status quo but its contributors were probably far less subject to a specific editorial stance than were contributors to the *Westminster*. The articles which appear in it, as we have shown, may be read at various political levels. All of them consider the politics of home life and all of them, despite appearances to the contrary, are aimed at social improvement, and at change, even if the polemic is a muted one. The intrusiveness of Caroline White's penetrating gaze is no different to that of Henry Mayhew's, whose *London Labour and the London Poor* was serialised in the *Morning Chronicle* (1851–2), and which, like White's article, might be equated with the idea of spectacle despite its reform agenda. Both could be said to be operating on Stead's premise that it is sensationalist journalism which gets results.

II

The titles of two journals, the *Home Circle*, and the *Home and Foreign Review*, suggest quite simply the differences implied in the word 'Home' as analysed in this chapter. The former addresses the ideologically framed private domain in which domestic government is a microcosm exemplified by the functional (or dysfunctional) household. The latter title, and others like it, address the ideological public domain in which political issues associated with English government, that is domestic government on a national scale, are opposed and compared to both European (Foreign) and colonial politics. The 'Prospectus' for the *British and Foreign Review*, for instance, states in 1835:

It is commonly said, that charity begins at home. Might we not add, that it too frequently ends there? With nations and individuals, domestic interests are apt to absorb those affections, the influence of which might be extended beneficially, without injury to the rights of those who from nature have the first claim upon them. . . . Selfishness, condemned in individuals, has been considered the privilege of communities; restrictions upon commerce have been thought the most effectual means of acquiring national wealth; and free institutions at home have been held to be best protected by crushing every germ of liberty abroad.

Indifference to the condition of every nation but their own, has been the peculiar reproach of Englishmen. (1)

However, the politics of home is played out in the *public* domain through a set of interconnected journals which have their own fraught history, the *People's Journal* (1846–8); *Howitt's Journal of Literature and Popular Progress* (1847–8); and the *People's and Howitt's Journal* (1849–51). The connection is the husband-and-wife writing and editorial team, Mary and William Howitt. The contrast between, say, quarterlies like the *Edinburgh Review* and monthlies like *Howitt's Journal* is an extreme one. The former so enduring, so very mainstream, the latter far more typical of the ephemeral nature of the periodical press at mid-century. *Howitt's*, like so many new periodicals, was desperate to build up a permanent and loyal readership while maintaining its political, social and religious principles. The choice of publishing moment could not have been more inauspicious, for similar kinds of periodicals by similar writers were flooding onto the newly literate market. By mid-century too, publishers were seeking popular 'names' to write for new periodicals. The *Home Circle*, as already indicated, offered a parade of well-known middle-stream literary names and its practice was similar to that of any number of other comparable titles.

Brian Maidment characterises journals like those with which the Howitts were involved as revealing 'possibly even a political and ideological alliance between progressive elements within bourgeois culture and intellectually ambitious sections of the artisan class' ('Domestic Ideology', 27). It is this political alliance which we wish to examine as it is manifested in the various articles, leaders, tales and poems which made up each number. These three journals, particularly the first two, which are dominated by contributions from the Howitts, belong to a very specific genre which Maidment labels 'popular progress'. He also notes elsewhere an 'impressive internationalism' located in both the numerous translations and the descriptions of 'continental social movements or ideas' the Howitts offered their readers ('Magazines of Popular Progress', 91–2).

The Howitts were jobbing journalists eking out a living as best they could, more often in debt than otherwise. Mary Howitt's weekly letters to her sister Anna Harrison over many years record long hours spent writing in a desperate attempt to keep themselves solvent. Nevertheless she was excited by the age in which she lived, and clearly immersed in the political issues of the day, writing to her sister in the winter of 1846:

Let nobody say that the age is not advancing in wisdom. . . . with the abolition of the Corn Laws will come free trade and that will do every thing for dear old England. . . . it is a glorious privilege to be living at this time for we shall live to see great and good things even beyond our most sanguine wishes, brought about if we are only favoured to live to the ordinary span of mortals. (Ms Ht/1/1/180/1&2)

The bourgeois position of the Howitts is manifest in this letter when Mary Howitt uses an expression like 'dear old England' and regards the age in such positive terms. Like Robert Chambers and William Tait, the Howitts envisioned a more egalitarian society, with equal opportunity for education, with shorter working hours, with greater 'mental cultivation' and 'domestic enjoyment' ('Address', 2). They greatly admired the independence of the American states; and they believed the French revolution to be a warning to government of the consequences of oppression and the neglect of education (2). They saw the periodical press as the natural vehicle for the propagation of their reforms agenda.

Probably late in 1845 the Howitts became involved both financially and intellectually with a new periodical called the *People's Journal*, edited by John Saunders, and embracing many of their own political ideals. The first number appeared in January 1846. Mary Howitt is very conscious of a readership in writing for the *People's Journal* at which the journal is aimed. She evinces a rather idealised even romantic sense of 'the People' and to what extent they become an actual readership is difficult to determine. She tells her sister she plans to 'write to Thomas Hodgson of the Mechanics Institute about it' and adds:

The People are to me intensely interesting – nothing would please me so much as to be esteemed and admired by them – I care not half as much for the rich and great as I do for the intelligent of the working classes. In a while I hope we shall live to see it – they will be very differently situated morally and intellectually than they are now and I will with heart and hand help on the good and great work of their advance. (Ms Ht/1/1/184)

Late in 1846 the Howitts and Saunders had a major falling out over money, the rights and wrongs of which it is difficult to determine at this distance. They believed he had failed to keep proper accounts and had mismanaged the journal (Ms Ht/1/1/181). They determined to start their own journal in opposition to John Saunders and the *People's Journal*. Called *Howitt's Journal*, the first number appeared in January 1847, with identical letterpress style to the *People's Journal*, identical political and social position, and an identical range of items including essays, poetry, short stories and woodcut illustrations. At the same time as their first numbers were appearing, the residue of their contributions to the *People's Journal* were still being published. Eventually the highly public dispute was resolved in Saunders's favour and the two journals were amalgamated under the combined titles. Notably, although bearing their name, there is no contribution by the Howitts to the *People's and Howitt's Journal*.

By 1847, the year in which *Howitt's Journal* first appeared, the Howitt name already carried a certain cachet. Their earliest publications were collaborations on volumes of poetry which they published in 1823 and 1827.[7] Subsequently Mary published short moral tales for children while William produced popular titles such as *The Book of the Seasons, or, the Calendar of Nature* (1831), praised by the *Athenaeum* in 'Book of the Seasons' as 'a book that cannot fail to raise the author's reputation as a literary man' (147). However, the reviewer goes on to admonish both Mary and William (despite the review being of a book by William alone) for displaying a 'too evident leaning to foreign literature' (147), revealing both the extent to which the couple were considered a team, and a conservative nationalism.

In their *Journal*, the combined signature of the Howitts sits over their editorial comments, but their individual names are signed to the short pieces, columns, poetry and so on. Similarly, many of the articles, stories and poems they accepted or commissioned also appear under each individual author's name. This suggests that many minor, more radical, and more short-lived journals depended on a 'star' system to encourage consumers long before this became common practice in the more mainstream journals. Perhaps too a journal's politics, its political frame, eschewed anonymity as a paternalistic mode operating against the 'good' of its readership. It is difficult to determine to what extent they wrote together for *Howitt's Journal* – that is, collaborated on each other's journalism – but Mary Howitt's correspondence suggests that when pushed for time they worked on each other's projects and consulted with each other. The collaborative nature of their work, however, never produced the kind of homogenised style so apparent in the *Edinburgh*.

Despite their literary partnership, gender, as the 'Contents' list shows, does seem to dictate, to some extent, the subject matter upon which they wrote for both their own and other periodicals. In their own journal, William still handled the more specifically political matter, while Mary ran the column for children and produced her short moral tales. Moreover, this division of labour was clearly signalled. 'The Child's Corner. Seasonable Tales for Children' carried Mary's name, while the series 'Facts from the Field – Game Law Tactics' carried William's. Nevertheless, in these more radical, less mainstream journals, gender is not the rigid divide epitomised by say the *Edinburgh Review*, rather it is a more flexible, less arbitrary factor. Female contributors to both *Howitt's Journal* and the earlier *People's Journal* often produced social and political essays, while male contributors wrote on flowers or offered children's tales and sentimental poetry without self-consciousness. Mary Leman Gillies published 'Associated Homes for the Middle Classes' in *Howitt's* and 'Antagonism of the Classes' in *People's*, Samuel Smiles published a biographical piece on George Sand for *Howitt's*, and Richard Horne addressed sentimental lines of poetry to Mary Howitt herself.[8]

Mary Howitt's correspondence indicates that *Howitt's Journal* was run from home and by the 1840s the family had a very established routine although it appears that William was always given precedence. When they move in 1847 to St John's Wood, Mary Howitt writes that 'we are beginning to fall into our usual places of work. William is in his little library' (Ms Ht/1/1/196). At some stage in the 1840s she writes in far greater detail of the difficulties in working from home at a point when conditions have clearly improved as far as she personally is concerned:

the thing I think which pleases me most is the circumstance of my being able to have there a little room to myself – a sort of little boudoir which if money was no object we could make very lovely but as it is, we shall manage as well as we can and where I shall be able to sit by myself and write and read in perfect seclusion. . . . It is good for all – say nothing of the necessity there is for a literary person to have their own sanctum. As yet I have written sometimes in one room, sometimes in another, but mostly in my own bed-room or the drawing-room, but neither of these are equal to having a little spot of one's own. (Ms Ht/1/1/356)

In 'Mother–Daughter Productions: Mary Howitt and Anna Mary Howitt in *Howitt's Journal*, *Household Words*, and Other Mid-Victorian Publications', Linda H. Peterson demonstrates that William and Mary offered a collaborative model of professional authorship (31). Peterson goes on to argue that Mary Howitt's letters express a 'sense of the site of authorship as the home' (32), and extending this, that 'Mary Howitt conceptualized her literary work as an extension of her familial role' (35). Howitt actually kept a record of the daily activities of her two youngest children which she published as *The Children's Year* (1847), claiming in the preface 'everything which it contains is strictly true' (quoted in Peterson, 'Mother–Daughter, Productions', 35). If, as Peterson suggests, Mary Howitt envisioned within her own household 'a family of writers, artists, translators and editors' (36), there were nonetheless two other 'families', two potential readerships, one middle class, the other working class, who were to be encouraged to consume their productions, to learn from them, and to develop a more egalitarian society as a consequence. The idea of the domestic, then, as a powerful political tool is epitomised in the Howitts's actual approach to periodical publication, even if that approach is class driven and a paternalistic/maternalistic model common in the period.

Consciously or subconsciously, the Howitts approached their readership in precisely this way, as experienced, observant parents offering 'home' truths, as their opening editorial or 'Address' in the first number of *Howitt's Journal* indicates. They declare that they are 'bound to no class, for we believe that in the cultivation of the whole, lies the harmony and the happiness of the whole' (1), but their style denies this at the outset. One strand of their potential readership is referred to consistently in the third person as 'the million', an amorphous, unindividuated mass, for whom the Howitts will labour to 'promote their education . . . to advocate their just rights, to explain their genuine duties' (1). Their key audience, to whom they use the more inclusive terms 'we' and 'us' and 'our', is a separate readership of like-minded people who have nevertheless to be educated into 'the recognition of those great rights which belong to every individual of the great British people' (1–2). While the Howitts are no radicals (rather they vehemently oppose advocating claims for one sector of the community at the expense of another) nevertheless their focus is very different from other similar journals, the *Home Circle* for instance. They believe in an ideal egalitarian future and in progress, and to this end their writing seeks to instruct their middle-class readership that the 'path of liberty and knowledge is the sure path of peace and general union' (2), rather than merely to amuse them.

Moreover, their contributors to the journal are styled 'workmen' who 'will soon, in the words of the old adage, be "known by their chips" ' (2) and it is perhaps this sense of themselves as fellow-labourers that gives a different inflection, even complicates, what might too easily be dismissed as yet another middle-class couple writing down to one level of a possible readership which may or may not even be purchasing their journal. Their perception of themselves as part of a fellowship of labour did not begin here. In 'Letters on Labour to the Working Men of England' published in the *People's Journal*, William Howitt recognises 'the workers of this country, men, women, and children' and exhorts 'working men, and working women of England' to reflect (210). His inclusion of women reveals his consciousness of female participation in the workforce.

The role of truthful parents is conflated with their role as journalists, and this emerges in the most seriously political segment of *Howitt's Journal*, a separately paginated column titled 'The Weekly Record of Facts and Opinions connected with General Interests and Popular Progress', which appeared at the back of each number of *Howitt's*, and was based very precisely on 'Annals of Industry' at the back of the numbers of the *People's Journal*. The Howitts, in the prefatory statement heading up the 'Weekly Record', declare that it is the intention of the editors to 'state candidly' their opinions 'on any matter of importance' and to 'form and guide public opinion, as every honest journalist should do' (1). This prefatory statement also attempts to break down class and gender divides by affirming that they solicit opinions of all 'be they rich or poor, be they masters or men, be they men or women' (1).

There is an implication in this opening statement that what the Howitts offer in 'The Weekly Record' is 'honest', an honesty equated with the idea of righteous parents, even though combining fact and opinion in this way seems discursively at odds with the usual separation of the two. Yet as Roger Fowler argues in his analysis of modern newspapers, leaders and editorials have an 'important symbolic function, seeming to partition off the "opinion" component of the paper, implicitly supporting the claim that other sections, by contrast, are pure "fact" or "report" '. Fowler goes on to point out that any discourse 'is always representation from a certain point of view' (208). The essay which follows the prefatory statement affirms that for the Howitts the 'Weekly Record' of *Howitt's Journal* 'will prove to be, perhaps the most important portion of it' (1). The Howitts's political point of view is informed in part by their Quaker background and their belief in progress, in what they term the 'great public virtues'. These include 'Peace, Temperance; the Extension of Schools and Libraries; the Early Closing of Shops; the Abolition of Slavery; the Elevation of Women' (1). But equally it is obvious from this list that their politics are domestic indeed and heavily inflected by both gender and class.

Indeed in January 1847 they celebrate as 'grand' the fact that in recent times two British prime ministers, outgoing and incoming, no longer focus exclusively on 'war and taxation'. This is opinion. They then report as a fact worthy of praise that the outgoing conservative prime minister has declared that 'Public Opinion is the ruler of England' and that the incoming prime minister, advocate of moderate reform, has declared that the British legislature will be confronted with three paramount questions: 'Ireland, National Education, and Sanatory [sic] Reform' (1). For the Howitts, this is a new dawning in the political world, where domestic issues take precedence, and for them the domestic moral exemplum, *love thy neighbour as thyself*, is now the reigning precept of social philosophy and a developing part of a national identity in which all can be 'zealous pioneers' (1).

By way of contrast, in February 1847 *Fraser's Magazine* published 'What are we to Expect?' expressing distrust of the Whig government and analysing the 'state and prospects of the empire' (244). While this broad vision narrows to focus on the very issues of the day as set out by the Howitts, in particular, Ireland and national education, the tone of the article is that of men speaking to men, more specifically of Tory speaking to Tory: 'readers will, doubtless, gather . . . that of the Whigs and of their principles we are as distrustful as we ever were' (252). The Howitts write of the crisis in Ireland that it 'is not now the time to go into the entire causes of this state of distress both in Ireland and the Highlands; the first and imperative thing is to relieve it' (2). Likewise, the author of 'What are we to Expect?' concludes that when 'people are dying of hunger, it is as cruel as it is useless to waste time in arguing about the best mode of supplying them with bread. Feed them first, and legislate on the subject of their permanent interests afterwards' (245). On the further remedies and modifications, however, the two journals diverge markedly. The Howitts urge that in Ireland there 'is something wrong in the tenure of land, in the treatment of the population by the landholders, which will want investigating' to determine on a 'lasting remedy', whereas *Fraser's*, while agreeing that 'care must be taken to provide against the recurrence of the calamity under which Ireland now suffers' (246) protests against the idea that landowners should be responsible for the people on their estates, because such support will reduce patrimony, and resorts to the usual stereotype of the idle Irishman – 'Pat is not the boy to oppress himself with hard work, if he can help it' (246) – to support a flimsy argument.

In 'English Journalism', which had appeared just two months previously, *Fraser's* had argued 'the necessity of giving to journalists a recognised position in the social and political scale' to prevent 'less distinguished writers' from giving 'a tone, and a colour, and a direction to the thoughts, passions, and creeds of many thousands amongst the partially educated and the easily influenced of our countrymen' (633). Doubtless the Howitts could be included in such a description. *Fraser's* commonplace expressions of fear about the working classes, who may rise up 'when want and stagnation darken the homesteads of our wealth' (633) throws into relief the positive approach of the Howitts who conversely, and in precisely the same time-frame, celebrate a new dawn and a metaphorical new world of 'zealous pioneers' (1). In resorting to such metaphorical language the Howitts designate England itself as so much territory to be recolonised and redomesticated, and its people to be brought out of a state of alienation back to this 'new land, the *Terra Incognita*, after which all ages and sages, all prophets and poets, have sighed' (1).

CHAPTER FIVE

Gender and cultural imperialism

In 1886 W. T. Stead in his critique of journalism for the *Contemporary Review* argues that the political power of the press is obvious and contributes in no small measure to the shape of the country. In 'The Future of Journalism' he claims:

Where there is the combination of the two elements, the distinct personality of a competent editor and the varied interests and influences of an ably conducted paper, it is not difficult to see that such an editor might, if he wished it, become far the most permanently influential Englishman in the Empire. (664)

Daniel Bivona has remarked in *Desire and Contradiction. Imperial Visions and Domestic Debates in Victorian Literature* that the question of empire influenced British culture enormously in the nineteenth, and in the early part of the twentieth centuries (viii). While agreeing with Bivona, we will argue in this chapter that the 'question of empire', like the 'woman question', with regard to both Mother country and Infant colonies, was contested, formulated, and framed within the pages of the periodical press, more often than not in precisely those gendered terms indicated by 'Mother' country.

It is due to this ongoing ideological debate over empire that its influence on British culture has been of such significance, a significance which probably resonated throughout much of the twentieth century as well. The flow-on effect on a sense of British nationalism, most commonly referred to in current scholarship as 'Englishness', and the effect on other nationalisms of colonisers and colonised, has been well critiqued but we will, nevertheless, be addressing this as a part of examining the role of the periodical press in disseminating what we broadly term 'Cultural Imperialism', even though, as Patrick Brantlinger has shown in *Rule of Darkness: British Literature and Imperialism, 1830–1914*, the word 'imperialism' itself was not much used before the 1870s (20–3).[1]

Thus the category of our title, 'cultural imperialism' will, for our purposes, embrace imperialism, orientalism and colonialism as being implied by that rubric and in this discussion the focus will be on the category as it is intersected by gender and gendered assumptions. These three terms are inevitably gendered terms anyway. The word 'imperialism' itself is almost always gendered male. Where women are sometimes complicit in supporting a male order, nevertheless they 'negotiate meanings within the context of dominant discursive fields' where the discourses 'are themselves challenged and reaffirmed by representations produced by both women and men' as Sara Mills argues in 'Gender and Colonial Space' (142).

The term 'orientalism' is subjectively female, especially because of the way in which its meaning is inscribed more consistently on female bodies, but also because the orientalist gaze subsumes the male object of the gaze into a feminised category of child-like passivity and helplessness. Reina Lewis in *Gendering Orientalism*, suggests that orientalism is characterised by the 'irrational, exotic, erotic, despotic and heathen' in contrast to an ideological European position, held by both men and women, that is the polar opposite to those terms (16).

Our final term, 'colonialism', on the other hand, is consistently formulated within the context of gendered middle-class domesticity and is, for this reason, the word most particularly explored by the press in the Victorian age, producing 'Mother' country and 'Infant' colonies which, in the fullness of time, will become 'Home' and 'sons of the empire'. It is for this reason that we read these two ideologies, home and empire, as the most significant in examining the practice of the Victorian periodical press, in which the myths of national identity and the idealised concept of home predominate as ideas to be formulated and propagated.

In 1830 William Maginn in 'Our "Confession of Faith" ' expresses similar sentiments: 'the policy of England should be insular, as she is an island, and colonial, as she is the queen of colonies, the nursing mother of empires' (7). This might almost be read as a blueprint for the future domestic reign of the young Princess Victoria. Maginn, in the same prefatory essay, boasts of English victories in Europe, of 'our own . . . inherited valour', and proclaims 'we have obtained that truest safeguard of national independence – the perfect certainty, on the part of our enemies, that any attempt to insult us is such an experiment as "drawing a tooth from an angry lion" ' (6). Such claims became commonplace.

Maginn voices here what Iain Chambers in 'Narratives of Nationalism. Being "British" ' has subsequently described as a 'tranquilizing image in which modern "Britishness" invariably stands in for the quiet authority and organic continuity of an English conservatism; a conservatism that is not simply political but also, and quite significantly, cultural in its effect'

(146). This 'quiet authority' can be located by implication, again in *Fraser's*, in Goldwin Smith's article 'Imperialism' (1857), in which he analyses imperialism as a philosophy. Dismissing the Roman Empire as 'a world of oppressed and plundered provinces, without a moral faith and without a God, sank down beneath a sensualist despotism' (498), and the French Empire, because it sprang 'from the corruption, not from the perfection, of society' (499), Smith writes in conclusion that empires such as these would be 'an anachronism, a monster, and a crime', something that every 'sensible, virtuous, and religious Englishman instinctively feels' (506). While he never mentions a British Empire, it is there nevertheless by implication in offering his models of failed imperialism. J. Castell Hopkins in 'Mr. Goldwin Smith' published in the *Westminster Review* in 1894 makes the connection directly, taking Smith to task for his pessimism: 'To him the Imperial position of England is a mistake, and the disruption of the Empire inevitable' (540). The forty-year gap reveals the manner in which the press could openly critique empire during its formative years, only to defend it late in the century when anxiety about its pre-eminence was at its height.

In locating Benjamin Disraeli's literary works of the 1840s as a starting point for *Desire and Contradiction*, Daniel Bivona cites him as a chief author 'of a nineteenth-century imperialist ideology tailored to appeal to the middle classes' (ix, 2). However, 'chief authors' are not the issue, rather it is the multiplicity of challenging voices, intersected by class and gender, which contributes to the formation and promulgation of an imperialist ideology. That ideology has its greatest impact at the moments (and these are various) in which it becomes domesticated. Connections between imperialism and the domestic were being made throughout the century. Frederic Harrison's essay, 'The Regrets of a Veteran Traveller', shows how imperialist ideology has become entrenched late in the century even while the expression of it acknowledges later modes and formulations in cultural imperialism. Harrison shifts from the language of high adventure (*Boy's Own* adventure) to the domestically mundane in one sentence, from 'peak and pass' to 'tea and tubs':

Morally, we Britons plant the British flag on every peak and pass; and wherever the Union Jack floats there we place the cardinal British institutions – tea, tubs, sanitary appliances, lawn tennis, and churches. (241)[2]

Harrison's summation is both individual and the result of an almost century-long process to which the articles, reviews, poems, short stories, serials, pithy paragraphs, editorials and illustrations of an infinite range of periodicals have all contributed. Indeed the extant material is so abundant that in addressing these issues we cannot, of necessity, access more than a bare representation of it. To this end we will, in this chapter, consider not only the content of periodical press items associated with the imperialist project but also the form they took, to demonstrate that because of its various shifting shapes, the message was, for this reason, so effectively disseminated across the Victorian age.

One simple example is this passage from Margaret Oliphant's 1858 article 'The Condition of Women' for *Blackwood's Edinburgh Magazine* in which one might not expect the issue of cultural imperialism to arise at all. Oliphant here argues against any special case for middle-class women's employment opportunities, citing what she terms that 'imaginary line of demarcation between men and women' and claiming that class affects the employment choices of both sexes, the educated class caught between 'the assured rich and the certain poor' who must be 'banished to the antipodes' (143). The argument that women have no special case to make is painfully familiar even today and ignores the fact that invariably in Oliphant's time, and well beyond, women's education was not equivalent to that of men. Oliphant, in making a case for men, adds:

In this vast London, which is the centre and focus of our extremity of civilisation, there are crowds of young men, trained to that pitch of bodily perfection and development which English public schools and universities, without doubt, keep up to a higher degree than any other educational institutions in the world – . . . who nevertheless, are as entirely at sea as to the best method of employing themselves and their faculties, as any woman with a feminine education equivalent to theirs could possibly find herself. Teaching, literature, art, which they have practised as amateurs to the admiration of their own families – or, last alternative of all, Australia or a curacy, lie before them, which to choose. (143–4)

Emigration, for Oliphant at least, appears to be a last desperate measure (for men) and yet just a page further on she asks whether emigration (for women) might not be the best expedient after all, and promotes Australia as 'the wealthy shores of our great young colony' (145). Rita Kranidis contends in *The Victorian Spinster and Colonial Emigration. Contested Subjects* that the emigration of Victorian women 'was comprised of a series of events that potentially can reveal the specifics of gender's relation to nation and empire' (1) and we argue that this series of events is nowhere more fully located, argued, debated and contested than within the pages of the periodical press.

Australia's beginning as a dumping ground for Britain's excess criminal population comes to be considered, along with other colonies, as a viable proposition for disposing of a supposed excess female population, most famously advocated by W. R. Greg in his article 'Why are Women Redundant?' for the *National Review* in 1862: 'of the 440,000 women who should emigrate, the larger number are wanted for the longer voyage to Australia' (444). Greg's position is contested fiercely by Frances Power Cobbe in 'What Shall we do with Our Old Maids?' She remarks, tongue in cheek, that she is not surprised 'to find the article in question quoted as the soundest commonsense' (595) and then brings together the two issues of surplus women and criminal transportation in a tellingly comic analysis:

> Their offence is on the increase, like poaching in country districts and landlord shooting in Ireland. The mildest punishment, we are told, is to be transportation, to which half a million have just been condemned, and for the terror of future evil doers, it is decreed that no single woman's work ought to be fairly remunerated, nor her position allowed to be entirely respectable, lest she exercise 'a cold philosophic choice' about matrimony. No false charity to criminals! Transportation or starvation to all old maids! (599)

This chapter will also in part focus on what England meant to the English[3] in terms of gendered cultural representation, as purveyed and staged by the periodical press. It will also address the transportation of such national identity to a particular colonial destination, and the way in which the periodical press contributed to the development of colonial identity. The colonial destination upon which we have decided to focus is Australia, a topic to which we will return later in this chapter.

I

Imperialism is tied to a sense of national identity and, more importantly, to the retention of national identity in the management of empire. In claiming that the question of empire was contested, formulated and framed within the pages of the periodical press, we want to begin by addressing the concept of national identity, of Englishness, as having a particular bearing on cultural imperialism. In *Being English. Narratives, Idioms, and Performances of National Identity from Coleridge to Trollope*, Julian Wolfreys argues that Englishness is not a fixed or unified state, but the 'effect of practices and discourses which are themselves not fixed' (5). Examples of this come at different moments in the century when the effect of imperialism, itself an unfixed idea subject to varying justifications and glosses[4] on the idea of Englishness, had become subject to some debate. The more simplistic attitudes promulgated in periodicals aimed at a lower-middle-class and working-class readership – such as these statements in 'Education in the Colonies and in India' from *Eliza Cook's Journal*, that the 'English race is destined to civilize as well as colonize the world' and the 'English race can only prosper as colonists, or as rulers of foreign peoples, through means of their systematic culture and superior moral discipline' (124) – suggest an innate sense of superiority in both sexes. Englishness as used here is not gender specific. However, these attitudes later give way to intensified argument about the cost of colonisation and the argument is framed in gendered terms that are specifically male.

James Froude, for instance, in 'England and her Colonies', written for *Fraser's Magazine* and published in January 1870, expresses anxiety that the colonies are being considered burdens on the English government (2) and weakening the 'English empire' (14) as he terms it. He remarks that although England has made use of the colonies for the disposal of convicts and for trade, 'when we cannot use them any more in this way we bid them go about their business, although they are Englishmen like ourselves' (6). For Froude, colonialism and empire (and his model is the Roman Empire) is still the simple answer to England's working-class population problems, declaring that England wants 'land on which to plant English families where they may thrive and multiply without ceasing to be Englishmen' (13). The issue is one of national male identity, and Froude believes it needs to be clearly established:

that an Englishman emigrating to Canada, or the Cape, or Australia, or New Zealand, did not forfeit his nationality, that he was still on English soil as much as if he was in Devonshire or Yorkshire, and would remain an Englishman while the English empire lasted. (14)

In E. D. J. Wilson's response, 'The Colonial Empire of England' published in *Dark Blue* (1871), Froude is taken to task for being unable to see sense. Wilson contends, in direct opposition to Froude, that in fact 'the North American and Australian colonies are not constituent elements of British nationality politically regarded, but independent communities loosely linked on to the mother country by what has ceased to be anything more than an imaginary tie' (770). The article goes on to critique the idea of an English empire as mere 'hollow pride' and 'the mask of illusory prestige' (775) and Wilson concludes that all the nation's forces must be concentrated on England and not the empire, to make England 'the centre of strength' (780). For Isabella Bird, however, writing in 'Australia Felix. IX – Victoria and Victorian Progress', the Australian colony of Victoria in 1877 represents a British triumph:

Enthusiastic loyalty, fervent attachment to the mother-country, and a tenacious clinging to the tie which binds her to it, are characteristic of the colony. But, so far as the parent State is pecuniarily concerned, not a shilling finds its way from the Imperial coffers into those of Victoria; . . . Victoria presents us at the antipodes with the most remarkable monument of British enterprise and genius for colonisation that the world has yet seen. (472)

Late in the century the tone is changing. Frederic Harrison in 'A Word for England', first published in 1898, grieves that the 'beloved name of my Fatherland is being driven out of use by the incessant advance of Imperial ideas' (277), and asserts, with Froude, that the 'style "England" no more excludes Ireland than it excludes Scotland, or Canada, or Australia' (278). Moreover, Harrison is sure that the words ' "Englishman" and "England" may properly describe every subject of our Queen, and every part of her dominions' (279). Iain Chambers argues that this 'narrowing of the national nomenclature' in the nineteenth century was no accident but rather a deliberate construction of an 'English' history, a national mythology which 'impregnated the whole debate on culture' ('Narratives of Nationalism', 147).[5] Harrison's intense anxiety, therefore, is more one of cultural semantics than politics. He wants the words 'England' and 'Englishman' to remain as terms of national identity, and offers no reasoned argument for this except that they are greater and truer than 'Great Britain' and 'Briton', and his wish is expressed quite belligerently, on a note that suggests to what extent the relationship of England to her colonies had changed at century's end, a change signalled in Wilson's article. Harrison writes: 'I will let no Scot, no Australian, no Rhodesian swagger me out of that name' (282).

Anxiety about England's greatness (analogies are continually made with the Roman Empire's decline and fall) are also expressed, at the century's end. In 1899, William Clarke, writing for *Young Man*, asks 'Is Britain on the Down Grade?', a title which makes it clear that Clarke has no problem with the terms 'Great Britain' and 'British Empire'. In words strikingly similar to those we hear today, Clarke asserts that 'there is no commanding vision in the Britain, in the civilized world, of to-day. Business and amusement absorb most of the time of men, . . . cynical indifference to every subject save money . . . – such is the tone of society, whether we are in London or Berlin or New York' (184). This article is significant, however, for the debate carefully constructed around it. Prior to publication (although this is not stated outright) the article was sent to a number of well-known, and some lesser, literary and political figures, including Conan Doyle, H. G. Wells and Frances Power Cobbe, for their responses.[6] Conan Doyle dismisses the article as 'unduly pessimistic' (222); H. G. Wells shrewdly observes that '[o]ur patriotism is mainly lyrical' and 'our press is less broad-minded' (222); and Cobbe, the only woman invited to comment, while celebrating 'the vast physical and mental advancement made by my own sex' (226) yet remains steadfast, that British soldiers and civil servants should continue 'that grand old programme, to "bear the white man's burden" through the world . . . because a necessity seems laid on our race to roll onward over all shores like a mighty tide' (226).

Cobbe's 'necessity' is merely another form of duty, and her vision of empire is a thoroughly feminised, domestic one, 'I knew Egypt before it was taken under the wing of England' (226). In his earlier quotation above Harrison uses the term 'Fatherland' in what appears to be an un-usual substitution for the more common Mother England, the term used most consistently in the articles we consulted. Kipling, for instance, in his late-century poem 'A Song of the English' (1893) has the colonial cities ad-dress England as 'Mother' and England's personified response includes the couplet 'The law that ye make shall be law and I do not press my will,/ Because ye are Sons of The Blood and call me Mother still' (177). The con-nection between 'Mother England', Britannia and Queen Victoria seems an obvious one and as Elizabeth Langland comments in 'Nation and Nationality: Queen Victoria in the Developing Narrative of Englishness', if Victoria 'is an icon for England, it is still mother England . . . Britannia' (21). Harrison is also not concerned at all about the term 'Englishwoman' which for him may possibly not even exist. Later in the century, England, says Langland, 'emerges as a feminine Britannia, the fertile soil of her English sons' achievements, and Englishness takes on an increasingly masculine construction' (14) and that gender 'creates a fault line along which national identity is precariously established' (17).

II

Englishness is always constructed in opposition to others; European oth-ers, indigenous others, colonised others. This opposition, developed as a simplistic superior/inferior dichotomy, is manifest in a wide variety of lit-erary discourses throughout the nineteenth century. The belief in English superiority is there every time a periodical suggests that the English can teach other nations justice and right, that it is their destiny, as the author of 'Education in the Colonies and in India' claims, to 'civilize . . . the world' (124). Similarly, the belief is there when Elizabeth Rigby, writing for the *Quarterly*, constructs the Englishwoman as the ideal in 'Lady Travellers' because whether 'as a traveller, or writer of travels, the foreign lady can in no way be measured against her' (102).

However, once orientalism enters into the equation then European women become, as Reina Lewis puts it, the 'beneficiaries of the structure of difference' and the Englishwoman, who, ironically, at home is positioned as 'other and inferior' (4, 5), discovers in the practice of orientalism,[7] and in her role as a coloniser, a bridge across the gender divide. Similarly, working-class colonisers of both sexes found in orientalism and colonialism a bridge across the class divide as well. Of course, it is vital to remain conscious of the frailty of any such structure and to be aware of the shifts and variations in the discourse. As Lewis writes of nineteenth-century imperialism itself, 'it was discussed, debated and contested as an issue of the day, present in everyday activities and diverse forms of cultural production – not just those that were "obviously" imperialist' (13).

What the periodicals do reveal is some broadening of informed knowledge across the century but at the same time certain orientalist ideas take hold and rarely shift, become framed indeed within ideology, and remain for that reason tenacious, despite all knowledges to the contrary. As an instance, many articles about China were published throughout the Victorian age, but for the most part there is little variation in their content. In fact, it seems that earlier articles were often plagiarised by the authors of later publications. The eighth instalment in a series on China published in the *Saturday Magazine* in 1837, titled 'China. No. VIII. Condition of Women in China' is an obvious, and perhaps only, source for 'Our Sisters in China' which appeared in the *Leisure Hour* in 1863. Both refer to the *She-king*, apparently an ancient Chinese classic; both leave the reader to assume that the *She-king*'s depictions reflect current social practice in China; both discuss the same issue, the degrading of girl-babies; and in particular both refer to the same fifth line 'She is incapable of evil or good'. Of this line the *Saturday* comments that it is 'strange' and 'If she does ill, she is not a woman; if she does well she is not a woman; . . . Virtue or vice cannot belong to woman, though her actions may be virtuous or vicious; that is to say, she is not allowed the rank of a moral agent' (39). The *Leisure Hour*, nearly thirty years later, abridges this:

A commentator on the fifth line of the first extract says, "If she do ill she is not a woman, if she do well she is not a woman," thus almost denying her moral agency. (199)

What is at issue, whether it is 1830 or 1860, is the domestic ideology that English women, in contradistinction, are indeed moral agents, that to them is assigned the moral policing of their homes, their husbands, their children, their servants. Both articles, in their titles, link the women of China to the women of England. The phrase 'condition of women' was commonly used from the 1790s on to denote the social condition of English women, and the term 'Our Sisters' as a title for the second article suggests the increasing missionary impulse, not surprising in a periodical published under the auspices of the Established Church through its publishing arm, the Religious Tract Society.

Periodicals do reveal considerable variation in their approach to issues of race, according to the politics of the journal. Some Victorian periodicals, despite a commonly held belief in our own day to the contrary, offer careful, intelligent thinking and considerable restraint in their assessment of both factitious orientalist ideas and the rights of indigenous people. In 1846 the *North British Review* protested strenuously in the article 'Australia' regarding aboriginal land rights, discounting the claim that indigenous people who do not cultivate the land are, therefore, not the rightful owners and accusing the British government of the day of being deluded by 'revolting and disgraceful sophisms' activated by greed and cupidity (291). While using such terms as 'savage' and 'uncivilized' of the indigenous people of Australia, the author nevertheless deems that there is no difference between hunting over land or ploughing and sowing it, as both activities are designed for subsistence. Moreover, claims of cannibalism and infanticide are dismissed as 'not well authenticated' (289).

Cannibalism and infanticide were, of course, popular sensationalist topics for some periodicals and any number of peoples and cultures accused of these crimes. Such discussions are often used to denigrate and demonise colonised people, and also to promote Christian missionary work as a shedding of light in darkness. The triumph of 'civilisation' so-called is often linked to Christianity and becomes a common theme, especially in church-associated journals like the *Leisure Hour*. The Reverend J. B. Owen's series 'Life in Australia' includes a chapter on aboriginal people in which every possible negative stereotype is produced specifically to create greater impact with a description of converted indigenes for whom Christianity is 'their great civilizer' (255). Illustrations were often employed to reinforce particular kinds of rhetoric.

The harem is another source of sensationalism throughout the nineteenth century and again the subject of very consistent misapprehensions promulgated both by the periodical press and later by the marketing and consumption of things oriental at the century's end. In 1891 the ex-patriate Australian writer Tasma (Jessie Couvreur) in 'Iftar in a Harem' for *Temple Bar* records both the traditional expectation, with a very pointed reference to *fin-de-siècle* style and consumption, and the existing social and cultural customs in Turkey at the century's end:

I may confess at once that my first sensation was one of keen disappointment. My imagination had pictured a kind of enchanted atmosphere of perfumes, jewels, and broideries. I had thought to see odalisques lounging upon silken cushions, fanned by barbaric slaves, reposing against a background as like Liberty's Oriental exhibition-rooms as possible. In reality I saw nothing of the kind. Djevdet Pasha's harem, I regret to say – or, rather, I don't regret to say – is too virtuous by half. The ladies, as I afterwards discovered, are mainly composed of his sisters, his cousins, and his aunts. (401)

Tasma, the epitome of the new woman, records without self-consciousness, 'I sipped my Turkish coffee, and lighted my Turkish cigarette under the direct protection of my friend the Pasha's daughter' (403). Despite her modernity, despite her claim that she is 'enlightened . . . upon many points' (403) about modern Turkey, the stereotyped version of the orient which Tasma imagines is a persistent image and her final summary of the 'present condition' of Turkey is that it tends to 'dissolution and decay' (406).

III

Jane Mackay and Pat Thane in 'The Englishwoman' have argued that her qualities discussed in the public forum were not generally perceived as specifically English but rather the qualities of a universal Woman (191). We differ markedly from this position to claim, in direct opposition, that a very specific idea of precisely what it meant to be an English woman was being constructed throughout the century, alongside the ideal English man, and that even certain characteristics common to both remain consistently to the fore. These ideals were absolutely necessary for the promotion and security of empire and a contributing factor to the successful imperialism of the Victorian age.

John Stuart Mill in his 1824 article 'Periodical Literature' for the new radical journal, the *Westminster Review*, complains that their rival, the long-established *Edinburgh Review*, panders to national prejudices, writing that for the *Edinburgh* 'English' and 'excellent' are synonymous terms. These synonymous terms will prove consistently enduring in the Victorian world. Mill contests what he labels 'the English standard' against which other nations are measured and often found wanting (521), a concept that has clearly taken hold by the time his article appeared in 1824. Nevertheless it was an idea that shifted and altered in structure and constitution and it came to be inextricably linked with the question of empire, and with orientalism, eventually posited as a standard towards which others could, and should, aim, although possibly always fated to fall short. Mill's protest in the *Westminster*

Review does, however, demonstrate the way in which ideologies might be weighed and found wanting in the press itself. Such protests possibly tempered and modified the forms which particular ideologies eventually took.

Despite Mill, the idea of English excellence persisted, taking on among its most dominant qualities those of self-help and independence. These qualities are clearly valued at the onset of the Victorian age and came to be regarded as much a part of the English standard for women, as for men. *Chambers' Edinburgh Review* in 1834 directly equates women and the state of the nation in a sentimental article titled 'Idea of an English Girl'. The English girl is a paragon and her sweet face, decked with maiden smiles, 'painted with perennial roses', assures men 'that England is still "right at the heart"'' (185).

Elizabeth Rigby, as previously noted, offers a very full description of the quintessential English woman then representing Britain at the very outskirts of the empire. Rigby attributes the Englishwoman's ability to travel 'to nothing less than the *domesticity* of the English character' (103), and also remarks on her ability as a settler, 'the Englishwoman's services being here most important' (105). In acknowledging women's contribution to empire, Rigby adds:

wherever there is room for rational tastes, orderly habits, and gentle charities . . . there we find the Englishwoman creating an atmosphere of virtuous happiness around her. . . There is no part of the world, however remote, from which she does not send forth a voice of cheerful intelligence. (105)

Independence and self-help as components of the English standard, for women anyway, still had to be nicely judged, and could still be contested, as the conservative organ, the *Saturday Review* reveals in 'English Girls', a review of *Timely Retreat; or a Year in Bengal before the Mutinies* (1858).[8] Clearly the by-now ancient spectre of French morals still haunts the ideological attitudes revealed in the *Saturday Review*, as does the continuing assumption of male supremacy. 'English Girls' begins:

One of the things upon which we have always most piqued ourselves as Englishmen is the unsuspected and unsuspecting freedom, the chaste and decent boldness, of our girls. How often have we fought the battle of our country's ways against Frenchmen, who can see nothing in the confidence we place in the purity and principle of our maiden countrywomen but stupid or shameful indifference to their virtue! (239)

However, this privilege for English girls may soon be lost, the *Saturday Review* fears, because of a new school of young ladies they designate 'Plucky Girls' who are no longer the passive ciphers of the *Chambers'* article. There is a hasty disclaimer of a kind, 'Not that we do not admire their curiosity, their courage, their contempt of difficulties, their power of enduring hardship and privation' (239), elements of the English standard endorsed in Rigby's earlier article, but the young women, the unnamed protagonists of *Timely Retreat*, have overstepped invisible but ever-present boundaries because they fail to appreciate 'what is respectable, graceful, dignified, amiable, or trustworthy in women' (239).

The 'Plucky Girls' transgress in very particular ways, as the following passage suggests, because they step outside 'the pale of civilized life':

Such ladies may assume that their claims to unblemished reputation are, in spite of appearances, to be accepted by society on their word. But neither their Colt's revolvers nor their impudent defiance of opinion will, we think, force this conviction on the world. The men who have most constantly and gallantly championed the decent and graceful and feminine liberty, the quiet courage, and the frankness, "thinking no evil", of our unspoiled girls, will by no means feel themselves called upon to defend the reputations of female swash-bucklers and adventurers from the sneering glosses of foreigners. (239)

This article is an obvious forerunner to Eliza Lynn Linton's 'Girl of the Period' articles for the *Saturday Review* discussed in the Introduction but is not by Linton, who had not started writing for the *Saturday Review* at this date.

The 'Plucky Girls' also offend against the English standard in their dealings with British colonised subjects. Their adventures have taken place in India and they have failed to set the right example in their conduct towards the local people. The reviewer accuses them of making ignorant comments which are 'flippant, vulgar, and above all inhuman' and of displaying a 'coarse insensitivity' and 'want of delicacy'. The racism to which the *Saturday Review* objects is, in part, a recent trend brought about by the Indian mutinies, about which there are many articles in the periodical press throughout 1858 and which the book's title clearly signals, and perhaps even cynically plays on. As George Stocking Jr observes in *Victorian Anthropology*, the mutinies sharpened racial resentments (63). The concluding rebuke is, however, less about racism than it is concerned with maintaining the English standard: '[t]hey should recollect that any misconstructions to which they wantonly subject themselves, fall, not upon them alone, but upon the sacred cause of the freedom, the dignity, and the usefulness of their sex' (239). The 'Plucky Girls' have not only strayed into the *Boy's Own* territory, but they have also failed to understand their proper 'duty', once there, in representing English women.

IV

The male equivalent to 'plucky girls', 'manly boys', does carry conditions with it. Early in the century there appears to be a general standard for men in which epithets like independence, self-sufficiency, courage, resoluteness and forthrightness are understood to operate, are givens which move independently across class lines but, as Mill points out in 'Periodical Literature', not across gender lines (526). Later these same epithets will be a standard for women as well but, as we have shown, within certain gendered limitations. However, as a rule, the periodicals work far harder to offer correctives to women at every turn, while the English man, because he does not carry the burden of the nation's morality, remains for the most part outside this intensive corrective impulse. This said, we should also note that anxiety about manliness tends to increase after the 1850s. The Revd. George Jackson writing the column 'Some Manly Words for Boys by Manly Men' for the *Boy's Own Paper* in 1897 locates manliness in the Bible, in English history and in empire:

The time would fail me to tell of Havelock falling amid the agonies of the Indian Mutiny; of Livingstone and Mackay, pouring out the precious treasure of their lives like water on the burning sands of Africa; of Gordon, meeting death with unblanched cheek in the fastnesses of far-away Khartoum. (127)

Throughout the nineteenth century the English man, because his sphere is the British empirical world, is most often defined in terms of emigration and colonisation, that is, in terms of what he can do for the honour of the nation and the British Empire. The last stanza of Eliza Cook's poem, 'The Englishman', re-issued in her magazine in 1851, and probably written between 1845 and 1850, amply demonstrates this:

> The Briton may traverse the pole or the zone,
> And boldly claim his right;
> For he calls such a vast domain his own,
> That the sun never sets on his might.
> Let the haughty stranger seek to know
> The place of his home and birth;
> And a flush will pour from cheek to brow
> While he tells his native earth.
> For a glorious charter, deny it who can,
> Is breathed in the words, 'I'm an Englishman.'
> (40)

Similarly for Froude, reflecting in 'England and her Colonies', the English 'are a race of unusual vigour both of body and mind – industrious, energetic, ingenious, capable of great muscular exertion, and remarkable along with it for equally great personal courage' (200).

Much earlier, however, in 1830, William Maginn in 'The Desperate System. Poverty, Crime and Emigration', condemned emigration as a trick of government to persuade the population that it was the only cure for present ills rather than the repeal of 'bad laws – of arbitrary measures – of oppressive monopolies – of despotic exactions – of insufferable favouritism – and of grinding taxes' (642). And such negative criticisms appeared side by side with encomiums in other journals praising emigration throughout the century in both the periodical and the daily press. Men, nevertheless, came to be defined within the frame of 'enterprise and self-reliance', of 'muscular Christianity',[9] and underlying these terms, of self-sacrifice.

In the early decades of the century, 'emigration' (be it voluntary or involuntary) was seen as the solution to any number of problems, unemployment, poverty, the Irish question, crime, overpopulation, gender imbalance and so on. In 1832 *New Monthly Magazine* published a comic item by 'A Compulsory Bachelor' titled 'What Will Our Spinsters Do? or, What Shall We Do with Our Spinsters?' The article is based on the current economic conditions which prevent marriage. In 1834 Christian Isobel Johnstone, writing for *Tait's*, produced a belated response to this titled 'What Shall We Do with Our Young Fellows?' Johnstone's response is as both a competitive fellow journalist and a woman reader. She asks 'how shall we place our genteel young fellows out in the world' (527)? She reads the issue as one of class and gender, and an ideological one directly affecting a particular English social standard: 'each of the sons is called upon by nature, and the customs of society (particularly of English society,) to achieve to himself a separate and independent station in life, equal, at least, to that in which he was born' (528).

As Johnstone points out, in the first twenty years of the nineteenth century 'the development of our powers, as a nation, was truly astonishing' creating an ambitious middle class keen to remain upwardly mobile and considering 'trade' beneath them:

Many a delicate youth has been sent out to our colonies with a poor and subordinate Government appointment, rather than enter a merchant's or trader's counting-house, within the genial influence of home; left to pine in the wilds of New South Wales, or the unhealthy climates of the East, far away from all that is dear and valuable to him . . . sacrificed . . . to the "grim idol" of gentility. (528)

The original question, as framed in the *New Monthly Magazine*, was intentionally comic and Johnstone's re-gendering of the question, as well as her re-framing of it as a serious response, is prescient in many ways of a debate that was to continue for some decades to come and which was to have great bearing on the lives of women and men generally. But it was prescient in other ways too – most noticeably in her decision to focus on young men as potential colonisers. For Johnstone, emigration, whether of men or women, is not really the best solution as her subsequent article, 'A Page for the Lasses' in 1835 indicates: 'we would advise no young woman to emigrate who has connections, or who can do even tolerably well at home' (128). Johnstone's negative attitude to emigration was a position opposed more and more firmly as the century progressed in any number of differing mediums and in any number of quite different kinds of periodical: from high Tory to the lowest of working-class magazines, designed for readers of all ages. *Tait's* itself, long after Johnstone's period of editorship had ended, addresses the issue again in 'Emigration and the Sexes', and, in particular, expresses concern about the large number of men who emigrate to Australia in comparison with women. This article focusses on the problem of regarding emigration as a 'business' and considers the political economist argument flawed that attempts to compare 'the human fabric to the social fabric' (509).[10] There were many such articles across the broad spectrum of the periodical press in which the gender imbalance in colonisation is seen as propagating an increase in prostitution at home and miscegenation abroad.

In 1848 the first number of the *Colonist* appeared, edited by W. H. G. Kingston and featuring his article 'How the Unemployed May Better Their Condition'. In Kingston's article emigration is a patriotic duty couched in determinedly religious and quasi-Biblical terms. Hesitant emigrants are told to 'manfully gird up their loins, take their staffs in hand, and go forth to lands where their industry will be rewarded' (4). In particular, however, Kingston addresses the 'Labouring Classes':

we ask you to believe that what we write is for your good; that when we say this, we have no other motive than the enjoyment of the true pleasure of doing what is right. . . When we say to you, emigrate, we do not say so to get rid of you, but because we believe it is one of the means by which our social ills may be remedied. (5–6)

The anger expressed by *Fraser's Magazine* in 'The Desperate System' eighteen years earlier, that emigration is too facile a solution to the societal problems of the day, makes even more sense in the light of this simplistic advocacy on Kingston's part. His overbearing paternalistic attitude, a kind of paterfamilias, is evidenced in which his readers are mere children to be told hard facts 'for your good'. Eventually the target audience for this kind of rhetoric will shift to what W. Jardine Smith describes, in 1872, as the 'middle middle class' (747). Eventually the popular juvenile journals of the last two decades of the century would bring all of these elements together into an ideological union, not only of 'Church, State, and military' (203) as John A. Mackenzie suggests in *Propaganda and Empire. The Manipulation of British Public Opinion, 1880–1960*, but also of consumerism as well, the one element which would aid and abet the spread of the developing propaganda which saw a new emphasis placed on race and gender as they intersect imperialist ideology.

The *Colonist* also carried a piece titled 'Character of a Good Colonist' in which the English standard is extended to a more precise formula specifically adapted to an imperialist imperative:

> To become a successful Colonist, a man should possess good health and strength, good spirits, and good humour, great forethought, great judgment, great perseverance, and great courage, and a firm trust in Providence. (29)

This is the formula which will contribute to the idea of the English man and the English boy in the wholesome Boy's Own tales of Kingston himself, including the many that he published in the Religious Tract Society's publication, the *Boy's Own Paper*, along with those of R. M. Ballantyne and others. Robert Dixon in *Writing the Colonial Adventure. Race, Gender and Nation in Anglo-Australian Popular Fiction, 1875–1914* observes that Kingston and Ballantyne were approved authors whose adventure novels would channel the 'natural excess of boys' natures' and inculcate 'the fundamentals of evangelical Christianity, Anglo-Saxonism and British imperialism' (31). Religion is, as we have shown, the predominating discursive practice which informs and enables the prose of the *Colonist*, and later, linked to romance, informs the narrative tradition of adventure stories for boys and girls. Mackenzie, in writing of the 'adventure tradition, replete with militarism and patriotism' of the 1880s, considers that 'adult opinion, politicians and social reformers, clerics and missionaries, parents and schoolmasters, found this tradition entirely acceptable, and fostered its growth' (199).

v

The decision to focus on Australia in this chapter has been determined by the dominance of writing and thinking about Australia in the British periodical press in the nineteenth century, dictated in part by the Gothic horror of its convict history ensuring its unpopularity as a migrant destination in the pre-Victorian period. *Chambers' Edinburgh Journal*, for instance, warns in 'Emigration' in 1832 that 'emigration towards that quarter of the empire is most improper' because 'New South Wales and Van Diemen's Land are crowded with a population formed of the offscourings of every town in England, Scotland, and Ireland – ruffians' (149). Subsequently, Australia then enjoys a sudden rehabilitation as a more attractive destination, on the discovery of gold.

This is not to say that the periodical press did not discuss Canada or the Cape of Good Hope, or New Zealand or India. There are many articles, tales, poems and other items about all of these places. However, India, for instance, offers too narrow a range for our discussion because it is structured in the Victorian era predominantly as a civil-service outpost and gendered strictly male. As the *Athenaeum* notes in 'Letter from Sydney', 'India, to be sure, is monopolized by the gentlemen of Leadenhall-street' (685). Canada and New Zealand were popular colonial destinations and are certainly well represented in the press in the early decades of the nineteenth century but do not seem to attract quite the kind of broad range of writing excited by Australia with its dubious beginnings, the romance of its antipodean distance and its unexplored possibilities in terms of both land and minerals.

The Australian gold rushes produced a gender imbalance within its various colonies' social structures which caused considerable anxiety in Britain and which the periodicals appear to have addressed with almost one combined voice. With its lower-middle-class readership in mind, *Eliza Cook's Journal* consistently published essays on the Australian gold discoveries, almost all of which reflect both on the wealth to the British nation and the domestic moral implications. We should make clear, however, that this was the rule, not the exception. Upper-middle-class journals with Tory leanings like *Fraser's Magazine* were as likely to sound warnings regarding the unstable moral and financial implications of a gold rush as were organs of the Established Church like the *Leisure Hour*. Indeed the latter published almost identically styled articles to those in *Eliza Cook's* in the 1852–3 period, such as 'Australia. II. – Its Gold-Fields', which warns of the 'moral contamination of the Australian gold-fields' (517) and promotes, instead, domestic emigration, as did many other journals published in the 1850s.

Just before the major gold rushes, however, in 1849, *Eliza Cook's Journal* published 'The Emigrant in Port Phillip', emigration propaganda for the newly formed Port Phillip colony (later Victoria) which is written up as a paradise of 'perpetual spring' where 'open and undulating plains . . . are capable of at once receiving the plough' (193). The author notes the discovery of gold but locates the information quite late in the article, on the last page, and gives it a moral inflection by striking a warning note:

The recent discovery of gold ore in the Australian pyrenees, north of Melbourne, is a new feature in connection with this colony. The real wealth of the country must ever consist in the fruitfulness of its soil, and the industry of its population. (195)

The stress on the work ethic, which British labourers are capable of because they are 'a people as hardy and industrious as is to be found on the face of the globe' (193), is a plea for domestication emphasised by the stated need for women to migrate along with men. This burden is taken up by a later article, 'Young Women in the Colonies' which declares that 'homes in the bush are often no homes; they want the cheering voice and the tidy help of women to make them cozy, clean, and comfortable, as homes should be' (241).

It is difficult to estimate to what extent such articles persuaded working-class and lower-middle-class readers to emigrate, but emigrate they did. Andrew Hassam in *No Privacy for Writing. Shipboard Diaries 1852–1879*, estimates 1.3 million free immigrants to Australia up until 1880 with a literacy level of between 70 and 80 per cent (xvi). Louis James, assessing the *London Journal* readership, notes that although women rarely have letters published in the *Journal*'s correspondence columns (his evidence is based on volume 7, 1848), when they do, their letters are on serious matters 'such as learning botany or how to emigrate' ('Trouble with Betsy', 365). He adds that emigration was the particular focus of volume 8 of the *London Journal*.

The increasing attractiveness of Australia as an emigrant destination and the issue of parental/governmental failure in England is illustrated by Isabella Fyvie Mayo's three-part story 'The Other Side of the World', published in the *Girl's Own Paper*, December 1881 to February 1882. While Mackenzie conflates 'juvenile' with a male literary tradition, we would suggest that the romantic colonial enterprise is, in fact, re-gendered in quite interesting ways in the 1880s, specifically to form a part of what he terms the 'new popular imperialism' (199). Mackay and Thane also argue that the gap between the nation's expectations of women and men was greater than the gap between women of differing classes in this period, that is, that 'gender differences were more significant than class differences' (193). This set of propositions is nicely demonstrated by Mayo's tale.

The story begins with a question: 'In all the wide world I wonder if there is a place where we are really wanted?' (Mayo, 'Other Side of the World', 145). Rita Kranidis, in discussing female emigration rhetoric in her 'Introduction' to *Imperial Objects. Essays on Victorian Women's Emigration and the Unauthorized Imperial Experience*, of which Mayo's opening question is a typical example, posits that the concern expressed in the question was projected onto 'redundant' women who were 'culturally excessive at the same time as they remained ideologically valued' but that, in fact, 'women's emigration was a response to the economic conditions and trade practices that ultimately situated England's wealth, finances, and brighter prospects . . . in . . . the colonies' (4). This being so, Mayo's tale is obvious propaganda, yet revealing all the varying conflicting positions regarding women in the period. For instance, Mackay and Thane's reading of the earliest numbers of the *Girl's Own Paper* suggests to them that there 'is no virtue for a girl in being restless or adventurous' (196). However, the decision to emigrate is in part written up in Mayo's tale as 'a breath of hope and adventure' specifically for girls (Mayo, 'Other Side of the World', 146).

Despite this hint of adventure, the heroines Bell and Annie are not 'New Women' but rather modern martyrs whose courage will nevertheless ensure that they do not cut sorry figures in Australia because of their willingness to work and their firm sense of duty, ideal qualities also expected of young middle-class emigrant men. Bell, in fact, expresses unlikely delight on learning that she may go out as an assisted emigrant because 'domestic work is exactly the work I want to do' (147). In explaining her decision to her parents Bell assures them she will work very hard, 'that her brother next in age might get the drawing-lessons he coveted so eagerly, and which might set free a real gift struggling within him, and so elevate and brighten all his life' (147). This declaration is perhaps the most disturbing feature of the tale because it explicitly supports the idea of duty and sacrifice on the part of the female child for the advancement of the male one, who is apparently not expected to make any effort for himself. It is difficult to determine to what extent anything published in the *Girl's Own Paper* simply reproduces 'dominant norms' and to what extent the position of its female authors might be marginal within 'the dominant spatial framework' (Mills, 'Gender and Colonial Space', 127–8). Perhaps Mayo's silence on this aspect of sacrifice may implicitly invite her readers to ask the inevitable question for themselves.

'The Other Side of the World' is obvious late-century gendered pro-emigration propaganda, of the kind that Mackay and Thane believe is aimed specifically at the middle class (205). Woven into the fiction are very specific instructions on how a young, respectable but impecunious woman might safely emigrate under the auspices of the Women's Emigration Society.[11] The Society points out that 'emigration is almost given over to men, thereby leaving an undue number of women in the mother country deprived of their natural duties and employments' (Mayo, 'Other Side of the World',

146) and assures our heroines that high-class families 'travel and settle in different parts of the world' (146). In an account of the public meeting which set up the Society, the reader is told that present were 'good and great men in many walks of life, ladies of rank, and influential colonists' (146). There is a telling absence of women of the middle class and lower, precisely those for whom the Society has been set up. Later in the tale it is suggested that some women 'might well prefer . . . the harder life and higher chances of a young community to the pampered menialism and rigidly limited range of an old civilisation' (258).

Bell and Annie discover Australia is a 'good opening for sensible young women fit for hard work and willing to do it' (Mayo, 'Other Side of the World', 290). Finally comes the tale's key statement which is centred on the idea of Englishness and the English standard yet simultaneously reassures the doubtful that class-bound restrictions may safely be left behind:

If English girls of a better class are to be found willing to leave home and friends, and to face all sorts of hardships, and to encounter great risks and difficulties to earn £20 per annum by doing *real servants'* work, simply because the public opinion of the strange country does not ostracise them for so doing, then I cannot help saying that English men and women, heads of households at home, and English girls of the better class seeking employment, have in their own hands the solution of the great 'domestic servant difficulty,' which, as mamma used to say, makes so much English female life one perpetual struggle and defeat. (290–1)

VI

The gold rushes had their inevitable effect upon the economy of Australia and for a few made the return trip 'Home' a possibility rather than a dream. For some the return was a permanent one, for others something much more akin to the grand tour in which Europe and Britain are sites of culture, of wonder and of comparison. It is important to consider what role in cultural representation returning emigrants might assign to themselves, and to what extent they saw themselves as inside or outside some kind of national or cultural equation. Australia, as the most distant outpost of empire, also seems best suited to considerations of this kind for our discussion.

Those who emigrated found their sense of national identity shifting. Early on some settlers began to think of themselves not only as 'English', but also as Canadians, New Zealanders or Australians, among others. The colonisers found themselves torn between two national allegiances as the following article by Catherine Helen Spence shows. In 1839, at the age of fourteen, Spence had migrated to South Australia from Scotland with her family. Apart from her various journeys back to Britain, she spent most of her life in South Australia. She was a noted feminist and made a major contribution to the achievement of women's suffrage in South Australia in 1896.

In 1866, while she was visiting Britain, she published 'An Australian's Impressions of England' with the *Cornhill*. Despite her claim to Englishness, the article is predicated upon a nascent Australian nationalism. In its very syntax, Spence's article opposes very decidedly, one place to the other, the social and political differences are highlighted and issues such as egalitarianism and universal suffrage reveal Spence's radical thinking:

In our case, we have an enormous territory sparsely peopled . . . and in the other case you have a small country dotted over with large and populous towns. . . With us we only produce the raw material. . . With you all invention is on the stretch to make as much out of the raw material as possible. . . In England all land is private property, and is in few hands. In Australia a great proportion of the land is unappropriated, and held by Government in trust for the people; . . . In England you have enormous wealth side by side with great want. In Australia labour and the rewards of labour are more equally divided. With you the suffrage is limited, with us it is all but universal. (110)

Spence's strongest words relate to the condition of women. While she admits that the daily work with which 'our colonial women' have to engage means they have no time to devote 'to literature, to art, or to philanthropy' their work nevertheless:

brings out an amount of common sense and consideration for others which is too apt to be wanting among the many thousands in England who have no taste strong enough to become a pursuit, and who on leaving school find that there is nothing for them to do. I certainly think that the position of the larger proportion of unmarried women in the United Kingdom is a most unenviable one. (119)

Having made these highly politicised contrasts, Spence reassures the *Cornhill* readers that 'English society is sound at the core, and that it is neither heartless nor altogether conventional' (120). It is in such samples as this that the various and varying cultural representations of imperialism in the nineteenth century are generated by the periodical press whose very diversity allows heterogeneity.

Britain in colonialist terms is always the 'mother-country', although often a parent failing in parental duty as well (see Bird's comment early in this chapter). Within the culture of the day, and as the century progressed, very particular ideological assumptions operated with regard to imperialism, but

Plate 8. 'A New Year's Family Party', *Judy, or the London Serio-comic Journal* 18 (1876): 117–18.

the most dominant of these, as we have demonstrated, was an emphasis on the domestic as a guarantee of future prosperity and the only means by which to achieve empirical consolidation. A cartoon titled 'A New Year's Family Party' appeared in *Judy, or the London Serio-comic Journal* (see Plate 8) on 5 January 1876. The caption reads, 'John to Jonathan. Jonathan, you may as well take your place at this table' (117–18). Revelling in the strength of empire, John Bull invites the United States to rejoin the family. What is notable in this cartoon is the domestic setting and the fact that empire is represented not only by male figures but female ones, and by indigenous people too, suggesting that there is possibly less anxiety about feminisation and race in the late 1870s than occurs in the late 1890s. In this regard the figure representing Australia is the most equivocal and perhaps the most disturbing: a young man, booted and at his ease, laconic almost, with an ominous whip under his chair, is central to the scene and after John Bull, the most dominant in this depiction of a 'family' group. He seems to occupy a space that is at once domestic (the family party) and yet undomesticated (the whip under the chair). His masculinity threatens.

CHAPTER SIX

Feminism and the press

When George Fleming wrote in 1888 of 'the loose-fibred habit of the feminine mind' in 'On a Certain Deficiency in Women', he echoed, rather belatedly, conventional views held by generations of nineteenth-century men and women who had been uncomfortably exposed to the radicalism of mid-Victorian women activists (406). Fleming's article for the *Universal Review* called on the cliché of the irrational, ignorant woman, her memory poor, her unoriginal thoughts randomly scattered like the litter of her sewing table. For Fleming an intelligent woman was even more rare than 'distinguishing talent' among men:

> among all the maids and matrons, among all these infinite results of infinitely diverging circumstance, this wilderness of wills and desires, of hopes, habits, schemes of life and plans of ambition, it would be an easy, if invidious, task to add up the number of these feminine minds which showed symptoms of a capacity for serious thinking. (401)

Instances of such views abound in the nineteenth-century periodical press. Indeed, that the issue of women's rights received so much attention, both positive and negative, from male and female writers within the pages of diverse, even rival, magazines suggests the importance of the press, both as a space for the contestation and elaboration of gendered discourses and as a vehicle for social change.

The profusion of comparisons between women and men evident in the press over several decades is itself one indicator of the intensity of social anxieties about changing gender roles. By 1888, at least in some quarters, the notion of an innate mental deficiency in women had been substantially challenged. The publication of an article by Emily Faithfull in the same journal six months later, 'The Progress of Women: In Industrial Employment', provides a very different sense of the social position of women in this period:

Imagine the amazement of our great-grandfathers and great-grandmothers . . . if they caught but one glimpse of what is going on at the present day, and saw 'our daughters' wearing collegiate caps and gowns and taking university degrees, working in telegraph and telephone offices, acting as law copyists, shorthand clerks, typewriters, house-decorators, landscape gardeners, journalists, doctors etc., while their elders serve as Guardians of the Poor and sit on our School Boards, lecture in public and advocate on the hustings the claims of the political candidate they support. (637)

Faithfull's piece was one of a series of regular articles on 'The Progress of Women' published in the *Universal Review* during 1888 which included articles by Millicent Garrett Fawcett and Florence Fenwick Miller. The inclusion of writers with opposing viewpoints was, of course, a well-established journalistic technique for stirring up public interest. The innovation of this series of articles by women well known to the public through newspapers and the periodical press is one indicator, however, that by the late 1880s publishers, editors and writers recognised that women formed a significant body of readers, consumers and commentators, and that women were important contributors to the periodical press as well as to society at large. The relative accessibility of the periodical press to women writers and readers also made it a potent medium for evolving perceptions of women in society.

This chapter considers some of the formations and representations of feminism in the mid- to late nineteenth-century periodical press in Britain, with particular reference to the women's press. We explore the close relationship between feminism and moral ideas associated with nineteenth-century British social reform, suggesting that for many feminists the promotion of broader social justice issues through the periodical press, such as public health, universal education and child welfare, also served as a mechanism for promoting the interests of women.

The development of feminist ideas through the periodical press was by no means a consistent or coherent process. Made up of a plethora of roughly congruent generic forms, the press provided the key medium for popular and corporatised public debate in this period. There were no official limitations on who could produce a magazine or constraints on what kinds of magazines could be produced. Views expressed within the pages of a magazine were clearly limited: by standard legal constraints, by the economic pressure of securing an interested readership and by prevailing ideological formations. For many special interest groups, however, from health reform associations to women's social clubs, the monthly or quarterly magazine offered a useful means of linking and gathering members, encapsulating ideas, reaching a wider potential audience and even questioning mainstream values. As the *Woman's Signal* observed in 'To Our Friends' in 1894: '"Love me, love my ideas," said a famous propagandist, "Love me, love my paper" is the watchword of the reformer' (1).

For women especially, the diversification of the press offered a valuable means of literary, artistic, social and political expression. That this was constructed, in part, as a dangerous breaching of the boundary between public and private social space has been closely elaborated elsewhere (see Poovey, *Making a Social Body*, and Flint, *The Woman Reader*). The refusal to allow this breach of the gendered boundary between public and private is exemplified by Queen Victoria's refusal to allow a young woman to write an article on the Royal Mews and Kennels, with the comment, quoted in Margaret Homans and Adrienne Munich, *Remaking Queen Victoria*, that, this 'is a dreadful and dangerous woman. She better take the facts from the other papers' (4).

This instance is one of several cited by Homans and Munich in order to show the gendered contradictions within Victoria's sense of her own absolute authority. It is also fascinating for what it suggests about the tensions between gender, domesticity and power. Victoria views the request with impatience and directs the woman to the presumably more masculine, certainly popularised, authority of 'the other papers'. Even if the comment is interpreted as an ironical dig at the presumptions of the daily press, its effect is to deflect the petition via Victoria's royal distance and power. Throughout her reign Victoria is at pains to maintain the balance between the integrity of her phallic status as Britain's imperial monarch and her emblematic role as archangel of the hearth. The Royal Mews and Kennels as a subject must be refused, partly because it is a masculinised space, partly because of its proximity to the royal household and the personal details it might reveal.

Victoria's pronouncement, made in 1892, also rehearses the idea that women writers for the periodical press are 'dangerous'. The unsuccessful writer herself lacks credibility: she is merely the obscure daughter of the supplicant. Her desire to write the article is 'dangerous' partly because it marks the presumption of the right of the subject to comment publicly upon the domestic life of the sovereign. This threat is intensified because of the writer's gender. As Florence Fenwick Miller observed in 'How I Made my First Speech', the act of a woman speaking in public or writing in the periodical press still posed a challenge to traditional views about women being confined to the domestic sphere (4).

Throughout the latter half of the nineteenth century, the periodical press remained a field of competing and sometimes curious tensions, particularly within the broad field of magazines for women. On the one hand, the magazine remained a 'domestic' item to be consumed, momentarily interesting or entertaining, easily put down: on the other hand, the magazine travelled into Britain's homes and minds, carrying with it opinions and ideas that evolved into the fashionable currencies of passing decades.

I

The 'woman question' was a major, often anxious, preoccupation within the nineteenth-century British periodical press. Although subject to attack as well as affirmation, by the end of the 1860s feminism had become an important, albeit contested, discourse within Victorian culture. The emergence of feminism can be perceived partly as one formative strand within the driving nineteenth-century ideal of progress – technological, economic, political and social. Moreover, feminism's public alignment with liberal social movements, with radical cultural transformations and with moral values associated with the great reform movements of the age provided it with an array of allies, modes of expression and diverse constituencies, for which the periodical press provided a form of connective tissue.

The term 'feminism', with reference to the Victorian period, must be somewhat loosely applied. Many key ideas associated with twentieth-century feminism, for instance, were not in full currency among women or among men during the mid-nineteenth century. Candida Ann Lacey argues in *Barbara Leigh Smith Bodichon and the Langham Place Group*, that Bodichon, the independent thinker and activist, was almost alone, even amongst her friends and colleagues, in placing the interests of women themselves above their more traditional concerns of home and family (9), while Philippa Levine refers in *Victorian Feminism 1850–1900* to the 'rejection of an overall formal organizing principle' as a key characteristic of the nineteenth-century British women's movement (160). Indeed, the broad advocacy of improved health, living and working conditions for women and of women's participation in public life was closely connected with, even embedded in, the great social reform movements of the nineteenth century in education, employment, health, suffrage and the law. Levine's observation, about the absence of a single-minded feminist programme, particularly applies to the key decade of development in nineteenth-century feminist consciousness – the 1860s – but her characterisation of feminism has, in some ways, remained the case throughout the twentieth century, perhaps partly because feminism itself embraces such a diversity of socio-cultural contexts, lived experiences and subject positions. The role of the periodical press in the women's movements of both the nineteenth and twentieth century reflects this multiplicity.

Organised feminism emerged in Britain during the 1850s and 1860s with the constitution of the Langham Place group, which included Barbara Bodichon, Bessie Parkes, Octavia Hill, Sophia Jex-Blake, Elizabeth Garrett, Emily Davies and Elizabeth Wolstenholme Elmy, among others. An important extension of the work of the women of Langham Place was the inauguration of the *English Woman's Journal*, which, in turn, gave rise to new generations of social and political magazines for women. As Parkes herself wrote in 1864, reflecting on the work of those associated with Langham Place:

> Ten years ago, although there was an earnest and active group of people, deeply interested in all that relates to female education and industry, and to the reform of the laws affecting the property of married women . . . . there was no centre of meeting, nor any one work which could be said to draw together the names of the ladies so actively employed. (quoted in Lacey, *Barbara*, 215)

Langham Place supplied that centre.

The origins of a philosophically and politically constituted feminism were, of course, much older than this. As the women associated with Langham Place contested social disadvantage, including the injustices of gender inequality, they drew in part on developments in human rights discourse as this had emerged from the American and French Revolutionary periods of the late eighteenth century. Most obviously it was Mary Wollstonecraft's *A Vindication of the Rights of Woman* that eloquently adapted the revolutionary principles of freedom and equality to the position of women. This was, as Linda M. Shires contends in 'Maenads, Mothers and Feminized Males: Victorian Readings of the French Revolution', a difficult heritage since 'the 1790s saw the boldest defenders of women and revolution disgraced' (72).

Given this shadowy legacy of public disparagement, early to mid-nineteenth-century feminists sought in various ways to work for women's political rights. Sometimes the means employed were, necessarily, indirect. Women writers and activists of this period even sought at times to mask the radicalism of their stance on the position of women, whether in a literature of domestic resolution, as Shires indicates, in the kinds of publicly recognised charities they chose to pursue, or through the adoption of a rigorous personal moral rectitude so as to circumvent potential public criticism.[1] As Shires argues, however, the influence of revolutionary politics on new generations of writers and activists was instrumental in producing a strong and effective women's movement during the 1850s and 1860s. The periodical press became a key mechanism through which this movement developed and disseminated its ideas.

For post-nineteenth-century commentators one of the central contributions of the Victorian women's movement was the way it began to raise questions about the naturalness of gender formations. Fleming's comments, as cited, and countless male writers before and after him express a common attitude. The notion that women could be educated professionals with independent opinions and individual voting rights appeared alien to mainstream values of domesticity and the assumed naturalness of gendered difference, yet it was partly the ideology of domesticity, and middle-class woman's presumed natural capacity for civility and common sense, that enabled feminist activists to further the political emancipation of women. This aligned with the reformist work across a range of social and political issues in which so many of Langham Place's supporters were involved. In discussing the increase in subscribers and readers of the *English Woman's Journal* in 'A Year's Experience in Woman's Work', Parkes noted in 1860 that at the beginning 'the ladies at that time subscribing to the ENGLISH WOMAN'S JOURNAL ... numbered a few hundreds. Many of these ladies were actively concerned in charity; and had founded, or supported, or visited, industrial schools, and small hospitals, homes for invalids, and refuges of different kinds' (115).

If the daily newspaper was the main medium for social and political discourse, the periodical press offered women a means of engaging with this public domain. By promoting a range of other social and moral causes through a diverse range of publications and by embodying a spirit of keeping the nation's house in order – variously clad in the mantles of matronly kindliness, feminine charity and even *noblesse oblige* – women were able to instigate major social, political and legal changes in the position of women. While it was precisely this dissembling that Bodichon, like many twentieth-century feminists, sought to overturn, several of her contemporaries, including Emily Davies and Frances Power Cobbe, believed that extreme positions and strong criticism would only alienate those upon whom their success depended, and even that other social issues such as women's education, health and employment were more pressing than that of women's suffrage. In 1866, Cobbe publicly expressed this view when she published a magazine article in answer to negative newspaper reports on the presentation of the Women's Suffrage Bill in parliament. Here Cobbe employed the conventional trope of the sensible and law-abiding domestic woman as an argument for her fitness in the political sphere:

Last summer *The Times* remarked that 'when working men desired to have votes *they* threw down the park palings, but that women have not shown their wish for the same privilege by any such proceedings'. Were we not on that same enchanted ground whereon all arguments are turned topsy turvy, we should have supposed that the mob who attacked the police and spoiled the public park, and the women who stopped at home and signed Mr Mill's petition, had respectively shown the one their *un*fitness, the other their fitness for the franchise of a law-respecting nation. (quoted in Lacey, *Barbara*, 399)

For Bessie Rayner Parkes as well, this exercise of middle class feminine sobriety was, as she wrote in reference to the writer Anna Jameson, an 'inner law of womanhood' (quoted in Lacey, *Barbara*, 216).

The election of John Stuart Mill to parliament in Britain in 1866 and his subsequent role in promoting women's suffrage in parliament is evidence of the potency of this surge of pro-feminist activism that took place during the 1860s. Mill's role in relation to the women's movement was always controversial (Lacey, *Barbara*, 105). As Lacey observes 'it was more Barbara Bodichon's belief in the political purchase of Mill as a publicist than her faith in him as a philosopher which . . . prompted her to capitalise on his position as an MP by asking him to represent the petition for women's suffrage' (4). Mill's association with the women's suffrage movement did, however, consolidate and authenticate the philosophical and ethical links between political democracy, social justice and women's rights, providing a touchstone for the kind of ethical and social framework upon which many members of the women's movement sought to build.

A two-part article by Bessie Parkes in the *English Woman's Journal* indicates the importance of Mill's role as a figurehead and speaker for the rights of women at the legislative level. Part One of 'The Opinions of John Stuart Mill' appeared in the September 1860 number of the *English Woman's Journal* and began by invoking Mill's masculine authority:

There is no name in England which carries with it so much weight . . . as that of John Stuart Mill, the philosopher, logician and political economist . . . What he has written is founded on reason, and stands like a solid rock amidst the shifting sands of public opinion. (1)

Parkes's essays on Mill provided ammunition for an exposition of the logical principles of woman's emancipation as articulated through Mill's social and political philosophy. The discussion raises a series of issues relating to the position of women in 1860, such as the importance of education in order to equip women for intellectual work, the claim for rational thinking as a genuinely feminine activity and the problem of achieving equal pay for equal work.

Mill conferred authority on such arguments by means of his position as a philosopher and parliamentarian. This enabled feminism virtual access to ideological power, with the key aim of achieving voting rights for women. Mill's position, however, tended to re-enact the gendered dynamic of discourses such as coverture and male patronage that Bodichon and others sought to overturn. Above all, the cultural work of Langham Place was to enable women in nineteenth-century Britain to seek access to 'the place of power', as Slavoj Žižek puts it in *The Sublime Object of Ideology* (147).

Žižek's discussion of power in the democratic context argues, with reference to Lefort, that the place of power must always remain symbolically 'empty'. Democratic government must be always available to change by the people through public elections, which are 'an act of symbolic dissolution of social edifice' (Žižek, *The Sublime Object*, 147). The 'place' of power in nineteenth-century Britain was, however, filled by the monarchy and its gendered offspring – primogeniture and the House of Lords. That the reigning monarch was a woman could be explained away by the notion that Victoria occupied sovereignty's phallic power by virtue of divinely imbued inheritance in advance of her sons, while embodying the feminine qualities of maternity, domesticity and fidelity. Victoria's occupation of the throne nevertheless represented an ideological ambiguity and implied the radical potential of a role for women in government. That women in nineteenth-century Britain were now claiming a place for themselves as participants within a democratic process offered a direct challenge to the naturalness of the existing order in political as well as gendered terms.

In the absence of electoral participation for women in the parliamentary process, the periodical press was a vital means of engagement in society, politics and culture. The *English Woman's Journal* was a crucial foundation for the working out of feminist programmes and ideas. Its primary role was to enable public discussion about the conditions in which women lived and worked, providing a space for both women and men to legitimately explore and re-imagine the role of women in society in relation to principles of social justice. In addition to articles that discussed the founding ideas of the women's emancipation movement, specific cases were investigated, such as the plight of needlewomen or governesses. In many cases the issues discussed could be interpreted as belonging to the feminine sphere of nurturing domesticity transplanted into the public and political realm. It was, in part, this discursive trajectory that enabled women to enter the social field and participate in social discourse in new ways.

As well as promoting the activities of women and celebrating the achievements of successful women the *English Woman's Journal* also encouraged debate in its 'Open Council' pages. These were 'intended for general discussion', and were always presented with an editorial disclaimer. Letters to the Editor published in 'Open Council' ranged from discussion of women's employment, corrections or notes on published articles and the promotion of events likely to be of interest to *English Woman's Journal* readers. Here and elsewhere in the journal the question of broader social conditions affecting children and men as well as women was regularly examined. Public health was a dominant theme, which was addressed through investigations of school kitchens, infant mortality, factories and prisons, often with a conviction and passion inspired by the privations of miserly institutions and their filthy conditions. In Parkes's 'Sanitary Lectures', about extracts from a course of lectures given for the Ladies' Sanitary Association, she noted 'many readers of the *EWJ* are deeply interested in sanitary reform' and attempted to satisfy the interested readers with the illuminating experiences of the Revd. John Armistead, Vicar of Sandbach in the creation of a new school kitchen where the school children 'received practical instruction in cooking meat and vegetables, and in making puddings, broth and gruels which are given to our sick poor' (47). Domestic ideology thus remained the unctuous medium through which social change was promoted, whether in reference to poverty or female education. The crucial issue of proper schooling was given attention in the *English Woman's Journal* in a variety of ways, frequently with attention to the education of girls and young women, with references to both mental and physical training. Edwin Chadwick's article on 'Physical Training', for example, supported exercise as beneficial for the intellectual development of both boys and girls. The emphasis in this article, however, was on female embodiment, rather than intellectual or professional opportunity. Exercise, Chadwick argued, had a special importance for girls, equipping them for their future role in life as mothers:

the evil effects of the common bodily constraints during long hours in school are seriously manifested on girls, and especially on girls of the higher and middle classes . . . Females subjected to long hours of sedentary application, either at home or at boarding school, are peculiarly liable to spinal distortion, to hysteria, and to painful disorders, which prevail to an extent known only to physicians – making life burdensome to themselves and wretched to their unhappy offspring. (263)

Chastened by their slavery to the usual ills of femininity produced by lack of exercise, unfit women are further condemned for their concomitant unfitness as mothers since poor physical health makes women unable to nurse their own children. At the same time Chadwick attends to the intellectual development of women by deprecating unsanitary boarding school conditions:

which enfeeble the body and predispose it to disease, make the mind the body's slave: sound sanitary measures tend to enfranchise the mind and make it the body's master. (263)

Although ideological contradictions abound in Chadwick's article, the emancipatory rhetoric in this latter excerpt was in keeping with the tone of the *English Woman's Journal*. Barbara Bodichon's article on 'Middle-Class Schools for Girls' in the same volume, for example, sought to promote education for girls while marrying this agenda to a broader one of schools reform and commenting variously on the voluntary education system, classroom conditions and the need for professional teacher training.

Bodichon's article openly addressed middle-class women and men whom she saw as those most empowered to contribute to changing educational conditions for girls 'of the middle class' (172). Her appeal for improvements in the quality of female education pressed some conventional moral triggers, such as the welfare of children and anxieties that attended public perceptions of the rising numbers of unemployed woman. Elsewhere Bodichon also nodded to the gendered ideology of motherhood as a woman's highest aspiration, perhaps partly to mitigate the radicalism of her argument, at the same time maintaining her clear stance on the practical necessities of educating 'middle class' girls and enabling them to become financially independent:

While the essential duties of these future women as mothers, house-keepers and governors of families must always be kept in view before and beyond every other object, the fact that most of the girls will probably have to work during some years for their own livelihood must not be lost sight of. (176)

Class issues emerged in various ways in the *English Woman's Journal* which largely affirmed the consolidation of the middle class as the social body most accommodated to pursuing national domestic objectives. For example, in the ongoing debate over the activities of the Society for Promoting the Employment of Women one correspondent to 'Open Council' questioned emigration as a solution for the problem of poor employment opportunities for middle-class women:

Madam, As I understand that your Journal penetrates as far as New Zealand, I take advantage of it to offer a few observations in reply to an article in a New Zealand newspaper, reproaching the Society for Promoting the Employment of Women, for seeking to enlarge the sphere of female occupations in England, instead of sending more women out to the colonies . . . information received on the subject of the want of women in the colonies, is most uncertain and contradictory. (141)

Moreover, the writer adds, the hearty working-class women who would be likely to find suitable employment in the colonies:

seldom, if ever, apply at our office . . . The applicants are either maid servants whose health will no longer enable them to do hard work . . . or else they are women of altogether a different class, tradesmen's daughters and others belonging to the middle ranks, whose fathers have been ruined or have died. (142)

In public response to this issue, in an article entitled 'A Year's Experience in Woman's Work', Bessie Rayner Parkes admits:

We have tried this year to induce several ladies to take advantage of the assisted passages granted to Canterbury, in New Zealand, the only place to which assisted passages are granted for educated women. But we found none willing to start . . . because of the vague uncertainty which awaited them on the other side. (120)

The *English Woman's Journal* was, nevertheless, actively working on home ground to produce social change. The journal offered something new to readers of the 1860s: a serious, informed and intellectually engaged publication that discussed the social position of women in Britain in relation to other major reform issues of the day, but without promoting a total inversion of gendered roles. The journal, its editors at Langham Place, and its contributors, held an important position as a locus for social and political action on several fronts. As Candida Lacey notes, the *English Woman's Journal* instrumentally supported the early work of Jessie Boucherett, Maria Rye, Isa Craig and Emily Faithfull in furthering opportunities for women in many fields (12). Further, Pauline Nestor comments in 'A New Departure in Women's Publishing: *The English Woman's Journal* and *The Victoria Magazine*', that the importance of the *English Woman's Journal* perhaps lay most of all in what it stood for: a 'foray by women for women into the world of print, principled and political in the broadest sense' (100).

The *English Woman's Journal* merged briefly with the *Alexandra Magazine* in 1864 in a move toward achieving a more popular audience but the enterprise was short lived. It was not long, however, before other magazines emerged built on the foundations of the *English Woman's Journal*, notably the *Englishwoman's Review* founded by Jessie Boucherett. In '"Amazed At Our Success": the Langham Place Editors and the Emergence of a Feminist Critical Tradition', Solveig Robinson points out that the *Englishwoman's Review* was the direct heir to the *English Woman's Journal* and took up the mission to examine 'the sources whence spring the evils which oppress women' (160). But the *Englishwoman's Review* was not alone. The second significant publication to emerge from the advent of Langham Place was the *Victoria Magazine* established in May 1863 by Emily Faithfull and Emily Davies. Later publications, such as *Woman's Signal* or the *Rational Dress Society Gazette*, also emerged as part of the new tradition in women's journals, often generated in response to single issues associated with living conditions for women, in these instances, temperance and dress reform respectively. The *Victoria Magazine*, however, aimed to engage a much broader level of public interest and was one of the most important women's publications of its time.

The relationship between Faithfull, Parkes and Bodichon has been given attention elsewhere in relation to the conflicts and negotiations between the different, and sometimes differing, branches of the women's movement (see, for instance, Levine, Rendall, Robinson). This relationship is not, however, the main focus of this discussion. Rather, our discussion now turns to the *Victoria Magazine* itself as a practical expression of feminist ideals.

II

In its early inception the *Victoria Magazine* drew on its close association with the *English Woman's Journal* and aimed for a broader coverage of issues, approaches and ideas. The magazine was initiated by Emily Faithfull as an extension of her mission as founder of the Victoria Press. The Press opened for private business in 1860 with the support of Bessie Rayner Parkes and the Society for Promoting the Employment of Women with the purpose of providing training, experience and paid work for unemployed women.

An article, 'Victoria Press', by Emily Faithfull appeared in the *English Woman's Journal* in 1860, where she identified its purpose as being an extension of the reform programme for women's employment and cited an account in the *Edinburgh Review* of 1859 of 'the actual state of female industry in this country [where] the notion that the destitution of women was a rare and exceptional phenomenon, was swept away' (121).[2] Faithfull's initial determination was to employ women at the Press as compositors and to train girls into the printing trade. She later sought to increase opportunities for this work by creating a magazine in which women could also be employed as editors and writers and which would give the work of the Press a new public profile.

The *Victoria Magazine* featured a regular series of articles on social issues such as prison reform and education for women's employment, but it also sought to entertain its readers in ways that had not been a priority for the *English Woman's Journal*, although it had not entirely neglected the need to be entertaining, occasionally including articles on travel and even on food. The *Victoria Magazine*, however, took this a step further, publishing art reviews and fiction as well as poetry, and articles as sensational and diverse as 'Bushranging in Australia' and the 'Fortune-telling practices of the Gypsies'. In this way it strove for a broader audience, to reach readers who were not immediately drawn in the first instance to women's political issues.

The role of woman continued to be discussed as a major theme in the magazine which took the reigning monarch, Victoria, as both its title and emblem. The Victoria Press had received Victoria's official blessing, and Emily Faithfull was appointed as 'Printer and Publisher in Ordinary to Her Majesty' in July 1862 (Nestor, 'A New Departure', 102). Victoria operated in two ways for the *Victoria Magazine*: firstly as the passive and stoical figurehead of national domesticity, while also performing the – at least implicitly – active role of national helmswoman. The question of Victoria's active participation in the government of British affairs was extensively discussed in the press of the day and this issue intensified as her reign progressed. In 1879, for example, 'The Queen as a Woman of Business' appeared in the magazine *Time* seeking to defend the opacity of Victoria's rule of Britain during the phase of her apparent withdrawal from public appearance in mourning for Albert:

> though the English Monarch be the crowning ornament of the Constitution, personally associated more with ideas of dignity and splendour than of toil, it is a grievous mistake to suppose that the lot of British Royalty is, has been, or can be exempt from labour. All the assistance which energy and ingenuity can lend to the accomplishment of work, her Majesty, indeed, commands. (41)

The notion of the Queen as a hard-labouring, behind-the-scenes business woman positions Victoria in closer relation to her subjects. The use of the word labour is also a reminder of the labour of childbirth, while references to the domestic management of the nation throughout the discussion eases the tension between the troublingly gendered distinction of active and passive feminine.

Earlier in the century, Victoria was also claimed as a figure of inspiration, as Homans and Munich observe, with reference to Victoria's iconic status as the national emblem of the domestic feminine:

> She meant different things to different groups, but her inspired performances ultimately made it possible for multitudes to think that they were doing the queen's work, whatever they did – from explorations to ethnography, to 'little' imperial wars, to having portraits made of their pets. (5)

The theme of Victoria's public role is also taken up in the *Victoria Magazine* in 1864 in 'Elizabeth and Victoria from a Woman's Point of View', comparing the reigns of Elizabeth I and Victoria. As with the later, and more urgent apologia for her in *Time*, the article positions Victoria as a potent monarch, foregrounding her femininity as the source of her beneficence and power. Elizabeth, on the other hand, is gendered masculine: 'with her masculine intellect, her iron will . . . and the utter blank of her domestic life' (99) rendering her a figure only able to be admired in retrospect.

Victoria is framed as the emblem of a suitably feminine (upper-middle-class) domesticity: 'who if not born a Queen might have been much like an ordinary gentlewoman; refined, accomplished, wise and good' (99). Her public withdrawal is at first defended: ' . . . the life of a nation is not its ceremonial but its moral life, . . . womanhood is higher than queendom' and those who doubt this are reprimanded for requiring 'not merely the thing itself, but the outward demonstration of it' (102). Yet, the article ends in an exhortation to Victoria to resume her public role in honour of those subjects who have shared her experience of widowhood:

You do but love as we love, suffer as we suffer. We understand it all, but still we ask you to bear it. Live through it, as many of us have done, expending wholly for others the life which is no longer sweet to ourselves. (103)

It is this spirit of exhortation to moral vitality and active womanhood that characterised the *Victoria Magazine* where women's work is reframed in gendered terms as the labour of national fruition. The field of nursing, in 'Miss Burdett Coutts' Experiment' for example, provides:

a sphere of work in which there is no immovable barrier, either of prejudice or law, in which women may fairly be tested as organizers, and in which, whether they succeed or break down, in the long run they must incidentally do incalculable good. (84)

Even the nominally paid work of the female parish missionary in 'A Poor Woman's Work': 'is no isolated and irregular effort, wasting some of its strength in the attempt to gain and hold an independent footing; it is linked to the whole power of our Church' (399).

From a review article of *Miss Parkes' Essay on Women's Work* (vol. 5) to 'The Reform Act and Female Suffrage' (vol. 10), social and political comment in the *Victoria Magazine* echoed many of the issues raised in the *English Woman's Journal.* Among the many social reforms with which both journals engaged was the move to open up educational opportunities for women. The *Victoria Magazine* featured articles on girls in schools and professional training for nurses and telegraph operators, and so on. As the decade passed, the emphasis on women in the trades and adjunct professions expanded to include discussion of women and universities. The dominant themes of women's employment and education were also interwoven with articles on welfare issues. Among these were the reform of female prisoners, proper evening entertainment for working girls and 'Women's Work in the Church', as well as reflections on the position of women in history such as P. F. André's translation of Laboulaye's *The Civil and Political Status of the Female Sex: From the Romans to the Present Day*, which was published serially.

In 'The Influence of University Degrees on the Education of Women', Emily Davies deconstructs the traditional masculine prejudice against sending women to university. This is based on the fear, she argues, that, 'women ought not to pursue the same studies as men; and that they would become exceedingly unwomanly if they did' (48). Worse still, as the argument is typically rehearsed:

Much learning would make her mad, and would wholly unfit her for those quiet domestic offices for which Providence intended her. She would lose the gentleness, the grace, and the sweet vivacity, which are now her chief adornment, and would become cold, calculating, masculine . . . unpleasing. (48)

Davies addresses these conventional terms of femininity by arguing, firstly, that the differences between men and women are exaggerated. She claims, moreover, that it is 'idleness' rather than education that is likely to produce mental illness, citing the famous British women intellectuals Somerville, Gaskell, Howitt and women in European universities, to prove the case (60).

The *Victoria Magazine* took a clear line on the issue of women's suffrage. One of the ways that it explored this theme was to discuss digest articles from newspapers and journals on the suffrage debate, for example from *The Times*, the *Spectator* or the *London Review*. In 'Feminine Suffrage and The Pall Mall Gazette', for example, the *Victoria Magazine* sharply deconstructed and debated key points on a proposal to advance the vote to widows and unmarried women:

The argument of the *Pall Mall Gazette* is, that unless the present proposal (to give the suffrage to spinsters and widows) is intended as the thin end of the wedge it is unintelligible and idle, and if it is so intended it is either disingenuous or inconsistent. There are two other phrases used in the same meaning . . . The advocates of still farther legislation in favour of women are supposed to intend something, which the writer calls "putting all women, especially all married women, on the same footing as men in all respects;" and again it is called "a general reconstruction of the relations between the sexes" . . .

It is unwise, as Macaulay observes, to lay down a wider principle than you really want to serve your present purpose. (211)

In this way the *Victoria Magazine* provided incontrovertible evidence that the public debate about suffrage was an active one in the mainstream press as well as its more radical enclaves.

On the question of suffrage, as well as those of education and work, the magazine thus served the work of the Victoria Press, promoting both an agenda of national improvement based on the consolidation of middle-class values and practices and a programme of relative democratic reform, mediating greater access to education and jobs for women of middle- and working-class backgrounds. The Press became a focus for various social and political activities – particularly following the cooling relations with Langham Place – including the Victoria Discussion Society which at times provided content for the magazine.

By 1869 *Victoria Magazine* had clearly begun to adapt to more contemporary forms of social comment, dealing with health issues such as tight-lacing and promoting modern women's clubs, even anticipating the lush interiors and glamorised gender inversions of the 1890s, in a review essay on George Sand's *Elle et Lui*. Its adaptive content, however, was not to ensure its survival beyond the early 1870s. The magazine had regularly included references to the position of women in America, seeing this as being a potential source of inspiration to its readers. In September 1872 Emily Faithfull spent seven months in America. On her departure a poem by Sophia Eckley was published in her honour in the *Victoria Magazine*. Its funereal motifs proved premonitory, at least for the magazine:

> So thou, brave champion of a noble cause,
> Shalt be remembered when the silent grave
> Must still thy voice; and friendship's sweet applause
> Shall on Fame's records thy pure name engrave,
> And say – She gave youth, strength, and life away,
> To plead the Cause of Woman, in her day.
> (Frontispiece)

For Emily Faithfull herself, this moment marked a transition. She was heralded in America as a champion of women's rights, but found her radicalism challenged by the freedoms available to women there. At the end of her tour of American factories and schools she spoke at a shipboard lunch in her honour, her words reported in 'Farewell Banquet to Miss Faithfull':

I yield to none of those who talk of home as woman's *only sphere* in the value I place on home life . . . I always believed myself to be a good liberal until I came to America: now I have been taught to realise my conservatism. (261)

The advent of the Victoria Press was an important moment in the narrative of gender and the periodical press in Victorian Britain: partly, as Nestor observes, because the magazine strove to carry 'the torch in the face of "the quietude of all the press" on the Woman Question' (102) and partly because it directly linked the platforms of education and social reform with the professionalisation of women's work.

Alongside these discourses of reform, changing representations of women's work in the periodical press offer a useful way of mapping transformations in Victorian feminism. Langham Place and the Victoria Press were critical agents in this process of transformation, actively striving to overturn the convention that paid work was demeaning for women and proposing the notion of equal pay and equal education for women as well as men. The *Victoria Magazine* comments in 'The Payment of Women' that 'women's work is inferior to men's – a fact that arises, we are willing to admit, from their usually inferior training' (85). The promotion of education, therefore, went hand in hand with advocacy of more equal working conditions for women who, it was daringly suggested, should be seen as having equal worth as individuals with men: 'That women can live more cheaply than men – if that be the case – is no reason why they should be worse paid if they do equally good work' (85).

Changes in attitudes to working women were slow to develop. In 1858 Thomas Henry Buckle in 'The Influence of Women on the Progress of Knowledge' differentiated male and female intelligence as 'inductive' and 'deductive' respectively, citing motherhood as the most powerful means by which women have, unwittingly, served progress in the masculine sphere of knowledge:

Unconsciously, and from a very early period, there is established an intimate and endearing connexion between the deductive mind of the mother and the inductive mind of her son . . . Thus it is that by the mere play of the affections the finished man is ripened and completed. (405)

Buckle, who presented himself as a liberal, did not digress from the trope of the domestic feminine, or from the presumption of male pre-eminence, and these were to remain powerful, although contested, notions throughout the Victorian period. Ten years later, for example, the *Victoria Magazine* derided the *Pall Mall Gazette* in 'Feminine Suffrage and the *Pall Mall Gazette*' for a quotation taken on 23 April 1868 from *The Times* newspaper that:

it is absolutely requisite to the peace of the family, and to the happiness of all the members of it, that the authority of the husband and the subordination of the wife and children should be decidedly maintained. (218)

By the end of the 1860s, the work of Langham Place was still struggling to permeate the mainstream. Changes were under way, however, for both middle- and working-class women in the fields of education and employment and through the roles women increasingly played in the development and promotion of a wide range of social reform movements.

The obstacles to professional employment experienced during the 1850s and 1860s by many of the middle-class women who became associated as activists with Langham Place, such as the medical practitioners Sophia Jex Blake and Elizabeth Garrett, served as catalysts in the programme to change public attitudes. By the mid-1870s more women were entering the professions, but still struggled for acceptance. At this time the writer and activist Florence Fenwick Miller, having completed her examinations at the Ladies' Medical College, moved from medicine to feminist activism because, she recalls in 'How I Made My First Speech', this remained the more necessary field for change (4).

III

The pressure from women for social change through the periodical press continued in new and evolving ways during the 1880s and early 1890s. Reflecting on the advances made by women in her own time, Millicent Garrett Fawcett gave the Married Women's Property Act (1882) and the Infant's Custody Act (1886) as evidence of the improved status of women, and observed in 'The Progress of Women in Political Education' that the women's emancipation movement:

has become more rapid, and it has become more self-conscious; but it never would have been what it is but for the momentum afforded by the steady, quiet pressure of the centuries behind our own . . . invisible, but immeasurably strong. (289)

Throughout the latter half of the nineteenth century the public role of women's philanthropy itself expanded, becoming a form of (usually) honorary career path which promoted greater gender and economic equality, public health, female suffrage and other political reforms as a preventative for social ills. For middle- and upper-class feminist writers and activists, such as Frances Power Cobbe, philanthropy was no longer a matter of random acts of individual charity, but a mission to 'relieve the miseries of mankind' (Lacey, *Barbara*, 13).

The promotion of women's interests through the press was not confined to the middle class. In 1889, working-class women had begun to galvanise around the issue of female labour exploitation. The feminist activist and writer Clementina Black records in 'A Working Woman's Speech' the story of the formation of a workers' union for female cigar-makers in Liverpool from a speech given by one of the union organisers. Threatened with pay reductions by the cigar factory the women went first to the manager and eventually came out on strike:

we all came out, every woman in the place – . . . they all stood together and the firm gave way. And I'm working there now. Well, then we went on with our union, and we had our troubles at first, I can tell you. (669)

The publication of Black's article in the *Nineteenth Century* – one among countless magazine articles on women and work in this period – suggests the emergence of greater public recognition of the obstacles and exploitation that women, particularly working-class women, encountered. Women's employment, education and suffrage were only the most prominent issues to engage pro-feminist writers. Other social reforms having direct impact on women's lives, such as public health, poverty, prostitution, sanitation and alcoholism, also provided mildly sensational topics for readers of the periodical press, although at times these contributions to public debates on social questions tended to reinforce class and other social prejudices, as when the *Victoria Magazine* in the 'Victoria Discussion Society' asks and responds: 'Where do we find drunkenness paramount? In the lower classes' (106).

Issues such as temperance, vegetarianism and dress reform gave rise to a host of single-issue journals and magazines, often motivated by a broader interest in improving conditions for women. Those who wrote critiques of social ills such as poverty, poor sanitary conditions, unemployment and male drunkenness were often motivated primarily because of the destructive effect these had on the lives of women and children. The *Rational Dress Society Gazette*, for instance, ran for two years and was a constant financial worry to its supporters, among whom were Constance Wilde, Charlotte Carmichael Stopes and Laura McClaren. Its aims were announced in the 'Preface':

The *Rational Dress Society Gazette* protests against the introduction of any fashion in dress that either deforms the figure, impedes the movements of the body or in any way tends to injure the health. (1)

As with so many cultural manifestations of the late-Victorian period, the *Rational Dress Society Gazette* floundered between radical critique, social conservatism and the desire for popularity, watering down its original firm position by bleating in the second issue that: 'We do not profess to do more than *suggest* a new form of dress' ('Preface', 1). The magazine carried advertisements for 'healthy' clothing of various kinds, including shoes and underwear, with occasional articles on dress in history or criticisms of current fashions. As one of its keenest contributors, Charlotte Carmichael Stopes argued for the inclusion of more advertisements, the naming of authors and even dared to inquire about payment (British Library Ms Add.58454, ff.1–38). The *Gazette* was, however, essentially the offspring of a group of well-meaning amateurs without the energy or resources to produce a more professional magazine and none of Stopes's suggestions were followed through. Many such single-issue magazines relied on the vibrancy of their parent organisations for their longevity. The Rational Dress Society had a long-lasting core of support but it was not a popular organisation with a broad-based membership. Successful publications tended to embrace more than one constituency or were connected to long-lasting issues or movements. By the middle of 1890, as subscriptions to the Society declined, the magazine was abandoned, although the idea was taken up in a new form with greater success some years later.

The *Woman's Signal* began its life, much as the *Rational Dress Society Gazette* had done, as the pet project of a small group of reformers – in this instance devoted to the twin principles of temperance and the advancement of women. It supported the aims of the Women's Christian Temperance Union, and in 'Our Policy' in its first issue Isobel Somerset portrayed it as the flashing beacon of moral activism, with a policy 'to help forward the concerted action of good women' (2). The magazine's feminism was thus inseparable from its moral and spiritual agenda. Initiated by Isobel Somerset and Annie E. Holdsworth, the *Woman's Signal* presented itself as one of the 'portals of reform' on women's and related issues: 'We cannot agree with those who hold that the individuality, talents, education and work of women find too large a place in the journalism of our day' ('Our Policy', 1).

Temperance was a long-standing personal crusade of the magazine's founder, Isobel Somerset, President of the British Women's Temperance Reform Association. Somerset, one of Britain's most wealthy women by inheritance, was also a supporter of the social advancement of women and Rosa Nouchette Carey in *Twelve Notable Good Women of the Nineteenth Century* notes Somerset believed that the *Woman's Signal* would be:

a paper which would interest and instruct the women in the home, and show them something of the movements regarding the uplifting of their sex . . . We take our stand by the side of Temperance and Social Reforms, the Purity Movement and Women's Franchise. (340–1)

Somerset saw the promotion of women's social and political rights as being directly linked with liquor reform. She states in 'Our Policy': 'we believe that the enfranchisement of women will be the enacting clause of those statutes that shall yet place the control of the liquor traffic in the hands of the people' (2). The earliest editions of the *Woman's Signal* gave substantial space to personal testimonies, fiction and general articles on this theme. The first issue, in particular, was studded with sensational titles such as 'Drink and Gold: the Twin Curses of West London' and headlines like 'The Devil's Fulcrum' and 'The Curse of Curses'. These articles linked alcoholism to problems then perceived as forms of wickedness including gambling, debauchery and crime.

As with the *Victoria Magazine*, the stated ambition of the *Woman's Signal* was to reach a broad public audience. Under the directorship of its second editor and owner, Florence Fenwick Miller, the magazine ran for a further four years, broadening its content and improving its visual style. A condition of Miller's directorship was that she continue to address the theme of Temperance in subsequent issues. She initially accepted this as one element in the progress of reforms associated with the women's movement. The magazine never achieved economic independence, however, and she later blamed Somerset's emphasis on Temperance for the magazine's ultimate demise. Miller remarked in her 'Editor's Farewell Address' in defence of her decision to terminate publication of the *Woman's Signal*:

I . . . undertook to allow a large slice of the paper to be made use of monthly, entirely at my expense, to print and publish the official notices and other matters of interest to the British Women's Temperance Association: alas! quite uninteresting to everybody else. (1)

Miller took over the management of the *Woman's Signal* towards the end of 1895. She had already appeared in the magazine's first issue in an auto-biographical article entitled 'How I made my First Speech'. It is fascinating to observe Miller's tracking in this article the political developments that occurred over the last half of the nineteenth century for women, and the potency of her own and others' contribution to this change. She writes that the 'laws about women under which I was born – less than forty years ago still' were tyrannous and unfair:

A married woman's earnings were not her own . . . her children were not recognised by the law as hers at all . . . Genuine contempt and hatred were felt and not concealed for the first women who asked for more equal laws, wider opportunities, better training, and more extended influence on public affairs for women. (4)

The story of Miller's own 'first speech', made in 1873 when she was just nineteen, is presented here as a difficult but necessary act: 'I simply joined the army that was slowly forming to fight for widening the sphere and improving the position of women' (4). The article is, above all, a statement for the importance of women's right to engage in public utterance, on the stage at public meetings and street rallies, in magazines, journals and newspapers. Miller herself was to practice all these forms of expression. Throughout her career as a writer and editor she encouraged younger women to find their own voices and engage with the ideas of the day on their own terms, arguing that gender should be no obstacle to women's equal participation in public as well as private life. The very act of 'speaking in public' is seen as a self-consciously political contesting of current values and legislature:

the very head and front of our offending . . . Only two years before I made my first speech, a public meeting in London was broken up by violence because Mrs Peter Taylor and Mrs Fawcett were to have addressed it. (4)

Miller's view on public speaking finds contemporary resonance in Žižek's anti-totalitarian idea, expressed in *The Sublime Object*, that in democracy the place of power must always remain open. Miller observes that democratic changes in women's roles and rights will not be easily accepted by the closed patriarchal order, but points to examples of the ways that change has already happened and will continue. For Miller, the magazine was an important extension of this work. Under her editorship the *Woman's Signal* embraced women's issues in the broadest sense, including articles on art, technical education, women in religion, notes on bills before parliament, recipes and poetry. She aimed for a more culturally sophisticated publication, with some emphasis on intellectual style and the New Woman. In one of her first issues, she published 'Character Sketch: Olive Schreiner' which demonstrated the breadth of issues that Miller was attempting to embrace. Miller's piece dealt with Schreiner's literary success as a woman, made references to the writer's radical views on marriage and discussed the politics of the South African colony: 'Olive Schreiner is taking a leading part just now in Cape politics. She detests very heartily and boldly the leading spirit in the development of the Transvaal' (1). Schreiner's position is seen as 'practically an attack on capitalism and private property' (1) and this vocal interest, as reported in the *Woman's Signal*, reflects Miller's sense of her own role in enabling radical women's voices to be heard, above all through the periodical press.

By the 1890s the debate on women's rights and roles had found firm footing within the mainstream as well as the radical press. Florence Fenwick Miller's role in public affairs, and as a member of the magazine-journalist fraternity, positioned her as a leading figure for feminism. She had an interesting and unusual career. Following her four-year stint as the editor of the *Woman's Signal* Miller continued a successful career in journalism, contributing widely to periodicals and newspapers, and became a leader writer for the *London Illustrated News*. Miller was also the subject of interviews and biographical articles often written as inspirational pieces for younger women. She was among several prominent women featured in the 1890s periodical *Young Woman: An Illustrated Monthly Magazine* aimed at the daughters of middle-class women who had been girls in the Girl-of-the-Period days.

Young Woman, edited by Frederick A. Atkins, offers an interesting contrast with the *Woman's Signal*. It regularly presented short biographical studies and interviews with enlightened women as 'role models' for girls: the writer, scholar and union activist Clementina Black, the publisher Emily Faithfull, the journalist Emily Crawford, and the writers John Strange Winter (Mrs. Arthur Stannard), Olive Schreiner and Katharine Tynan. Entertainment, often with instructional or even political asides, came in the form of articles ranging from domesticity to science and travel articles by well-known pro-suffrage women including Tynan, Miller and Adeline Sergeant.

Young Woman appeared to encourage the development of independent-minded and active young women, but its politics was at times confounded both by the discourse of the domestic feminine and by the awareness of the practical limitations of women's lives. In 'Our Contributors' Club' Mrs H. M. Stanley commented on the benefits of natural history as a hobby:

I would advise parents to encourage their girls to live *out* of themselves: to get them microscopes, or aquariums, or even hedgehogs, squirrels, owls, or bats, if it will quicken in the girl an all-absorbing interest in life, and rouse a love for the dear little room at home, where you may be "scientific" and untidy, and messing to your heart's content. (25)

Here, the writer both urges readers to undertake study, observation, exploration and interests beyond conventional accomplishments but returns them to the 'dear little room', the safe space within which such activities and their untidy outcomes can be hidden from the rest of the world.

In many ways the *Young Woman* was distinctively declarative in its liberal view of the position of women, but it allowed its liberalism to be mitigated. It adopted the strategy used by a number of women's magazines in this period, presenting several short pieces by keynote writers from different perspectives. On the subject of 'The Ideal Husband', for example, Lady Jeune wrote: 'The new woman has appeared, and in her new-found strength she is redressing the inequalities of four thousand years . . . What men laughed at and ridiculed at the onset has now become an accomplished fact' (23). John Strange Winter, on 'The Ideal Husband', with her tongue planted firmly in her cheek announces:

the ideal husband will from the very first make his wife his friend, his chum, his other half. . . . he will not worry nor interfere about small domestic details; and even if owing to some accident . . . he has had a bad dinner, he will not make himself more disagreeable than he can help; for he will remember that to a good wife it is pain untold to see her husband served with a dinner which is not above reproach. (119)

If the *Young Woman* occupied the more stylish end of the publication range during the 1890s its competition was a host of new liberal, pro-reform magazines such as the *Humanitarian, Shafts* and the *Woman's Tribune*, laying the groundwork for the increasing radicalism of magazines associated with the suffragette movement of the early twentieth century.

As women began to enter trades, schools, universities and the professions the pressure for women's suffrage grew and the periodical press remained a crucial medium of expression and debate for this and other social re-form movements. There was, however, as the legislative history of the suf-frage movement shows, steady and often strident institutional resistance to change. The magazine *Punch, or the London Charivari* – an institution in its own right – is perhaps one of the most potent and long-lasting barometers of masculine antagonism towards women. The cross-currents and contra-dictions within the gender politics of *Punch* can provide a useful means of tracing some of the transformations and resistances in attitudes to femi-nism, although it must be remembered that this magazine's main aim was always to be satiric about the status quo. The use of negative female tropes as a means of condemning the anti-suffrage Goldwin Smith in 'To a Male Scold' is a case in point:

'Oh! Goldwin Smith, great Goldwin Smith,
Who set such store by manly pith,
You have a most effeminate fashion
Of getting in a towering passion!

Your last attack's a regular rough rage
Excited by the Female Suffrage . . .
I seem to see your angry jaw set
Against the pleas of Mrs. Fawcett . . .
The way in which you whirl and twirl
Reminds one of an angry girl
Not of a man composed and bold.
Women you flout? Then do not scold;
For that is quite a woman's way
And imitating her won't pay.   (21)

The Victorian period was, above all, a time of unprecedented development and change: economic, industrial, geographical and political. The
movements of reform that emerged in this period – from expanding legal
and political rights to public sanitation and education – were, in many ways,
linked to this pattern of change with broader structural reforms helping
the discourses of liberalism and social change to emerge on several fronts,
including that of feminism.

As we argue throughout this discussion, the periodical press was a major
sphere for the working out of social attitudes towards women, a subject that
received intense, even at times disproportionate attention by both supporters and attackers of women's rights. Perhaps partly because of its diversity
of opinion and capacity to embody multiple standpoints, the periodical
press was a central means of expression for mid-nineteenth-century feminists, providing a venue for social comment. The periodical press provided
women with an outlet for promoting causes, debating contemporary issues,
passing on information to the public, attracting organisational membership
and a forum for establishing and developing new ideas. This was not without its difficulties, however. The periodical press, even more directly than
the novel, permitted women to earn money while remaining at home, thus
troubling widely held conceptions of the domestic sphere as a sacred place
free from professional (female) activity.[3] Further, as Patrick Brantlinger observes in *The Reading Lesson*, the press was the focus of some degree of social
anxiety for its capacity to give voice to dissident social groups, producing
fears of radicalism and unrest (23).

The emergence of organised feminism in the mid-nineteenth century
was conveyed in the press through diverse and evolving representations
of femininity and masculinity and was regarded variously as an aspect
of social progress or decay. Frequently, magazine editors capitalised on
the implicit salaciousness of the woman question by presenting opposing
views. The press was, therefore, as with other cultural fields, subjected to the

pressure of ideological homogeneity. Its status as an item of consumption further reinforced this homogenising process. But, as we emphasise from the outset, this was neither uniform nor coherent.[4] Through the work of women in the nineteenth-century periodical press, the key tropes of representation through which the idea of the feminine was uttered were gradually unsettled, countered and broken down into more multiple and accessible forms.

CHAPTER SEVEN

Gender, commodity and the late nineteenth-century periodical

This chapter addresses two manifestations of late nineteenth-century magazine culture in Britain: the brief flourishing of the journals of art and literature associated with decadence, and developments in fashion magazines for women. The proliferation of the periodical during the nineteenth century, combined with its increasing specialisation, suggests that the split between popular and high-aesthetic culture began to be broken down by the mass production of the periodical press in all its forms.[1] Here we consider how these two forms of the late-Victorian periodical are linked by the rise of the magazine as commodity in the nineteenth century, and the extent to which gender emerges in this period as a discourse of consumption. A rapid expansion of the periodical press occurred during the early decades of the nineteenth century, followed by a sudden decline during the 1860s.[2] This decline was reversed towards the end of the century, exemplified by the great increase in the number of magazines targeted at women readers.

The rise of the magazine as commodity intersects with a number of key nineteenth-century discourses, including education, work, commerce and class. As Thomas Richards notes in *Commodity Culture of Victorian England* (1990), for example, the 'icons of Victorian commodity culture all originated in middle-class periodicals' (7). This chapter continues to explore the ways that women from different social groups participated in consumer culture as readers, writers, subjects and purchasers of magazines. Here we also refer to the evolving shape of Victorian masculinity and discuss some of its challenges. The mode of the periodical itself can be seen as one expression of a late-Victorian discourse of social and cultural transformation through which categories of gender are apparently contested. The periodical has a particular relation, moreover, to tropes of the feminine, with its attending bodily associations of regularity, production and change.

I

The value of the notion of periodicity as a trope for gendered discourse is strikingly apparent in the case of the woman's fashion magazine where the publication's purpose as commodity is so closely engaged with reinscribing a text of femininity.[3] In ' "A Material Girl in a Material World": the Fashionable Female Body in Victorian Women's Magazines' Kay Boardman refers to the woman's magazine as a locus for nineteenth-century representations of the female body and consumer practices, arguing that:

> the spectacular image of the female body in women's magazines with its emphasis on consumption, display and leisure and its relationship to burgeoning consumer capitalism becomes almost a metonymy for capital, for spectacle and for modernity in popular Victorian discourse. (94)

Perhaps more than any other genre of the periodical press, the fashion magazine draws attention to the elements that create it as a perpetual site of consumption: its repetition, the textual brevity of its use and appeal, and its foregrounding of the body as the locus for a set of discourses of consumer culture. As a spectacular practice, to invoke Guy Debord's 1983 work *Society of the Spectacle*, the magazine is constituted as the object of a gendered consumer gaze, but is also the site of a semi-sustained multivocality, shaped by changing generic forms and conflicting desires. This notion will be examined more closely in relation to some key magazines of the British *fin de siècle* but can be exemplified more generally here, by way of introduction, by the manner in which late nineteenth-century fashion magazines often shift from treating women seriously as intelligent beings interested in health, education and professional life, to portraying them as inarticulate creatures repeatedly seized by passing fancies to possess the latest fashion item. It is made further evident in the literary and art magazines of the 1890s where representations of both masculinity and femininity are foregrounded in frequently contradictory and cross-referential ways.

Gender thus emerges as a discursive vehicle for the practices of late-Victorian commodity consumption. Indeed, an interesting three-way relationship can be seen between the emergence of masculine decadence as a fashion movement, Victorian fascination with the commodity and the expanding late nineteenth-century periodical press, particularly as it gathered momentum during the last two decades of the century.[4] The magazine, in this period, can be seen as a compendium of proto-modernity with all its goods on display. Even in its more self-consciously literary versions, the late nineteenth-century magazine operates as a virtual emporium, offering an endlessly repeated source of fascination and delight, with its collections of articles, pictures, advice columns, advertisements and reviews.[5] In fact, the success of the popular magazine relied on the diversity of its appeal. Gender, as we have argued, is central to this discourse of consumption. The aim of the press, however, was also to reach a wide audience by diversifying magazine content, suggesting at least on a superficial level, the recognition and targeting of different social groups and identities as a means of attracting a wide readership.

With the expansion in popular magazines for women in the latter part of the nineteenth century came an intensified elaboration of the feminine as trope of commerce. This can be demonstrated in the way that the idea of 'woman' was glamorised through commodity fetishism in advertisements for feminine items from hats to corsets, and in the fashion columns of the popular daily press. The trope of the feminine as a mode of exchange was not, however, merely confined to the woman's magazine as part of a wider doctrine of separate spheres for men and women. In the context of the late nineteenth-century periodical press, the female body was also the key to the economic relation between the fields of commerce and art, and to the crossing of notional boundaries between them. Kathy Psomiades argues in *Beauty's Body: Femininity and Representation in British Aestheticism* that within Victorian aestheticism the representation of 'femininity allows for the difficult and vexed relation between the categories of the aesthetic and the economic' to be both signalled and masked by a gendered eroticism (3). Psomiades's argument is based on a study of Victorian aesthetic literature and art, but her recognition of the interlocking tensions between art and commerce can usefully inform a discussion, for example, of the woman's fashion magazine, where the category of the feminine works to glamorise and eroticise commodity consumption.

The feminine is at its most performative and recognisable within the genre of the fashion magazine, but it can also be traced through complex tensions within the periodical press more generally. Consciousness of feminine identity is a recurrent theme that runs across the genres of magazine culture, taking multiple forms and preoccupying illustrators, poets, fiction writers, essayists and reviewers in different ways. The feminine attracts attention and contradiction, often inviting its apparent boundaries to be challenged. From the 1860s, constant lampooning of the 'unfeminine' occurs in numerous forms from cartoons to non-fiction prose. At the same time the establishment of the feminine as a naturalised category tends to deflect its recognition as an economically motivated trope. As Thomas Richards has observed, and as has been discussed earlier, the presiding gendered identity of the age, Victoria Regina, herself emerges as a feminine commodity (71–118).

We would not want to suggest, however, that the commodification of the feminine is a straightforward process in which the expression of gendered difference as a mode of consumption simply fixes women as cultural objects. The idea of 'woman' as commercial *tabula rasa* was frequently contested by the way that her intellectual and professional role in society was widely discussed and debated within the periodical press. The commodification of the feminine may also be seen as central, if problematic, to the creation of women as cultural players and as consumers themselves. Ros Ballaster, Margaret Beetham, Elizabeth Frazer and Sandra Hebron in *Women's Worlds* have shown, for example, the way in which gender issues were central to the construction of women as active participants in this social and economic exchange, arguing that 'it is no accident that the late nineteenth-century boom in magazines addressed specifically to women coincided with the increasing importance of advertising revenue in the financing of the periodical press' (80). The use of feminine tropes, for example, as a press marketing strategy in one sense allows women to enter the marketplace, as it also binds them in other ways to passive and conventional forms of social existence. In *The Gender of Modernity* Rita Felski explores the contradictions within the discourses surrounding female consumption, observing that on the one hand:

consumption was presented as a necessity, indeed as a familial and civic duty for the middle-class woman . . . on the other hand, the growth of consumerism was seen as engendering a revolution of morals . . . which could in turn affect the stability of existing social hierarchies. (65)

From quite early in the nineteenth century women participated in the periodical press in substantial ways, as writers and as subjects, even though the recognition that women were beginning to enter the public sphere through the periodical press was publicly viewed as a breach of moral nature and convention. Mary Poovey argues in *The Proper Lady and the Woman Writer: Ideology as Style* that any association between women and money still carried the taint of sexual exchange. She writes:

Writing for publication, in other words, jeopardizes modesty, that critical keystone of feminine propriety . . . cultivates and calls attention to the woman as subject, as initiator of direct action, as a person deserving of notice for her own sake. (37)[6]

As one observer firmly expressed it in 1871 in an article in *Temple Bar*, 'Woman's Proper Place in Society', woman's mission 'is within doors, not out of doors; not in the market place, but in that more sacred and tranquil interior of which the hearth is the altar and the shrine' (178). Later in the century the participation of women in the periodical press remained active and contested. This participation was framed by a discourse in which the boundaries of the feminine seemed to be in question while, paradoxically, the use of the feminine as a mechanism of commerce relied on a set of discursive markers that were apparently fixed and coherent.

Such negotiations over the representation of femininity are, then, crucial for an examination of gender and commerce in the late nineteenth-century periodical press. Representations of the masculine, however, also played an important part in the gendered discourse of the *fin de siècle* and were used to promote the periodical press. Although overt attention was much less frequently directed to the question of gender in masculine terms in commercial texts of the period, there are some clear instances in which broad notions of male social identity are subjected to close and often contradictory definitions, ranging from those of male effeminacy,[7] including the dandy, aesthete and decadent youth, to those of the intellectual auteur and colonialism's adventure hero. While men were frequently positioned differently from women, as the participants in an equal dialogue about culture, rather than as passive consumer or embodiment of discursive practices, the masculine was by no means coherently represented. Arthur Symons's *Savoy*, for example, while framed almost exclusively for a male audience interested in 'good literature', achieved its social cachet partly through the sexual ambiguity of Aubrey Beardsley's elaborate designs. Moreover, the combination of the *Savoy*'s literary sensibility and its anti-femininity served to identify the magazine in a particular way as a problematic masculine product, marked, even feminised, by the taint of early-nineties decadence. In the introduction to *A Magazine of Her Own?*, Margaret Beetham comments that it 'would be impossible to write a comparable history of magazines which defined men in terms of their masculinity' (3). While the text of gender is unquestionably constructed as the text of the feminine in the nineteenth-century periodical press, and beyond, Beetham's statement signals the extent to which ideological significations of the masculine are, at times, so paradigmatic as to seem invisible. We aim to take up this issue here in order to explore some of the ways that both masculinity and masculine difference can be said to have had a commercial function for the late nineteenth-century magazines of art and culture such as the *Yellow Book* (1894–7) and the *Savoy* (1896).

In the second part of this discussion, we attempt to engage with the often vexed relationship between aesthetic and popular culture in the periodical press by investigating different aspects of the representation of gender within both these cultural realms. The split between culture and commerce is exemplified, primarily, by the *Yellow Book*, edited by Henry Harland and Aubrey Beardsley, and by women's popular magazines such as *Woman's Life* and *Woman At Home*. In order to mediate the boundaries between culture and commerce we begin with a brief discussion of the magazine *Woman's World*, edited by Oscar Wilde. Reference to the *Woman's World* allows us to interrogate the connections between the decadent preoccupation with gender and artifice and to consider the central part that the idea of 'woman' played in the promotion of fashion magazines. *Woman's World* foregrounds the way that categories of gender and generic categories of the magazine both operate as contested discourses within the broader cultural and economic field of the periodical press. *Woman's World* can also be seen as a site of transfer between magazines of high culture and the popular women's press, offering an important example of the ways that representations of gender both traced and traversed the boundaries between the two periodical modes. The persona of Oscar Wilde, with its own ambiguities, contradictions and transformations, was central to this process. Our discussion will conclude by examining some key representations of gender in the popular women's press of the 1880s and 1890s.

II

If the *Yellow Book* was considered 'the Oscar Wilde of periodicals', as Walter Graham observes in *English Literary Periodicals* (265), it did its best to disassociate itself from that particular signifier of decadent identity – not that it was able to escape the persona of Wilde altogether as the frequently cited incident leading to Aubrey Beardsley's dismissal as art editor of the magazine shows. Questions of public perception and reception were central to the *Yellow Book*'s identity and approach for both social and economic reasons. In this respect the magazine was part of the broader commercial conditions of periodical publishing, well established by the mid-1890s.[8] Seven years earlier it was the social cachet of Oscar Wilde's public identity[9] that prompted Wemyss Reid at Cassell to invite him to become editor of the *Lady's World*, one of the company's in-house magazines.

The woman's magazine is important for this discussion in several ways. It directly foregrounds the concept of gender, presents an ideological view of the feminine that is at once extreme and contested, and speaks to the category of the feminine within a context where deference to masculine authority is not a necessary precondition of female expression. In *Making A Social Body*, Mary Poovey draws on the concept of relative autonomy, as evolved by Louis Althusser and Pierre Bourdieu, to articulate the 'relative' or partial nature of autonomous institutional practices in a way that can serve to elaborate the shifting ideological tensions and transformations within the cultural field of the periodical press: 'the concept of relative autonomy enables us to register both a historical process – the gradual disaggregation of domains and the specification of relationships among the institutions that reified this disaggregation – *and* a continuing structural interdependence' (13).

As with earlier genres of the periodical, discussed in previous chapters, a further significant aspect of the late-Victorian woman's magazine is its multivocality, that is its capacity to encompass ideology and difference within the same textual space. Multivocality can unsettle and affirm prevailing social values. The woman's magazine can appear, for example, to transcend class boundaries by referring to experiences common to all women, but also reinforces stereotypes of women as concerned with trivial subjects such as appearance and gossip. For Oscar Wilde, the focus of these magazines on fashion, costume and public identity intersected with his interest in the symbolic power of the public image. Indeed, his editorship of the *Woman's World* enabled him both to extend his identification with high literary culture and to further promote his public persona through the development of a market for the popular consumption of literature and art, a process which he had begun through his tours for D'Oyly Carte.

The *Woman's World* was a remodelling of Cassell's fashion magazine for middle-class women, the *Lady's World*, first published by Cassell in 1887.[10] Edited by Wilde in 1888 and 1889, the magazine ran for a further year without a star editor, until it was withdrawn from publication at the end of 1890. As Anya Clayforth observes, Wilde's alteration to the title, from 'lady' to 'woman', reflects the emergence of a new market of female readers in the late nineteenth century and shows in some interesting ways the extent to which the trope of Victorian woman was changing and contested (88–9). In its general content *Woman's World* explores the representation of woman in different forms and social contexts, responding to well-established nineteenth-century debates about the social role of women in terms of a range of clichés: as Coventry Patmore's domestic Angel, as Eliza Lynn Linton's Girl of the Period, as the Queen of Ruskin's domestic garden, or as *Victoria Magazine*'s Queen of social reform and as the New Woman of *fin-de-siècle* fiction.

The preoccupation of the woman's magazine with the reification of a marketable 'ideal' woman raises the potential question of the 'ideal' man – an issue raised in many other types of journals – and points to the interactions between popular culture and literary discourse. The magazine addresses the trope of woman by featuring articles on famous women in history, celebrating the fashionable accoutrements of femininity, and even attempting to create obscure women into celebrities, as in the case of Marie Corelli's piece 'Shakespeare's Mother'. Elsewhere the magazine followed the popular practice of profiling famous women in history: Mme de Recamier, Mme de Maintenon, Cleopatra, oriental women poets, as well as British and European royalty. *Woman's World* recognised the achievements of women and published new poetry and prose by women writers, many with established literary reputations including Olive Schreiner and Amy Levy, but it did so in a way that was characteristic of the contradictions and multiple subject positions of the woman's fashion magazine. Serious discussion of literary and social issues was accompanied by fashion notes and prettily decorated illustrations, while the portrait of the Princess of Wales in her academic robes mixed with the rather more rampant figure of Ellen Terry as Lady Macbeth. The feminine operates in the magazine both as a trope of art – through the figure of the female artist such as Sappho, Kauffmann, Browning and Rossetti – and as commodity, linking material consumption and visual representation. Aestheticism itself is thus constructed here not as an invasion of high cultural journalism, as Osbert Burdett suggested in *The Beardsley Period*, with reference to the *Yellow Book*, but as a recasting of the popular commercial mode to incorporate aestheticism as a form of cultural exchange that is popularly available for exercise and consumption.

Woman's World delved into a range of fashionable topics, in particular addressing the politics of the 'woman question' by featuring articles advocating women's educational and political rights, such as those by Millicent Fawcett, 'Woman's Suffrage', and Laura McLaren, 'The Fallacy of the Superiority of Man', which were challenged by anti-suffragists like Lucy M. J. Garnett's 'Reasons for Opposing Woman Suffrage'. Its promotion of dress reform and sport for girls and celebration of the work of women in the arts constructed a view of women's contribution to mainstream culture as historically important. It also followed the common practice of fashion magazines marketed for women in discussing professional opportunities for women, although in the case of *Woman's World* the representations of women and work tend to be marked by class politics, Morell's 'The Umbrella' for instance (155). Articles on such topics as women field workers or lady shopkeepers, for example, are presented in very different terms from the magazine's promotion of medicine, teaching and academic study as suitable occupations for middle- and upper-class women. Indeed, as Ros Ballaster *et al.* observe, the cultivation of a middle-class readership identification with middle-upper-class practices and values was a common characteristic of the fashion magazine. Alfred Harmsworth's mid-1890s weekly magazine *Home Chat* exemplifies this. While it was aimed at middle-class women, Ballaster *et al.* point out that *Home Chat's* occasional subject matter and its by-lines by women with aristocratic titles:

> carried a double promise to female readers. On the one hand they allowed the readers the pleasure of asserting their equality *as women* with those supposedly far above them . . . and paradoxically, they offered them a peek into the world of the very rich. (105)

Both class and personality were marketable commodities in the world of the magazine and the *Woman's World* used both to its advantage. Wilde actively sought contributions from key society figures, well-known writers and illustrators, as is demonstrated by his letters to various 'names' of the age (Wilde, *Selected Letters*, 68). His own voluminous presence figured through a regular column initially entitled 'Literary and Other Notes' which reviewed books and commented on social events. The social notes were later dropped and the column contracted to literary reviews, but by the middle of 1889 Wilde had lost interest altogether and even the reviews disappeared. Individual contributors were named both in the contents list, by their formal married names or titles, if they were women, and at the end of each piece by personal names. The widespread practice of capitalising on the cult of personality was a guiding principle of many articles published in *Woman's World*, enacted through a parade of famous female personae, but above all via the figure of Wilde himself as the presiding masculine genius of feminist cultural sophistication and reform.

Wilde attempted to create a publication that, he claimed, would 'deal not merely with what women wear, but with what they think, and what they feel' (*Selected Letters*, 68), and his own identity lent the magazine an air of intellectual credibility. He sought to achieve this by incorporating the popular topics of fashion and society with the more serious issues of gender identity and cultural history. Wilde commissioned essays by several writers on the history and significance of women's fashion items, treating fashion as a subject for serious discussion. These include S. William Beck's 'A Treatise on Hoops' and 'Gloves Old and New', Constance Wilde's piece on 'Muffs', referring to their depiction in major works of art, F. Mabel Robinson's 'Fans' and Wilde's feature review, 'A Fascinating Book' on Lefebre's *The History of Lace*. Wilde was to utilise some of this gendered cult knowledge of the history and mystique of the commodity in his novel *The Picture of Dorian Gray* (chapter 11). The elaboration of this contemporary discourse on fashion, gender and the commodity through the periodical press was taken up in parodic terms in Max Beerbohm's *Yellow Book* article, 'A Defence of Cosmetics'.

This treatment of fashion as a discourse is suggestive of Wilde's interest in the transformations and ambiguities of social and sexual identity that characterised the more theatrical moments of *fin-de-siècle* culture. Indeed, the whole question of 'gender' works more broadly as a topical subject in *Woman's World* where its contributors appear to be questioning the naturalness of gender identity by referring to masculine, as well as feminine, dress practices, an issue that Wilde had expressed interest in elsewhere. Wilde observed, for instance, that:

the uniform black that is worn now, though valuable at a dinner-party, where it serves to isolate and separate women's dresses, to frame them as it were, still is dull and tedious and depressing in itself, and makes that aspect of club-life and men's dinners monotonous and uninteresting. (*Selected Letters*, 91)

This treatment of costume and masculinity in *Woman's World* is exemplified by such pieces as Emily Crawford's 'Women Wearers of Men's Clothes', Ella Hepworth-Dixon's 'Women on Horseback' and Beck's descriptions of historical changes in the gendering of social dress codes in 'Gloves Old and New' (88). To a limited extent this challenged the naturalness of gendered difference by pointing to transitions in the cultural significance of dress and other fashion items.

The magazine's interest in gender from a variety of perspectives offers a useful point of reference for Wilde's negotiation of literary culture, social transformation and the marketing of public identity in the *Woman's World*. To some extent, as the *Yellow Book* drew the veil of light entertainment over the seriousness of decadence, *Woman's World* can be said to engage in a similar kind of veiling, its use of fashion and popular women's culture serving to cover its more unsettling discussion of the fashioning of gender roles. *Woman's World* was not unusual, however, in its attempt to address issues of interest to a broad range of women readers. Other magazines, for example, Arnold Bennett's *Woman* or Annie S. Swan's *Woman At Home*, also discuss the role of women in social life from various points of view. Further, while *Woman's World* at times seems radical in its advancement of women, interpolating the voices of women into contemporary social and cultural discourse, this process is circumscribed by the generic identification of the woman's magazine as marginal, and by the economic imperative for the publication to conform in a broad sense to middle-class gender ideology. The social and political discussions in *Woman's World* on the history of costume, women writers or female enfranchisement were framed, indeed by Wilde himself, in ways that indicated these topics were not meant to be taken too seriously. This was signalled in the tone of Wilde's literary reviews, in the inclusion of social and cultural ephemera, and in the textual framing of the 'fashion' periodical as a genre of popular culture. His reviews in 'Some Literary Notes' of women writers, for example, refer to 'little volumes', 'nice stories', 'poetesses', 'admirable decorations', to Violet Fane's 'temper of wonder' (2:223), or in 'A Note on Some Modern Poets', to Mabel Robinson's 'fascinating spring lyrics' (111). At the same time, Wilde had prefigured his vision for the magazine as one that 'men could read with pleasure' (*Selected Letters*, 68) indicating a blurring of boundaries between the gendering of the periodical genre, momentarily allowing *Woman's World* to be associated with the more entertaining forms of 'authentic' public discourse carried on among men in organs of the press from the *Pall Mall Gazette* to the *Saturday Review*. This was most obvious in the regular articles on fashion: 'The Latest Fashions' by Mrs Johnstone and 'Paris Fashions' by 'Violette'. Above all, the magazine's conservatism is evidenced by its representation of the feminine as marked by availability, in particular by its availability for consumption through the propagation of materialism, as conveyed through numerous written pieces and illustrations on dress and other consumables from wedding chests to feather fans. The advantage, however, of this concentration on the feminine as a discursive entity was the foregrounding of gender as an area of cultural negotiation which reflected the interests of many of the magazine's contributors including women writers such as Charlotte Carmichael Stopes, Olive Schreiner and Laura McLaren, among many others. While the issue of gender was appropriated by the commercial field in the form of the woman's fashion periodical, this also became a means of widening access to the debates about the social roles of men and women, if packaged in a way that not only entertained the reader but also appeared ultimately to conform to prevailing values.

In the year following Wilde's departure from the editor's office *Woman's World* adopted a more conventional approach, including sewing patterns and other domestic items. Interestingly, these alterations were not successful in increasing sales, perhaps suggesting that the new female readership Wilde had identified in 1887 had begun to look to new kinds of publications for their reading material. Just as, in its attempt to aestheticise material culture, *Woman's World* was only briefly useful to Wilde as a means of evolving his public identity as a writer and London literary figure, ultimately the magazine's progressive standpoint was only useful to the publishers, Cassell, as a market strategy for reaching a newly emerging female readership. As with Cassell, several publishing companies capitalised on this new market, as demonstrated by the activities of publishers and editors such as George Sala, George Newnes and Alfred Harmsworth who produced numerous penny magazines aimed at women readers. *Woman's World* remains notable, however, for the way its representations of gender served to connect both the commercial and the cultural fields. In this sense, through its interest in fashion, public identity, literary culture and social transformation, *Woman's World* is among those magazines that anticipated and, arguably, even created the economic conditions for the less popular but influential cultural magazines of the 1890s.

III

Writing in 1925, Osbert Burdett in *The Beardsley Period: An Essay in Perspective*, characterised the cultural quarterlies of the 1890s, the *Yellow Book* and the *Savoy*, as an attempted invasion of commercial publishing, arguing that these magazines were seen as radical partly because they challenged the economic basis of the popular press: 'It was the uneasy sense that . . . disinterested work might be able to enter the commercial field and appropriate a corner of it, that constituted the excitement that the *Yellow Book* aroused' (258). Burdett's notion that the commercial field was challenged and even disrupted by the emergence of the economically 'disinterested' publishing enterprise is, of course, only one element in the notoriety that these journals achieved. The aura of scandal that accompanied the early issues of the *Yellow Book*, for example, has been extensively associated with its reputation for a willingness to publish material relating to sexual identity and desire: what Katherine Mix in *A Study in Yellow* calls its 'shocking but profitable modernity' (198). This is exemplified by Arthur Symons's poem 'Stella Maris', which appeared in the first issue. Joseph Bristow notes in 'Sterile Ecstasies: the Perversity of the Decadent Movement' that both '*Granta* and the London-based *Critic* poured scorn on this monologue about a chance encounter with a prostitute' (74).

The way in which the *Yellow Book* mystique has been perpetuated is demonstrated by Fraser Harrison's observation in *The Yellow Book: an Illustrated Quarterly* that:

the identity of woman, and, more specifically, her sexuality, were, however, issues that dominated either overtly or by implication, an enormous number of *Yellow Book* stories. This can hardly have been the result of Harland's commissioning so many women writers, for these themes obsessed both the men and the women alike, and neither group displays more or less radicalism than the other. (28)[11]

Burdett also observes that, 'the periodical has always been commercial in England' (257), and his attention to the commercial/industrial context of the periodical press is useful partly because it draws attention to the breaching of conventional boundaries between culture and commerce. It also alerts us to the novelty and brevity of the life of the cultural magazine, its characteristic momentarity and its appeal to a variously interested readership as a desirable feature of the magazine. Indeed, his use of terms associated with desire, such as 'excitement' and 'arousal', suggests the idea of the magazine itself as a sexualized commodity. As with Holbook Jackson's study of the 1890s (*The Eighteen Nineties: a Review of Art and Ideas*), or Richard Le Gallienne's reminiscences of the same decade (*The Romantic Nineties*), Burdett's *The Beardsley Period* was written from the vantage-point of twentieth-century Modernism. From this perspective the late nineteenth-century periodical, in association with the mood of the *fin de siècle*, could begin to be read as a proto-modernist genre, emerging amid succeeding waves of representation or cultural movements that corresponded with the developments in commercial mechanisation and production. The magazines associated with *fin-de-siècle* decadence in Britain, such as the *Yellow Book*, the *Savoy*, or the less well-known *Dome*, offered a novel publishing phenomenon, the literary and cultural commodity, in which an association with the feminised practice of commodity consumption was central in establishing the air of fashionable sophistication that helped to promote them.

It was this novelty that characterised, in particular, the relationship between the *Yellow Book* and its public following, along with its relatively low prices and apparent sexual adventurousness. This magazine's broad public following was essential to its cultural and historical impact. Bridget Elliott remarks in 'Sights of Pleasure', for example, that 'one of the more interesting aspects of the *Yellow Book* was the large number of lower-middle-class readers who purchased it' (96). Elliott cites reviews in the *National Observer*, *Granta* and the *Pall Mall Gazette* as evidence for this, but does not comment on the class positioning of such magazines in relation to the *Yellow Book*. Max Beerbohm's ironical 'A Defence of Cosmetics' with its posed celebration of 'Artifice' as 'Queen', Ella D'Arcy's story 'Irremediable' with its frank depiction of a failed marriage and Aubrey Beardsley's extreme images of actresses are some of the earliest and most frequently cited examples of the journal's flagrantly decadent sensibility. Beerbohm remarks, in contemplation of the horrid spectacle of men in 'paint', that to 'lie among the rouge-pots' will inevitably 'tend to promote that amalgamation of the sexes which is one of the chief planks in the decadent platform' (78).

For all its playful satire the piece is conventionally gendered. The market politics of the *Yellow Book* underwrote this apparent decadence. As Laurel Brake in 'Endgames: The Politics of *The Yellow Book*' argues, the magazine's sensationalism functioned 'in the marketplace as a new journalism technique of enhancing sales' (59–60). Its effect in the first instance, however, was to alienate the reviewers, although not the purchasers of the magazine. Elizabeth K. Helsinger has, moreover, noted in another context in 'Consumer Power and the Utopia of Desire: Christina Rossetti's "Goblin Market"', that the conventionalism of associations between women and consumer practices were well established, observing that in eighteenth- and nineteenth-century upper- and middle-class culture, 'women were themselves a sign of luxury' (191).

The sensationalism of the early editions of the *Yellow Book* was not only a product of the references to sexuality or to gender transformations such as the 'new woman'. Commerce itself contributes to this idea of the magazine as a text of sensationalism in the way it is foregrounded as a theme in the magazine. Most importantly, for the purposes of this discussion, it is the engagement between gender and commerce that forms a central discourse in the *Yellow Book* and this is at its most 'scandalous' in those examples where the feminine enters the marketplace. This occurs, for example, where women are shown to participate in the literary and non-literary marketplace as active players, compromising the boundaries of the conventional feminine. One of the most interesting and neglected instances of this intersection between the feminine and the marketplace is Kenneth Grahame's short story 'The Headswoman', about a young Frenchwoman of the sixteenth century, Jeanne, who decides to adopt her father's profession of town executioner. This is an hereditary position, but Jeanne's right to inherit is placed in question by the fact that she is a woman.

'The Headswoman' is a class-conscious satire on major 'decadent' themes. The story pokes fun at both Mayoral bureaucracy and the 'new woman' narrative, adopting a tone of masked avuncularity in its rendering of Jeanne's gender-free, socialist labour-market philosophy: 'to be dependent on no one. I am both willing and able to work, and I only ask for what is the common right of humanity . . . a fair day's wage for a fair day's work' (27). Although one town councillor protests that this 'is unheard-of', Jeanne's graceful but businesslike manner prevails.

'The Headswoman' combines many of those elements for which the *Yellow Book* acquired its popular, if exaggerated, reputation: art, death, desire, theatricality, commerce, the 'new woman' and things French. Jeanne's work places her literally in the marketplace of a French township, centre stage with the executioner's axe in hand, where she performs for her audience in a thoroughly dignified and ladylike way:

Instead of objecting, as they used to do, and wanting to argue the point . . . the fellows as is told off for execution come skipping along in the morning, like a lot of lambs in Maytime. And then the fun there is on the scaffold! The jokes, the back-answers, the repartees! And never a word to shock a baby! (35)

The business of death is, therefore, Jeanne's way of life and there is an obvious association here with the story of Salome, a popular trope of the destructiveness of *fin-de-siècle* feminine power.[12] As the 'new woman' executioner she occupies a public arena, breaching the conventional gender boundary between public and private and confronting the view that, as one character puts it, women are hopelessly 'delicate organisms' (31). The rational radicalism of Jeanne's position is, however, undercut by the mock-seriousness with which the story is told. Moreover, the assertion of feminine delicacy is authenticated when, feeling unwell, Jeanne sends a note to the Mayor, explaining that she has a 'nervous headache' (33).

Jeanne proves her steadfastness, nevertheless, when the young nobleman she is in love with is accidentally brought to the scaffold. The public exchange that takes place between them, while comical for its apparent unsettling of gendered conventions, may also be interpreted as performing an inversion of female sexual inexperience and reinforcing a transgressive link between female commercial activity and sexual knowledge. As Jeanne says to her nobleman as he is brought to the chopping block:

"any little advice or assistance that I can offer is quite at your service; for the situation is possibly new, and you may have had but little experience."

"Faith, none worth mentioning," said the prisoner, gaily. "Treat me as a raw beginner. Though our acquaintance has been brief, I have the utmost confidence in you."

"Then sir," said Jeanne, blushing, "suppose I were to assist you in removing this gay doublet, so as to give both of us more freedom and less responsibility?" (39–40)

When the mistaken identity is revealed, Jeanne at first insists that the execution should still take place as she still has her job to do, regardless of bureaucratic inefficiency. Jeanne's performative professionalism earns her marriage to the nobleman and the adoption of a domestic life, re-establishing a conventionally gendered order of things and alleviating any possible masculine anxieties about dismemberment or castration that the idea of the female executioner might suggest.

This story by Grahame is only one of several *Yellow Book* contributions that address the theme of gender, sexuality and commerce. One of the journal's major ontological preoccupations, the vagaries of the world of the late-Victorian periodical press, is expressed in several stories in which the desire of the male writer for publication on the London literary market places him in a feminised relation to the literary magazine and its editor. In these instances the writer is depicted variously as martyr, as in Henry James's 'The Death of the Lion' which was published in the inaugural issue (1894), or as supplicant and victim, as in James Ashcroft Noble's 'The Phantasies of Philarete' in which an invalid writer's gushingly sentimental review of a novel proves to be fatal to its author. The *Yellow Book*'s self-consciousness is reflected in numerous ways, here most obviously in the 'series of articles on "Fin-de-Siècle" Fiction' that the fated writer is promised (200). It was the work of art editor Aubrey Beardsley, however, that initially created the image of the ambiguous professional woman as a keynote of *Yellow Book* style. Beardsley's images of actresses, the 'femme fatale' and other women of the night, were sexualised figures of public and economic exchange that drew attention to the boundaries of both gender and art.

The perception of decadence as a cult of artifice is well rehearsed in discussions of the little magazines of the 1890s, where attention to costume, personality and fashion are often seen as unsettling assumptions about the naturalness of gender roles (see Chris Snodgrass, 'Decadent Parodies: Aubrey Beardsley's Caricature of Meaning'). Aubrey Beardsley's position, as art editor for both the *Yellow Book* and subsequently the *Savoy*, was central in the construction of decadence as a symptom of late-Victorian reactionism, characterised by androgynous figures decorated with imperialism's oriental souvenirs. Decadence was not, however, the only 'cult' that shaped the emergence of magazines such as the *Yellow Book* and the *Savoy*. The cult of personality was an important factor in the promotion and economic viability of many magazines, as we have demonstrated with regard to earlier examples. It was especially important to the magazines of decadence and aestheticism where the persona of both editor and publication itself became, at times, iconoclastic. Although his work was influential and widely imitated, his images of actresses and other sexualised women drew widespread criticism from contemporary newspapers and journals in reviews of the magazine's first issue. Criticism also came from mainstream periodicals such as *Westminster Review*, *Granta* and the *Spectator*, as Mix and Elliott have also both noted. The identity politics of the *Yellow Book* were indeed firmly embedded in early 1890s preoccupations with gender and artifice, in particular with the fashioning of appearances. This was, however, only one of the journal's strategies for creating a place for itself in the periodical market. Publishing practices such as the extensive use of visual alongside literary material, the presentation of multiple points of view – so typical of the popular press in this period which reflected the broader cultural shift in British society away from a homogenised masculine elitism – and the element of novelty, were crucial to the *Yellow Book*'s public identity and early popularity. Robert M. Booth speculates in 'Aubrey Beardsley and *The Savoy*' whether the *Savoy* failed because of its lack of advertisements: in combination with its low price: 'a great deal was being given for very little money' (83). In other words, the *Savoy* failed partly because of its lack of participation in the commercial process and partly because of the lack of a mainstream audience. Of course, the *Yellow Book* had already met with its demise, ultimately for the latter reason.

Bridget Elliott observes that Beardsley's attempt to merge the popular with the aesthetic failed, partly because it violated 'fundamental cultural assumptions that defined art as the property of a social elite and amusement as the popular recreation of the masses' (97). Elliott also argues that this attempt was finally unsuccessful, creating irritation rather than enjoyment for the magazine's readers and once again foregrounding the magazine's financial priorities (97). The *Yellow Book*, nevertheless, has a central place within the gendered discourse of late-Victorian publishing, both as a medium for a new economy of ideas about social and sexual identity and as an attempted site of exchange between the cultural and commercial fields. The magazine's pictorial art reproductions, for example, serve not merely as markers of its artistic sophistication but also show its broader relationship with the popular British periodical press (Brake, 'Endgames', 39). The *Yellow Book* both produces and gives attention to the commodification of authorship, as it also manufactures the tropes of gender, art and desire for commercial ends.

The role of the pictorial illustration in identifying the popular periodical as commodity is perhaps most intensely exemplified in the preoccupation with image and style that characterised the development of the late nineteenth-century woman's fashion magazine. In both popular and cultural magazines the negotiations over definitions of gender were achieved through the use of text as well as image. It was the visual production and content of the *Yellow Book*, however, that framed its identity politics and helped to establish it as a periodical icon. Some *Yellow Book* artists left when Beardsley was sacked and subsequently worked for the *Savoy*. Those who remained associated longest with the *Yellow Book* included Charles Conder, Walter Sickert and Patten Wilson. After Beardsley's departure the work of a greater number of women artists was employed. An interesting example of this was the inclusion of reproductions of work by Scottish artists Frances and Margaret Macdonald in the July 1896 issue of volume 10. The magazine accommodated the idea of the working woman and the 'new woman'. It was also willing to publish modern and experimental art. While the Macdonalds may have been influenced by Beardsley in their blurring of the boundaries between art and design, their images of the female body expressed a muscular contrast, even antagonism, to Beardsley's pictures of the 'femme fatale', suggesting that the conventional link between women, nature and childbirth offered a source for imagination and art, rather than caricature.

The *Yellow Book* was by no means strikingly radical in feminist terms. Beardsley's depictions of women, such as the actresses Ellen Terry and Mrs Patrick Campbell, tended to act as reflectors of cultural anxiety rather than to suggest the cultural emergence of women as complex desiring subjects and active participants in social life. This is not to suggest, however, that the position of the *Yellow Book* with regard to the figure of the 'new woman' was antagonistically fixed. Indeed, in its post-Beardsley phase, the work of women writers and artists was given substantially more attention than in many other periodicals. From its inception it published the fiction work of its co-editor Ella D'Arcy, although, according to Barbara Onslow in *Women of the Press in Nineteenth-Century Britain*, D'Arcy also 'proof-read, paginated, arranged the pictures, and indexed the magazine' (152). Her conditions of employment replicated a long sexist tradition and were far from 'new'; her remuneration was poor and she lacked any real power over editorial decisions. Nevertheless, later editions were notable for names of writers such as Ada Leverson, Constance Mew and Vernon Lee: further evidence, perhaps, of the magazine's interest in promoting itself to the 'new' woman reader and suggesting further linkages between commerce and the plasticity of gendered identity and desire. Indeed, the *Yellow Book* was founded as a celebration of the sensationalism associated with the late nineteenth-century discourse of the 'new': new journalism, new literature and art, 'new' women and men. Ella D'Arcy, Vernon Lee and Ada Leverson were among its 'new women' writers of social satire, while several key modernist writers, W. B. Yeats for one, were first featured in its pages. The journal was also notable for its art reproductions by those working in new styles, as with the early anticipations of art nouveau by Margaret and Frances Macdonald, published in 1896. The magazine featured discussions about, and images of, women, published the work of women writers, and took in its stride subjects such as feminine desire, prostitution, adultery and illegitimate pregnancy. Essays by male writers such as Beerbohm and Harland, stories about women and desire, and images of women as objects of public attention are further evidence that the *Yellow Book* sought to use gender as a device to spark popular interest.

Paradoxically, through title and format, the *Yellow Book* attempted to embrace the sign of the 'book', apparently making an appeal to cultural conservatism (Brake, 'Endgames', 59). Moreover, it is worth noting that pieces such as Henry Harland's articles signed by 'The Yellow Dwarf', Henry James' 'The Death of the Lion' and James Ashcroft Noble's 'Phantasies of Philarete', criticised the vulgar practices of popular magazine journalism. The narrator of James's 'Death of a Lion', for example, condemns the 'editors of magazines who had introduced what they called new features . . . periodical prattle about the future of fiction' (38). Rather later in the journal's production, Arthur Waugh's 'The Auction Room of Letters' sarcastically describes the work of 'the literary man who offers his goods for sale' as 'snippet literature' (225). At times the *Yellow Book* also adopted the tone of the nineteenth-century mandarin quarterly with its privileging of gentlemanly disquisitions on literature and art. In particular this genre is evidenced in the writings of Max Beerbohm, Richard Le Gallienne and Henry Harland. The attempt to construct itself as desirable by intersecting the powerful cultural formations of both 'book' and 'magazine' suggests the editors' desire to reach a broad, socially diverse readership and thus of its proximity to commerce. This approach was not, of course, confined to the *Yellow Book*. Bridget Elliott remarks, for example, that during this period the 'proliferation of literary products tended to erode a cultural consensus that had been based on shared upper-middle-class patterns of consumption' (96). As Elliott further notes, however, the book itself became transformed in this period as both an object of commodity-fetishism and repository of cultural capital, assisted by the rise of the single-volume novel (72).

The construction of the *Yellow Book* as a magazine tainted with luridly decadent associations undoubtedly owes much to the parodies of *Punch* which had always tended to depict in tandem its weedy images of decadent aesthetes with the severe and bespectacled 'new woman' as opposing faces of the same social aberration. In its depictions of masculinity the *Yellow Book* could, however, be curiously ambiguous, embracing a playful attitude to gender that was, nevertheless, underwritten by heterosexual convention. If Max Beerbohm could pretend to complain in 'A Note on George the Fourth' that 'our sexes are already nearly assimilate' (249), by 1897 the writer Stanley V. Makower in 'Three Reflections' had no hesitation about cashing in on the 'lodging-house myth' (128) of the cross-dressing Countess: the exception that proves the 'rule' of authentic femininity. Makower's Countess Cunégonde de Blum de Cavagnac, resident of the floor below, turns out to have extremely large feet and loud habits, including the blowing of an enormous nose – suggesting that all is not as it seems. The suspicion that the 'Countess' might not be quite as much a 'woman' as she appears is confirmed when the narrator happens to lean out over his balcony:

> I saw a very strange sight.
> A Lady with bare arms, and a loose black gauze thrown round her shoulders, was standing with her head bent forward and all her hair down. It hung in loose, damp strips from round a bald patch in the middle of her head, upon which it was my ill fortune to gaze. While she held the gauze across her shoulders with one hand, with the other she was frantically waving a bright scarlet Japanese fan backwards and forwards against her wet hair. (127)

The 'Lady' is never thoroughly investigated, only offered as a kind of eccentric adventure in social life. Makower's attention to the accoutrements of femininity – the long hair, the fan, the shawl and bare arms – is interestingly contrasted with the authentic signs of the masculine – the large feet and loud nose – and with the servant's corroborating comment that the Countess is 'a funny woman'. Femininity, it seems, can be put on but masculinity is authentic.

The *Yellow Book*'s flirtation with transgressions of gender and desire undoubtedly provided it with free publicity, but this went only as far as the publishers deemed it to have commercial effect. Its 'jaundiced' complexion and literary excursions into the sexual adventurism of the *fin de siècle* were only too easily linked to the social terrors that feminism, decadence and Oscar Wilde appeared to have unleashed. This was famously demonstrated by the magazine's conservative response to the publicity surrounding the case of Oscar Wilde when it sacked Aubrey Beardsley because of his past association with Wilde. This event has now become a commonplace signifier for the demise of the 'gay' nineties. That commercial viability was important to the publisher of the *Yellow Book* was made further evident when John Lane terminated the magazine because it was no longer marketable. Its tone became more subdued after April 1895 immediately following the Wilde crisis when its contributions suddenly manifested a preference for sober moral tales and Victorian sentimentality. The *Yellow Book* would continue to provoke controversy, however, in relation to the way it positioned itself in the marketplace as an organ of serious literary criticism and as a journal of the 'new'. Moreover, it actively reclaimed the myth of scandal about itself. It sought to achieve this partly by inventing a new representative persona, and one that was calculatingly gendered, the 'Yellow Dwarf', who represented the satirical voice of the male literary critic.

As 'The Yellow Dwarf', Henry Harland made three feisty contributions to the journal, including a reminiscence in 'A Birthday Letter' of the first issue of the magazine which had provoked such strident public response from 'all the newspapers in England: 'the noise was deafening . . . *Wasn't* it a jolly company?' (120). According to Katherine Mix in *A Study in Yellow*, the Yellow Dwarf was presumably created in order to reclaim some of the popularity created by the cultural adventurism associated with the first issues, and to reinvigorate flagging magazine sales (230). This was done, however, in a way that was problematised by the Yellow Dwarf's supercilious attitude to the bourgeois elements in the journal's readership. In 'Dogs, Cats, Books, and the Average Man' for example, the Yellow Dwarf critiques the literary culture of the age: 'I actually know nice people who have read Mr. Conan Doyle! And I have actually met nice people who do not read Mr. Henry James! And that is all the fault of the Average Man' (22–3). In addition, Harland exploited the mystery of his identity to visit attacks on several contemporary authors who had previously failed to treat the *Yellow Book* with respect. Harland thus created a 'scandal' out of the secret of his identity but the commercial effect was short-lived, perhaps overshadowed by more disturbing social secrets of the day.

IV

The expansion of the periodical press in the nineteenth century was an important factor in the generation of a new public discourse: the relationship between culture and commerce. The nexus between representations of the feminine and material consumption in late nineteenth-century fashion magazines offers a useful vantage point from which to consider this theme in relation to the broader issues surrounding gender and the periodical press. Antagonistic preoccupation with the feminine was a well-established theme within journal publication early in the nineteenth century. Further, the woman's magazine provided a commercial mechanism through which the feminine proliferated in new ways, both as product and as changing discursive entity while acknowledging that the role of women in the late-Victorian economy of magazine publication was complex (Ballaster *et al.*, *Women's Worlds*, 75–107). The rise of the woman's magazine as a commodity, however, enabled women more control over their own participation in the virtual public space of the periodical, as writers, editors and artists and, as readers, through advice columns or letters.

The linking of women with commerce remained, nevertheless, an area of social anxiety. The role of advertisements drew particular attention to the association between gender and commerce. Women's magazines relied on advertising to survive and frequently featured advertisements on both covers as well as on the same pages as articles. This practice foregrounded the financial motive of these magazines. David Reed observes in *The Popular Magazine in Britain and the United States, 1880–1960*, that advertising played a crucial and increasingly dominating role. By the end of the 1880s, for example, Newnes's popular journal *Tit-Bits* filled 29 per cent of its content with advertising. The commercialisation of the periodical press was, however, a development that threatened to undermine journalistic credibility and this anxiety became intensified where it was linked with the woman writer and consumer. As the popular magazine *Woman* reported in a 'Note' on 17 January 1894:

A Woman Journalist has created quite a flutter in the dove-cotes of Lady-Journaldom by her letter to the Times on 'Ladies' Journals'. It appears . . . that certain "ladies' journals are run purely in the interests of advertising agents and advertisement canvassers and that at least one of them is actually edited by an advertisement canvasser". (5)

This passage expresses a clear intersection between gender, materialism and the periodical press. It associates the woman's magazine with a realm – 'Lady Journaldom' – occupied by the female journalist: a contradictory figure who aspires to the condition of serious journalism, but is also constrained in her femininity and her professionalism by the characteristic commercialism of the genre. That the outraged 'Woman Journalist' herself is a creature of uncertain status is signalled by the quotation marks around her title. More unauthentic still are the 'Ladies' Journals' accused of product puffing. Here *Woman* is at pains to distance itself from 'the many heinous offences' (5) of magazine advertorials. These publications are not, it indicates, the kind of journal that any real 'lady' would want to read. Although *Woman* admits that it carries advertisements necessary to its survival, it nevertheless seeks to 'assure our friends that, in accordance with our determination at the outset to strike out an original line, our founders decided to have a real Editor, and not a mere tool in the hands of an advertisement department' (5). In practice, however, the woman's magazine, particularly those such as *Woman's World* or *Sylvia's Journal*, tended to tread the line between editorial respectability and economic motive by self-consciously appropriating materialism as a form of cultural expression. Julia Prewitt Brown takes up the point in *Cosmopolitan Criticism* (1997), that for Wilde, journalism represented the decline of art in modern culture, citing his statement in 'The Decay of Lying' that 'we have sold our birthright for a mess of facts' (71) but Wilde puts late-Victorian consumer culture to work, first in *Woman's World* and later in *The Picture of Dorian Gray* by suggesting that life itself has become a form of embodied representation.

While the expansion in magazine culture, including the women's fashion press, was one aspect of a much broader increase in late nineteenth-century material culture, the promotion of consumption itself became a matter of concern for the self-conscious popular magazine. As Alfred Harmsworth's *Answers* observed, for example in 'Answers to Correspondents', 'Modern journalism seems to be a succession of crazes' (220), providing an object-lesson in simple capitalist economics which *Answers* defines as 'the competition that kills' long-term profitability (220). As if to demonstrate its economics, *Answers* became the main rival to Newnes's popular compilation journal, *Tit-Bits*. The effect of this kind of discussion of advertising and marketing strategies served to confer a disinterested credibility upon the commentator, while actually foregrounding popular consumer practices and providing a form of entertainment for the reader.

Aimed at a mixed audience of travellers and commuters, male and female, *Answers* follows the practice of many of its contemporaries in expressing a mix of opinions and attitudes that reflected the assumed values of its potentially diverse readership, most notably with reference to gender. The journal's 'special Lady Commissioner', for example, who is billed on the front cover of number 13 (16 February 1895) as having 'some of the most extraordinary adventures ever undertaken by a woman journalist', is posed against references, also on the cover, to weak-willed women 'drunk' on smelling salts. In case these headline examples of late-Victorian womanhood should prove too louche, the journal provides a commentary in 'Answers to Correspondents' on the virtues of an ideal wife, ostensibly written by the journal's male readers, although, according to Reed, almost certainly written by Harmsworth himself (89). While this section is constructed by Harmsworth as a repertoire of independent voices and opinions, one coherent view clearly dominates: the woman 'they want to marry' is 'not a new woman' but a 'thorough domestic helpmate' (226).

If representations of women in the broader popular press drew on a set of largely contradictory clichés, these were equally at work in the featured content of women's magazines themselves where the feminine was represented with greater specificity and attention to detail. The cover page of the magazine *Woman's Life* offers one example of the way in which self-promotion was combined with promotion of material consumption by women, through the glamour of feminine fashion items and upper-class practices. Featured contents of the first volume which appeared on the covers of numbers 1 and 5 included such titles as 'Little Fortunes Spent in Shoes', 'Round the West-End Shops', 'Shopping in Search of Novelties' and 'Where Society Women Learn to Cycle'. The magazine's title 'Woman's Life' can even be seen, therefore, as a metonym for the gendering of material culture.

Two problematic and striking representations of the material feminine recur throughout the woman's magazine of this period in references to the cycling woman and advertisements for female corsetry. The taut relationship between commercial viability, gender ideology and the emergence of the 'new woman' consumer is perhaps most effectively encapsulated in an advertisement printed in *Woman At Home* in 1896 for 'The "Rational Corset" Bodice' cited by Dulcie Ashdown in *Over the Teacups*:

The 'Rational' Corset Bodice: Ladies who study their health and mothers who study the health of their children will find the 'RATIONAL' Corded Corset Bodice far superior to the ordinary hard, stiff Corset, from which it is distinguished by its great pliability and the ease with which it can be washed. (213)

Advertisements for female undergarments were common in magazines of the period, sometimes even appearing on the cover page. Sharp, Perrin and Company's advertisement for the 'rational' corset bodice was calculated to appeal to the sensible, even scientifically minded woman through its references to practical hygiene. At the same time the advertisement stresses conformity to the embodied characteristics of the essential feminine, from girlhood to motherhood.

As shown in our earlier discussion of the mainstream popular press, the degree to which women's magazines carried expressions of social and gendered difference varied considerably, as did the 'authenticity' of this practice. Many of the contributions in *Woman*, for example, while presented as the work of multiple authors, were written by the editor Arnold Bennett (Ballaster *et al.*, *Women's World*, 47). Annie S. Swan's *Woman at Home*, however, made a virtue of posing a question and then presenting arguments from several points of view written by named identities on a range of subjects from 'Platonic Friendship' (359–61) to 'What is the Best Cycling Dress for Women?', by Lady Jeune, Viscountess Harberton and Mrs Norman. A sense of engagement with a range of readers' and writers' voices is also conveyed in Annie Swan's regular column 'Over the Teacups'. Often discussions were performed by well-known public figures, whose views on women's issues were sometimes divergent: in the instance of 'Platonic Friendship' the four-part series included pieces by Eliza Lynn Linton and Florence Fenwick Miller. The three-part series on cycling dress provides a useful case study for the way in which gender ideology was both reproduced and under construction. In Section III, Mrs Norman's 'frank' position that 'nothing but custom' stands in the way of 'assuming a suit of knickerbockers to-morrow' (623) mediates Lady Jeune's earlier attention to the difficult details of finding a graceful cycling costume in Section I: 'No one will maintain that a woman was ever intended to wear trousers. Her figure is not adapted for it in any way' (620). For the second commentator, Viscountess Harberton, the fashion for cycling is 'an instance of our marvellous power of getting accustomed to something new' (622). While the novelty of cycling leads her to the daring position of advocating a costume suitable for any daytime activity – 'women's present dress is only really suitable for invalids who spend most of the day on the sofa' (623) – conventional modesty remains a prevailing concern. The Viscountess, therefore, recommends the Syrian skirt, worn 'so that the folds fall over as far down the leg as is compatible with freedom from risk of catching the pedals' (622). Mrs Norman, however, rapidly moves her discussion away from the indelicate subject of legs altogether, remarking: 'in truth I am more concerned with the upper-wear than the other matter' (623).

As with the 'rational' corset bodice, the figure of the cycling woman acts here as a trope for the issues of gender, consumption practices and the woman's magazine. The significance of the public discourse surrounding the late nineteenth-century female cyclist has been previously referred to in several discussions of the 1890s New Woman, most notably by Marilyn Bonnell in 'The Power of the Pedal: the Bicycle and the Turn-of-the-Century Woman' (215–39), and in Ellen Gruber Garvey's study of gender and consumer culture in the American periodical press, *The Adman in the Parlor: Magazines and the Gendering of Consumer Culture, 1880s to 1910s* (107).[13] Garvey argues that magazine advertisements 'linked bicycles with codes of femininity' (109) as a means of controlling rather than liberating the female body. There were, however, clear differences in the development of the British and American periodical press, particularly with reference to the acceptability of advertising and other commercial practices (Reed, *The Popular Magazine*, 14 and 100).

References to the female body, direct or indirect, are also evident in advertisements of the popular British periodical press where the figure of the cycling woman was used in various ways, from selling bicycles to bread. Ashdown notes an advertisement for Bermaline malt extract bread 'as used in the Queen's household' (211), further evidence of the way gender operates as a cultural economy in popular magazines of the late nineteenth century. The image of the cycling woman also appeared in proximity to advertisements for corsets, insurance and even sanitary towels. These were advocated in a way that appeared to promote feminine pleasure and mobility. The Hartmann's 'hygenience towelette', for example, was advertised as 'invaluable for ladies travelling', while the Sickness & Accident Assurance Association Ltd offered 'a new system of . . . Insurance for Women' with 'Ordinary cycling risks covered' (quoted in Ashdown, *Over the Tea-Cups*, 211).

The tension between freedom and restraint expressed in advertisements as well as in articles discussing cycling, costume, corsetry and dress reform suggests that the feminine body was itself a contested field. These magazines do not merely trade on the trope of the feminine, they also reconstruct popular culture in terms of a feminised material production. As this chapter has argued, the use of gender as a commercial and ideological strategy was not confined to the genre of the woman's magazine, or even that of the mainstream popular journal, but was also adopted by the magazines of elite and avant-garde culture within a rapidly evolving technological, economic and social context. The mode of the magazine can be seen, further, as a representational 'social body' with multiple parts, voices and social functions, reflecting the vibrant and contested culture of late-Victorian Britain.

Conclusion

At the beginning of her book *Sexual Anarchy: Gender and Culture at the Fin de Siècle* (1990), Elaine Showalter meditates on the various kinds of 'borderlines' that were disrupted as the nineteenth century approached its end and prepared to cross over into the new. It is in this interstitial *fin-de-siècle* cultural territory, this 'no man's land', that we find the established borders of sexual difference coming under threat in more fundamental ways than in previous decades. For this was a time when, as she notes, 'all the laws that governed sexual identity and behavior seemed to be breaking down'; when, quoting Karl Miller, 'Men became women. Women became men. Gender and country were put in doubt. The single life was found to harbor two sexes and two nations'; when 'both the words "feminism" and "homosexuality" first came into use, as New Women and male aesthetes redefined the meanings of femininity and masculinity' (3). Looking back at that transitional historical juncture from our own 'borderland' condition at the turn of another century, it seems pertinent to reflect on such moments of transit as times when, according to Homi Bhabha in *The Location of Culture*, 'space and time cross to produce complex figures of difference and identity, past and present, inside and outside, inclusion and exclusion' (1). It is in the borderland of the century, when boundaries are at once so momentous and so permeable, that Bhabha locates those '"in-between" spaces' which 'provide the terrain for elaborating strategies of selfhood . . . that initiate new signs of identity' (1), and it is in this transitional decade that the gendered binaries which have been the focus of this study of the periodical press seemed finally to begin to lose their rigid definition and to make way for more complex models of subject formation.

We have sought to pursue the many ways that representations of gender inform the dominant themes in Victorian culture and society conducted through the periodical press from 1830 to 1900. The attention given in the press to gender identity and gender issues can be seen both as the engagement with a long-standing discursive currency and as a touchstone for numerous nineteenth-century anxieties about social transformation. With the daily newspaper, the periodical press was, we argue, a central medium for ideological exchange. As the chief form of nineteenth-century public media, it locates and manifests a great tension between diversity, congruence and polarisation of opinion, offering a methodological meeting place between historicity and textual analysis. As we have earlier suggested, the periodical press itself occupies the fraught position of embodying the binary politics of gender in certain ways. In one sense the periodical press can be seen as the domestic partner to journalism's more rugged forms of social and cultural reportage, such as the daily newspaper. This gendered binary also operates within the field of the periodical, with the 'masculine' magazines being seen to be engaged in broad public issues, high culture or social satire, while the 'feminine' magazines deal primarily with household matters, popular culture and fashion. Nevertheless, in line with Showalter's identification of a broader culture of gender transgression, this separation of spheres within the press industry itself begins to break down towards the end of the century, a process which is reflected in the myriad elements of the press as multiple but connected sites of discourse.

In *The History of Sexuality*, Michel Foucault makes the crucial point that:

Discourses are not once and for all subservient to power or raised up against it, any more than silences are. We must make allowance for the complex and unstable process whereby discourse can be both an instrument and an effect of power, but also a hindrance, a stumbling-block, a point of resistance and a starting point for an opposing strategy. Discourse transmits and produces power; it reinforces it, but also undermines and exposes it, renders it fragile and makes it possible to thwart it. (1: 100–1)

Several fine studies of Victorian gender ideology in the past two decades have drawn on Foucault's genealogical re-envisioning of the grand narrative of history to emphasise with him the disruptions, discontinuities and discursive instabilities of historical change. Some, like Mary Poovey, Nancy Armstrong and Elizabeth Langland, have made use of cultural ephemera and trivia, traditionally accorded the 'status of junk' to quote Nancy Armstrong in *Desire and Domestic Fiction: a Political History of the Novel* (258), in their production of a new materialist history that takes account of domestic culture, for example, to offer a more nuanced account of gender. They have uncovered ambiguities and contradictions in fictional and non-fiction prose narratives that speak of counter-hegemonic forms of resistance. It is our contention that the periodical press, more than any other cultural resource, so fundamentally ephemeral and heterogeneous a cultural form, yet so ubiquitously influential and representative, offers an unrivalled field for this kind of critical work.

Our aim, then, has been not to demonstrate a seamless story of progress, either in terms of an unfolding history of gender, or of women and the profession of journalism, but to read that narrative as comprising multiple and competing discourses. This book has argued that the periodical press, because of its uniquely heterogeneous, multivocal form, and its pervasiveness and currency as a medium for cultural exchange, was fundamental to both the construction and the dismantling of gender in Victorian Britain. Its aim has been twofold: to examine the expression of gendered identity and politics within nineteenth-century British periodical literature; and to explore the role of the periodical press as a mechanism of social discourse, serving both to generate and to contest powerful ideological formations. It began by examining the roles of writer, reader, publisher and editor. The first section foregrounded the reinscription of gendered identity for both men and women, demonstrated the constraints on women as press participants and offered many examples of women who overcame these constraints as writers, illustrators, editors and publishers. The discussion continued by considering the periodical press both as agent and interrogator of constructions of gender within nineteenth-century British culture. Concepts of home and nation, the discourse of the colonial adventure, the steady emergence of feminism from the late 1850s onwards, the rise of market forces in shaping cultural expression have been key areas for examination in this study. We have explored the way these issues intersected with debates and tensions surrounding gender stereotypes, eliciting numerous fascinating instances of the reproduction of gendered discourse, and the development of counter-discourses, in relation to both masculinity and femininity.

One of the strongest initial impressions gathered from a study of the nineteenth-century British periodical press is that of volume and diversification, as several scholars of the field have noted.[1] As the century progresses, the number of magazines not only increases exponentially, it also reflects the enormous range of social organisations, hobbyists, cultural interests and forms of expression at work in the culture of the period. As the press gathers momentum throughout the nineteenth century, the magazine becomes not only a widespread public medium for expressing and exchanging views on social issues, such as 'the woman question' or 'the Irish question', it also becomes a point of identification and a voice for different cultural philosophies and interests, social groups and advocates of social or political issues. This is sometimes reflected in a general stance which ranges from the establishment journals such as *Fraser's Magazine* or the derogations of difference as exercised in *Punch*, to the alternative reformist positions taken by the *Humanitarian* or the *Woman's Signal*. As evidenced in our chapter on editorship, the more specific identification of magazines is sometimes centred around an individual or name, as in the cases of *Eliza Cook's Journal* or *Howitt's* magazine, or else can be reflected in the emergence of single-interest magazines as with the *Rational Dress Society Gazette* or the hobby magazine *Wheeling*.

The great variety and number of magazines can, however, be misleading. Fascinating and revealing as these are when examined in detail it is also important to consider how the periodical press functioned as a media phenomenon in mid-late nineteenth-century Britain and we have pursued this question by elucidating key discursive strands. These can be seen as finding expression through the periodical press in the form of both recitative and dialogue. The periodical press operates in this sense as a space enabling individual ideas to be voiced and dialogue to take place, a process which is crucial for social development and change. The great reform movements of the nineteenth century were conducted through the periodical press, as much as in public meetings and proposed legislation, providing a written and visual forum for passionate debate which could often engage those, particularly women, for whom attendance at public meetings was often impossible, while direct representation in parliament was almost completely unavailable.

The nineteenth-century British periodical press, with its diverse opinions, contrasts, overlappings, ruptures and reattachments, can be seen, therefore, as the formation of a network of virtual, as well as actual, communities, enabling marginal interventions in mainstream debates, providing evidence of a society in transition. For all its multiplicity, however, the press was as much a reflection and reinstatement of existing ideology as a source of resistance. The voices of magazine editors and contributors were not always progressive, although they were a part of continuing social change. Even the more radical publications often exemplified the compromised transitions of late-Victorian gender politics.

The partial progress of gender politics is well demonstrated in Janet Hogarth's 1897 article for the *Fortnightly Review*, 'The Monstrous Regiment of Women'. Hogarth's title refers to the forceful tide of women, particularly middle-class women, entering the work force, a powerful and unsettling trope that had been ironically invoked at the beginning of our period

('A Blast Against the Monsterous Regimente of Womene', 1835), and which was once more to give rise to responses in the *Fortnightly Review* and elsewhere. Hogarth prefaces her remarks with a short satire on the position of the woman worker and her construction as a social menace:

There are few aspects of the Eternal Feminine more disheartening to contemplate than the alarming increase of that monstrous regiment of women which threatens before very long to spread throughout the length and breadth of this city of London. It is no exaggeration to say that every day, almost every post, brings to any one with the faintest chance of getting employment for his fellow-creatures, appeals for work so piteous that they might melt a heart of stone. What is to be done? There is a prejudice against Lethal chambers, though they offer such a tempting and immediate solution . . . Still if we must turn our backs upon this attractive remedy, there remains the far harder and more thankless task of attempting to reduce this monstrous regiment to something like discipline and order. For at present it has little of the regiment about it but its name; it is simply an innumerable host, blindly bent on forcing its way into the professions. (926)

As Virginia Woolf was later to do in *To the Lighthouse* (27), Hogarth ironically alludes to Tennyson's 'The Charge of the Light Brigade' (1854):

Clearly someone has blundered. Or perhaps it would be truer, as well as kinder, to say that the leaders of the host have not yet sufficiently recognised how important it is before proceeding further to take stock of their resources, and to draw up an definite plan of campaign. What, after all, have women accomplished during the Victorian era, and what, under more enlightened direction, may they hope to accomplish? (926)

Hogarth continues by recommending teaching as the best and most obvious profession for women: 'the safest of all professions; it gives the longest and most regular holidays – no trifling matter to a sex whose work is liable to such curious ups and downs, and which is so little calculated as yet to stand a long-continued strain' (929). Her aim is to promote and encourage professional opportunities for women – she ends by recommending the establishment of a 'Central Bureau for the Employment of Women' – yet she depicts 'the average girl' as incapable of independent thinking and directs the would-be female worker towards a limited range of professions, calculated to be least likely to displace men in already established professions.

In particular, Hogarth warns young women of the dangers of attempting a career in journalism for which young men are so much more suited 'to the inevitable strain and unwholesome conditions of the journalist's life' than young women:

if only they knew of a little more of the position and prospects of the average woman-journalist, of the desperate struggle to make both ends meet . . . I do not say she may not make a living, but she will have to content herself with a kind of journalism, far enough removed from literature – with the chatty article, or the women's papers, with the *Forget-me-Nots*, the *Home Notes*, the *Nursery Chats*, and the hundred-and-one scrappy periodicals which have so successfully hit off the taste of the rising generation, that they bid fair to reduce England once again to a condition of illiteracy. (928)

Hogarth's position echoes that of numerous male magazine editors confronting the increasing entry of women into journalism, and into the work force more generally. The fear of educated women displacing men in middle-class professions was a widespread source of anxiety and resistance to women entering higher education and the work force. Numerous instances of this anxiety abound. In a review of David Ritchie's *Darwinism and Politics* published in his column 'Some Literary Notes' in the *Woman's World*, Oscar Wilde cites Leslie Stephen's rebuttal to John Stuart Mill, noting that: 'women may suffer more than they have done, if plunged into a nominally equal but really unequal contest in the already overcrowded labour market' (390). Wilde's review reports Ritchie's questioning of the contradictions in separating the values of home from those of government, paraphrasing his rather frivolously presented argument that the entry of women into politics would mean 'the moralisation of politics' (390), but does not challenge Ritchie's agreement with Stephen's views about women in the labour market or comment on the correlative implication of the entry of women into the work force as heralding an improvement in working conditions.

Social roles for women and men in the nineteenth century were slow to change; the development of gender ideologies was 'uneven' (Poovey, *Uneven Developments*, 3). There could be no question that by 1900 women had entered public life and were there to stay. But it was to be many years before women entering the profession of writing could free themselves of the legacy of Victorian gender ideologies. Three decades into the new century, Virginia Woolf still found it necessary to kill the Angel in the House in order to write a critical review of a male author, as she wrote in her essay 'Professions for Women' (II: 284–9), and in *A Room of One's Own* still felt oppressed by the 'shadow shaped something like the letter "I"' that lay across the masculine page (130), suggestive of a unitary gendered writing subject that bore no resemblance to her own sense of identity as a constellation of subject positions, defined by plurality and fragmentation. For Woolf, subjectivity embraced, amongst other things, mutations between genders, an idea most radically realised in her eponymous hero/ine Orlando, but more generally explored and articulated in the experimental discursive forms of her own fictional prose. It was the masculine forms of fiction, according to Woolf, and of poetry that were most resistant to the incursion of the female imagination. It is, then, interesting to recall that, like so many of the women writers discussed in these chapters, she began her professional literary career, as 'Professions for Women' reminds us, writing reviews for the periodical press. A generation on from her journalist father, Leslie Stephen, who was, as we have seen, such a powerful voice in the nineteenth-century periodical, the press could equally accommodate the style and views of the writer who would, in *To the Lighthouse*, so mercilessly use him to expose the iniquities of the patriarchal family and the Victorian gender economy.

Notes

INTRODUCTION

1. We are grateful to Delphine McFarlane for this and the following reference. Of course, articles about foppishness may be found much earlier still. See, for example, the anonymous letter to the Editor, 'On the Effeminacy of Some of the Male Sex', *Lady's Magazine* (1738): 82–3.

2. It is not until the 1890s that the dandy is given serious and sympathetic treatment. See, for example, A. S. Forbes's, 'Dandyism', *Temple Bar* 88 (1890): 527–34.

3. See Regenia Gagnier, *Idylls of the Market Place: Oscar Wilde and the Victorian Public*.

4. See also Laurel Brake, *Subjugated Knowledges: Journalism, Gender and Literature in the Nineteenth Century*.

5. Important critical and bibliographical work on the Victorian periodical press upon which we have drawn includes Patricia Anderson, *The Printed Image and Transformation of Popular Culture 1790–1860*; Laurel Brake, A. Jones and Lionel Martin, eds., *Investigating Victorian Journalism*; Laurel Brake, *Subjugated Knowledges*; Laurel Brake, Bill Bell and David Finkelstein, *Nineteenth-Century Media and the Construction of Identities*; Lucy Brown, *Victorian News and Newspapers*; Kate Campbell, *Journalism, Literature and Modernity: from Hazlitt to Modernism*; Marysa Demoor, *Their Fair Share: Women, Power and Criticism in the Athenaeum, from Millicent Garrett Fawcett to Katherine Mansfield, 1870–1920*; Linda K. Hughes and Michael Lund, *The Victorian Serial*; Joanne Shattock, *Politics and the Reviewers: The* Edinburgh *and the* Quarterly *in the Early Victorian Age*; Joanne Shattock and Michael Wolff, eds., *The Victorian Press: Samplings and Soundings*; Larry K. Uffelman, Lionel Madden and Diana Dixon, *The Nineteenth-Century Periodical Press in Britain: A Bibliography of Modern Studies*; J. Don Vann and Rosemary T. VanArsdel, eds., *Victorian Periodicals and Victorian Society*; Michael Wolff, John S. North and Dorothy Deering, *The Waterloo Directory of Victorian Periodicals 1824–1900*. See Bibliography for numerous articles on individual journals.

6. For fuller discussion of the 'Girl of the Period' phenomenon, see Elizabeth K. Helsinger, Robin Lauterbach Sheets and William Veeder, *The Woman Question: Society and Literature in Britain and America 1837*, 1: 103–25; and Valerie Sanders, *Eve's Renegades: Victorian Anti-Feminist Women Novelists*, 130–43.

1. THE WRITING SUBJECT

1. Eliza Lynn Linton was, incidentally, herself a contributor to *Tinsley's Magazine*.
2. The former descending from Joan Rivière, 'Womanliness as a Masquerade' (1929), reprinted in *Psychoanalysis and Female Sexuality*, ed., Hendrik M. Ruitenbeek (1966); the latter from Judith Butler's *Gender Trouble: Feminism and the Subversion of Identity* (1990) and 'Critically Queer' (1993).
3. See Margaret Beetham, *A Magazine of Her Own?*, 21. See also Marysa Demoor, *Their Fair Share: Women, Power and Criticism in the* Athenaeum, *from Millicent Garrett Fawcett to Katherine Mansfield, 1870–1920*, 21.
4. See also Adele M. Ernstrom's interesting discussion of text and illustration in 'The Afterlife of Mary Wollstonecraft and Anna Jameson's *Winter Studies and Summer Rambles in Canada*'.
5. See Demoor, *Their Fair Share*, for a fascinating and scholarly account of the women who wrote for this particular weekly, as well as insights into broader questions relating to women's role in journalism in the period.
6. 'John Ruskin's *Modern Painters*, Vol. III' in 'Art and Belles Lettres', *Westminster Review* 65 (1856): 625–33; Elizabeth Rigby, '*Modern Painters* I–III', *Quarterly Review* 98 (1856): 384–433; E. F. S. Pattison, 'John Ruskin, *Lectures on Art and Catalogue of Examples*', *Academy* 1 (1870): 305–6. On Lady Morgan, see Leslie A. Marchand, *The Athenaeum: A Mirror of Victorian Culture*, 203–6, 328–34.
7. Not so magazines for boys and young men. See, for example, Maurice Phillips, 'A Famous Editor and Journalist. A Chat with Mr. P. W. Clayden' in which the profession of journalist is unequivocally gendered masculine.
8. Eve Kosofsky Sedgwick comments on '[t]he apparent floating-free from its gay origins of that phrase "coming out of the closet" in recent usage', in *Epistemology of the Closet* (72).
9. See, for example Mrs. E. Rentoul Esler's column 'Between Ourselves. A Friendly Chat with the Girls. Mrs. Oliphant'.

2. THE GENDERED READER

1. See Lynne Warren's discussion of this problematical notion in 'Women in Conference: Reading the Correspondence Columns in *Woman* 1890–1910', especially 122.
2. The gustatory analogy was a common one. We find Edward Dowden using the same metaphor in 1889, in 'Hopes and Fears for Literature', though with a more negative inflection: 'Our caterers nowadays provide us with a mincemeat which requires no chewing, and the teeth of a man may in due time become as obsolete as those which can still be perceived in the foetal whale' (168–70).
3. The phrase was widely used, particularly in journals directed at the working classes, such as the *Dublin Penny Magazine* and the *Working Man's Friend*.
4. Some, like those of Louis James, *Fiction for the Working Man 1830–50: A Study of the Literature Produced for the Working Classes in Early Victorian Urban England*, David Vincent, *Literacy and Popular Culture, England 1750–1914* and Simon

Eliot, *Some Patterns and Trends in British Publishing, 1800–1919*, have a historical, materialist or sociological focus; others, like those by Kate Flint, *The Woman Reader*, Jon Klancher, *The Making of English Reading Audiences, 1790–1832*, Garrett Stewart, *Dear Reader: The Conscripted Audience in Nineteenth-Century British Fiction* and Patrick Brantlinger, *The Reading Lesson: The Threat of Mass Literacy in Nineteenth-Century British Fiction*, concentrate more on the representation of the reader as topos and the rhetorical analysis of readerly conscription.

5. To boys of all ages, it seems. Age range categories are interesting to note from the competitions held in both the *Boy's Own Paper* and the *Girl's Own Paper*. In the *Boy's Own Paper* they include an adult (twenty to twenty-four years) and an 'Over-Age Section' in which one certificate winner is forty-one years old. Letters from readers in both are mostly fulsomely grateful to the magazine for its advice and its beneficial effect on their lives.

6. See *Girl's Own Paper* 4 (1882): 184–5 for chapter 1. And see Simon Eliot, *Some Patterns and Trends*, on girls reading *Robinson Crusoe*.

7. On the language of the social explorers, see Fraser with Brown, *English Prose of the Nineteenth Century*, 88–97. Jonathan Rose is more sanguine, believing that 'the history of the common reader, at least after 1800, is recoverable' ('How Historians Study Reader Response: or, What did Jo think of Bleak House' (195)).

8. Cited in Beetham, *A Magazine of Her Own?*, 11. See also Lynne Pearce, *Feminism and the Politics of Reading*, particularly her introduction, for a discussion of the feminist politics of reading that draws productively on film theory and work in media and cultural studies.

9. Beetham notes that 'magazines routinely complained that "both with manuscripts and books our table has been groaning"' (20) (*Lady's Magazine and Museum* 7 (1835): unnumbered).

3. EDITORSHIP AND GENDER

1. See also Lynne Warren in 'Women in Conference' (131).

2. See Brian Maidment's essay 'Victorian Periodicals and Academic Discourse' in *Investigating Victorian Journalism* for a discussion of this problem.

3. For a full and very provocative analysis of Lewes's article, see Mary Jean Corbett's *Representing Femininity. Middle-Class Subjectivity in Victorian and Edwardian Women's Autobiographies* (1992), 60–2.

4. The *Windsor Magazine* was specifically designed for men and women. It is notable that the military metaphor has here been romantically medievalised.

5. See for example 'Copley's Life by his Granddaughter' (1884); or 'The Annals of a Publishing House', Margaret Oliphant's history of William Blackwood and Sons (1898). Books about notable women by women are also represented, memoirs of Sarah Coleridge by her daughter (1874); of Anna Jameson by her niece (1879); of Caroline Fry by her two daughters (1879).

6. *Nineteenth-Century Women Poets*, ed. Isobel Armstrong and Joseph Bristow with Cath Sharrock, notes that Cook's father was a wealthy merchant but that despite her middle-class background she was 'entirely self-educated' (359).

7. Mrs Sarah Trimmer (1741–1810) conducted the *Family Magazine* (1788–9) and the *Guardian of Education* (1802–6), a periodical criticising and examining books for children and educative books (*DNB*).

8. We are indebted to Alex Tyrrell for allowing us access to his manuscript article 'Samuel Smiles and the Woman Question in Early Victorian Britain' prior to its publication in *Journal of British Studies*.

4. GENDER AND THE 'POLITICS OF HOME'

1. The term 'domain' is used here as defined by Mary Poovey in *Making a Social Body*, in which she signals 'the transformations that occur when land becomes property: territory is appropriated; boundaries are drawn; rules governing usage are established; unequal privileges are codified by law and then naturalized by repetition' (4).

2. Some competitive titles include *Domestic Economist* (1850); *Family Economist* (1848–60); *Family Friend* (1849–1921); *Family Journal of Useful Knowledge* (1848); *Home Companion* (1852–4); *The Home* (1851–3); *Home Friend* (1852–6); *The Home Magazine: a Journal of Entertainment and Instruction for Everyone* (1856–66) and many more.

3. The naming of contributors is quite common in certain periodicals so that while the *Fortnightly Review*'s practice might be termed 'innovative' from its inception in 1865, it is only so with regard to the major reviews (see Mark Turner, 'Defining Discourses: the *Westminster Review*, *Fortnightly Review*, and Comte's Positivism', 279).

4. 'On the Social Position of Women' warns that 'the exhortations and vituperations of writers professing to befriend the weaker sex are calculated to lead women to consider men almost as natural enemies' (271).

5. A reference to the outbreak of various revolutions on the Continent in 1848.

6. Two decades later Frances Power Cobbe comments on landlords who fail to provide 'needful repairs or facilities for decency and cleanliness' (155) in 'The Indigent Class – their Schools and Dwellings'.

7. Respectively, *The Forest Minstrel and Other Poems* and *The Desolation of Eyam: The Emigrant, a Tale of the American Woods, and other Poems*.

8. Respectively, *Howitt's Journal* 1 (1847): 270–3; *People's Journal* 1 (1846): 53–4; *Howitt's Journal* 1 (1847): 128–30; and *Howitt's Journal* 3 (1848): 400.

5. GENDER AND CULTURAL IMPERIALISM

1. John Ruskin's Inaugural Speech as the newly appointed Slade Professor of Fine Art on 8 February 1870 ends with a call to English men to embrace imperialism, although he does not use the word: 'And this is what [England] must either do, or perish: she must found colonies as fast and as far as she is able, formed of

her most energetic and worthiest men; – seizing every piece of fruitful waste ground she can set her foot on' (xx: 42). Linda K. Hughes in 'History in Focus. 1870', *A Companion to Victorian Literature and Culture* cites Ruskin's speech as indicating 'the degree to which empire permeated every facet of Victorian England' (44–5).

2. The collection in which this essay appears contains a prefatory 'Note' to the effect that the articles 'have appeared in America and in Reviews and Journals at home' (v) but does not name which periodicals.

3. At various periods in the nineteenth century the terms 'British' and 'English' were used indiscriminately, but the latter predominated and that is the term we will use. For further discussion, see among others Eric Evans, 'Englishness and Britishness: National Identities, c.1790-c.1870', in *Uniting the Kingdom? The Making of British History*; Simon Gikandi, *Maps of Englishness: Writing Identity in the Culture of Colonialism* (New York: Columbia University Press, 1996); and Robert Colls and Philip Dodd, eds., *Englishness: Politics and Culture, 1880–1920* (London: Croom Helm, 1986).

4. These are Raymond Williams's terms (*Keywords*, 159).

5. See also Chambers's *Border Dialogues. Journeys in Postmodernity*, 17.

6. These responses are included in the Bibliography under William Clarke.

7. See Edward Said, *Orientalism* (1978) and the many subsequent debates, discussions and contestations of this general theory in which the 'Orient' is a Western construction, a misrepresentation, or as Reina Lewis puts it, a 'self-referential process of legitimation that endlessly asserted the power of the West to know, speak for and regulate the Orient better than the Orient itself' (Lewis, *Gendering Orientalism. Race, Femininity and Representation*, 16).

8. By sisters Harriet Maria and Madeline Anne Wallace Dunlop, who are not named in the review.

9. The term 'muscular Christianity' dates from about 1857 and is directly associated with Kingsley. This new kind of masculinity was characterised by 'sensitivity, steadfastness, conscience, and doing good – the celebrated ideal Christian gentleman' (10) as Christopher Parker puts it in *Gender Roles and Sexuality*.

10. See Rita Kranidis, *The Victorian Spinster*, for a detailed and erudite exposition of this topic.

11. Carmen Faymonville in '"Waste Not, Want Not": Even Redundant Women Have Their Uses' suggests that the Women's Emigration Society, operating between 1880 and 1884, helped approximately 200,000 women (81).

6. FEMINISM AND THE PRESS

1. Ironically, the eventual collapse of Langham Place was brought about in no small measure by sexual scandals linked to Matilda Hays, sub-editor with Bessie Parkes of the *English Woman's Journal*, and Emily Faithfull's involvement in a notorious divorce case.

2. This is a reference to Harriet Martineau's 'Female Industry', *Edinburgh Review* 109 (1859): 293–336.
3. On the novel, home and professionalisation of women's work, see, for example, Monica F. Cohen, *Professional Domesticity in the Victorian Novel: Women, Work and Home* (1998).
4. We are indebted to Mary Poovey's elaboration of this point in *Making a Social Body: British Cultural Formation, 1830–64* (1995).

7. GENDER, COMMODITY AND THE LATE NINETEENTH-CENTURY PERIODICAL

1. See Rita Kranidis, *Subversive Discourse: The Cultural Production of Late Victorian Feminist Novels* (1995), 31.
2. Carol T. Christ, 'The Hero as Man of Letters', *Victorian Sages and Cultural Discourse: Renegotiating Gender and Power*, ed. Thais Morgan (1990), 21.
3. Major studies of gender and the woman's magazine include Ros Ballaster *et. al.*, *Women's Worlds: Ideology, Femininity and the Woman's Magazine* (1991); Margaret Beetham, *A Magazine of Her Own?: Domesticity and Desire in the Woman's Magazine, 1800–1914* (1996); Cynthia White, *The Women's Periodical Press in Britain, 1946–1976* (1977).
4. See, for example, Ros Ballaster *et. al.*, *Women's Worlds*; Margaret Beetham, *Magazine of her Own?*; N. N. Feltes, *Literary Capital and the Late Victorian Novel* (1993); Thomas Richards, *The Commodity Culture of Victorian England* (1990); and Rita Felski, *The Gender of Modernity* (1995).
5. Boardman compares the magazine with the emporium, as does Ellen Gruber Garvey in the introduction to *The Adman in the Parlor: Magazines and the Gendering of Consumer Culture, 1880s to 1910s* (1996), 1.
6. Poovey also comments on gender and authorship in Chapter 4 of *Uneven Developments*.
7. For a discussion of the culture of male homoeroticism in this period, see Joseph Bristow, *Effeminate England: Homoerotic Writing After 1885* (1995).
8. For a discussion of the rise of the British art market see John Seed, '"Commerce and the Liberal Arts": the Political Economy of Art in Manchester, 1775–1860', *The Culture of Capital: Art, Power and the Nineteenth-Century Middle Class* (1988).
9. On the subject of the construction of Wilde's public persona see Gagnier, *Idylls of the Market Place* (1987); and Katharine Worth, *Oscar Wilde* (1983), 6.
10. For a more extensive consideration of *Woman's World* see Laurel Brake *Subjugated Knowledges*, 134–42; Anya Clayforth, '*Woman's World*: Oscar Wilde as Editor'; and Stephanie Green, 'Oscar Wilde's *Woman's World*'.
11. For further discussion of the notoriety associated with the journal's identity see: Laurel Brake, 'Endgames: The Politics of *The Yellow Book*'; Bridget Elliott, 'Sights of Pleasure: Beardsley's Images of Actresses and the New Journalism of the Nineties', 71–101; and Regenia Gagnier, *Idylls of the Marketplace* (1987).

12. See Bram Djikstra, *Idols of Perversity: Fantasies of Feminine Evil in Fin-de-siècle Culture* (1986). It is also worth noting that Wilde's play *Salomé* had been banned from production in 1892.
13. See also Patricia Marks, *Bicycles, Bangs and Bloomers: The New Woman in the Popular Press* (1990).

CONCLUSION

1. Among these scholars are Brake, Brantlinger, Maidment, Pykett, Reed, each cited previously in this study.

Appendix: the periodicals

REFERENCE WORKS CONSULTED

A—Ellegård, Alvar. *Darwin and the General Reader: the Reception of Darwin's Theory of Evolution in the British Periodical Press 1859–1872*. Göteborg: Distributors Almqvista Wilsell, 1958.

AE—Ellegård, Alvar. *The Readership of the Periodical Press in Mid-Victorian Britain*. Göteborgs Universitets Arskrifft, 1957.

B—Beetham, Margaret. *A Magazine of Her Own? Domesticity and Desire in the Woman's Magazine, 1800–1914*. London: Routledge, 1996.

BLC—British Library Catalogue

BUC—British Union Catalogue of Periodicals

CVLC—Herbert F. Tucker, ed. *A Companion to Victorian Literature and Culture*. Malden, Mass.: Blackwell, 1999.

CW—White, Cynthia L. *Women's Magazines 1693–1968*. London: Michael Joseph, 1970.

E—Edwards, P. D. *Dickens's 'Young Men'. George Augustus Sala, Edmund Yates and the World of Victorian Journalism*. Ashgate: Aldershot, 1997.

EC—Crawford, Elizabeth. *The Women's Suffrage Movement. A Reference Guide 1866–1928*. London: UCL Press, 1999.

IVJ—Laurel Brake, Aled Jones and Lionel Madden. *Investigating Victorian Journalism*. New York: St. Martin's Press, 1990.

JR—Rendall, Jane, ed. *Equal or Different: Women's Politics 1800–1914*. Oxford: Basil Blackwell, 1987.

N—Nicoll, Mildred Robertson, ed. *The Letters of Annie S. Swan*. London: Hodder and Stoughton, 1945.

NCM—Laurel Brake *et al.*, eds. *Nineteenth-Century Media and the Construction of Identities*. Basingstoke: Palgrave, 2000.

O—Onslow, Barbara. *Women of the Press in Nineteenth-Century Britain*. London: Macmillan, 2000.

PB—Brantlinger, Patrick. *The Reading Lesson. The Threat of Mass Literacy in Nineteenth-Century British Fiction*. Bloomington: Indiana University Press, 1998.

R—Reed, David. *The Popular Magazine in Britain and The United States 1880–1960*. London: British Library; University of Toronto Press, 1997.

S—Sutherland, John. *Longman Companion to Victorian Fiction*. London: Longman, 1988.

T—Turner, Mark W. *Trollope and the Magazines: Gendered Issues in Mid-Victorian Britain*. Houndsmill: Macmillan Press, 2000.

VPR—*Victorian Periodicals Review*. Various articles on specific titles.

VPVS—Vann, J. Don and Rosemary T. Van Arsdel, eds. *Victorian Periodicals and Victorian Society*, Toronto: Scolar, 1994.

W—*Wellesley Index*

WD—*Waterloo Directory of Victorian Periodicals 1824–1900*.

Descriptions are based on our own observations, supplemented by the above reference works. Unless otherwise stated the cost per issue is the price at which the periodical was first offered to the public. Costs changed when stamp duty was reduced to 1d. in 1836 then abolished in 1855, and the tax on paper was removed in 1861.

Ainsworth's Magazine (1842–54), cost 1s.6d., published monthly in London by Hugh Cunningham. Politically conservative and domestic, offering serialised fiction, short stories, light essays and a ladies' page. Designed and edited by Harrison Ainsworth to compete with *Bentley's Miscellany**. [BLC, S, *VPVS*]

Alexandra Magazine and Women's Social and Industrial Advocate (1864–5), cost 6d., published in London by Jackson, Watford & Hodder. Politically feminist, but recognised contemporary domestic ideology. Edited by Bessie Parkes, editor of the *English Woman's Journal**, then by Jessie Boucherett. Became *Englishwoman's Review*, 1865–1903. [BLC, JR, VPR]

All The Year Round (1859–95), cost 2d., published weekly in London by Charles Dickens, replacing *Household Words**. Politically liberal and middle class, offering fiction, poetry and articles on the social and political issues of the day. Edited until his death in 1870 by Dickens, assisted by W. H. Wills, and subsequently by Charles Dickens, Jr. [A, AE, BLC, S]

Athenaeum (1828–1921), cost 8d., reduced to 4d. (1855), published weekly in London by Henry Colburn, and very popular. Unaffiliated politically, it reviewed theology, history, travel, science, fine art, literature and fiction and reported on art exhibitions, opera, theatre and learned societies. Edited by Sir Charles Dilke, 1830–46, and purchased by Charles Wentworth Dilke in 1869. [A, BLC, EC, VPR]

Aunt Judy's Magazine (1866–85), published in London, founded and edited by Margaret Scott Gatty until 1873, then her daughter Horatia, 1873–85, initially with her sister Juliana Ewing. Politically conservative and middle class, designed specifically for adolescent girls, it contained fiction and items on natural history, indoor amusements and reviews of books for children. [BLC, O]

Belgravia (1866–99), cost 1s. (1870), published monthly in London by John Maxwell, and designed for novelist Mary Elizabeth Braddon, the first editor. Acquired by Chatto & Windus in 1876. No specific political or religious affiliations but competed with *Temple Bar** and the *Cornhill**. Primarily a fiction magazine, with racy sensation stories and chit-chat, but some didactic criticism exploring contemporary issues. [A, AE, BLC, S, VPR]

Bentley's Miscellany (1837–68), cost 2s.6d. (1860), published monthly in London by Richard Bentley, it had no specific political or religious affili-ations and offered fiction, reviews and short articles. First editor Charles Dickens, succeeded in 1839 by Harrison Ainsworth, then Bentley from 1841 with a slide in standard. Incorporated with *Temple Bar** in 1868. [AE, S, T, *W*]

Blackwood's Edinburgh Magazine (1817–1980), cost 2s.6d. (1860), published monthly in Edinburgh by Blackwood and Sons. Politically Tory and con-servative it was initially designed to compete with the *Edinburgh Review**, but its monthly format with miscellaneous offerings placed it firmly in the magazine category. William Blackwood, then his son John, closely managed the magazine with the editors. [AE, S, *W*]

Bow Bells (1862–97), cost 1d., published weekly in London by John Dicks, offering topical essays, a ladies' page and needlework patterns. Initially printed as a broadsheet divided into four columns, with tiny print, it stan-dardised to quarto from 1864. Illustrations were a feature. [*VPVS*]

Boy's Own Paper (1879–1967), cost 1d., published weekly in London by the Religious Tract Society. Politically imperialist, evangelical and conservative, with quality illustrations. It offered adventure fiction, poetry, informative pieces and correspondence columns. First edited by James Macaulay, then George Hutchison. Its sister publication, *Girl's Own Paper**, was created in response to demands from *BOP*'s female readership. [BLC, *CVLC*, S]

British and Foreign Review; or European Quarterly Review (1835–44), cost 4s.6d., established by Thomas Wentworth Beaumont and published quarterly in London by Richard and John Edward Taylor, 1838–44. Politically between Tory and radical, focussing on political and personal freedom. Edited by John Mitchell Kemble, 1836–44. Reviews were more political than literary in the early years. [BLC, *W*]

Cassell's Magazine (1867–1930), *Family* added to title (1874), cost 1d., published weekly in London by Cassell and Co. Politically conservative and aimed at a family readership, profusely illustrated, offering a range of general interest articles and fiction from notable authors. Later much more of a miscellany. [A, S, T]

Chambers's Edinburgh Journal (1832–1936), from 1854 *Chambers's Journal of Popular Literature, Science and Arts*, cost $1\frac{1}{2}$d. (1860), published weekly in Edinburgh and London by William and Robert Chambers. Politically designed for self-improvement among the working and artisan classes focussing on useful knowledge, temperance and moderation, but also included tales and occasional serials. [AE, BLC, PB, S]

Children's Friend (1824–1930), cost 1d. (1861), published monthly in London by Seeley, Jackson & Halliday and S. W. Partridge. Politically conservative and religious. First series edited by William Carus Wilson. From 1861 high-quality print and woodcuts offering a range of short, pithy moral tales and poems, and general knowledge items. [*WD*]

Colonist (1848), published in London by Trelawney William Saunders, edited by W. H. G. Kingston, later a contributor to *Boy's Own Paper**. Politically imperialist and conservative, didactic in tone and aimed at the 'Labouring Classes'. [BLC]

Contemporary Review (1866–ongoing), cost 2s.6d. (1870), published monthly in London by Strahan & Co., then Henry S. King & Co (1866–82). Politically liberal promoting social reform and broadly evangelical, readers tended to be upper to middle class. Edited by Henry Alford, Dean of

Canterbury (1866–70) then James Thomas Knowles and Alexander Strahan himself, who also published *Good Words* and *Sunday Magazine*, among others. [AE, BLC, *W*]

Cornhill Magazine (1860–1975), cost 1s., published monthly in London by Smith Elder until 1916 then quarterly by John Murray. Politically liberal, avoiding morals, politics and religion, rather designed to offer first class illustrated fiction and short articles. First edited by W. M. Thackeray, later editors included Leslie Stephen and James Payn. After 1896 it became more nationalistic. [BLC, S, *W*]

Critic (1843–63), cost 1d., published weekly by the Penny National Library Office. A quality literary miscellany, independent of any particular political or religious affiliations, but supporting Disraeli and the Young England Movement. [A, BLC, VPR]

Cycle Magazine (1895–7), published in London, edited by C. P. Sisley, the title tells you all. [BLC]

Dark Blue (1871–3), cost 1s., published monthly in London by Sampson Low. Politically liberal, advocating social and educational reform, especially women's education. Conceived and edited by John Christian Freund, offering historical, geographical, political and social essays focussing on Europe. High contributor payments, costly illustrations and publisher, contributed to its failure. [BLC, *W*]

Dome (1897–1900), cost 1s., published quarterly in London by Unicorn Press. An illustrated quarterly focussing on art, architecture, literature, drawing, painting and engraving, and music, including reviews and notices. [BLC]

Dublin Penny Journal (1832–6), cost 1d. published weekly in Dublin. Conducted by P. D. Hardy, designed to compete with the SDUK's *Penny Magazine* by claiming to offer topics more suited to the Irish working classes. [BLC, *WD*]

Dublin Review (1836–1969), cost 6s. (1860), published quarterly in London by William Spooner, then C. Dolman (1838–44), then Thomas Richardson and Son (1844–1863), thence various others. The leading Roman Catholic journal in Britain with orthodox affiliations. A standard review quarterly, first edited by Michael Joseph Quinn, the proprietor was Daniel O'Connell until 1847. [AE, BLC, *W*]

Eclectic Review (1805–68), cost 1s.6d. (1860), published in London by Jackson, Watford & Co. Politically liberal, representing religious dissent, particularly Congregationalist and Baptist, it offered essays on general literature, featuring Biblical topics and church politics. [A, AE, BLC]

Edinburgh Review (1802–1929), cost 6s. (1860), published quarterly in Edinburgh, then London, by Archibald Constable, then Longmans. Politically a Whig-liberal journal, with an upper-class, conservative readership, style and publishing format barely changed across the century. Strictly a review quarterly with long erudite articles on the noted publications of the day. Editors included Francis Jeffrey (1803–29), Macvey Napier (1829–47), William Empson (1847–52) and Henry Reeve (1855–95). [A, AE, BLC, *W*]

Eliza Cook's Journal (1849–54), cost $1\frac{1}{2}$d., published weekly by John Owen Clarke, then Charles Cook from 1851. Politically progressive addressing a working-class and artisan readership. Eliza Cook's occasional leaders and addresses to readers suggest she was editor. The journal offered short stories, articles, poems (mostly Cook's own) and reviews, focussing on women and the domestic, as well as emigration, and regularly employed women writers. [BLC, VPR]

Englishwoman's Domestic Magazine (1852–77) then *Illustrated Household Journal and Englishwoman's Domestic Magazine* (to 1881), cost 6d., designed and published in London by Samuel Beeton. Politically conservative and domestic, with fashion and women's pages edited by Isabella Beeton. Samuel Beeton edited 'Conversazione' and other columns. Every issue included a fashion plate and embroidery pattern, both in colour, as well as black-and-white illustrations. [B, BLC, O]

English Woman's Journal (1858–64), cost 1s., published monthly in London by the English Woman's Journal Co. Shareholders included Barbara Bodichon, Matilda Hays and Maria Rye. Politically feminist and dedicated to women's causes, founding and chief editor was Bessie Rayner Parkes with Matilda Hays. It included reviews of publications, and articles specifically addressing the woman question, but also literary and cultural reviews not directly related to that topic. Succeeded by the *Englishwoman's Review* and *Victoria Magazine**. [EC, JR, VPR]

Family Economist. A Penny Monthly Magazine Devoted to the Moral, Physical, and Domestic Improvement of the Industrious classes (1848–60), cost 1d., published in London by Groombridge & Sons. Initially aimed at a working-class readership, with many articles, poems and stories on emigration. In 1855 inserted *Entertaining* into the title to capture a middle-class readership. [BLC]

Fraser's Magazine (1830–82), cost 2s.6d. (1860), published monthly in London by James Fraser, Nickisson, Parker, then Longmans from 1863. Liberal conservative with broad Church associations, but more radical under Froude's editorship (1860–74). First edited by William Maginn, offering a mixture of reviews on literature, history and colonial politics, comic illustrations and poems, with a lively humorous tone, it became more subdued under others. [AE, BLC, *W*]

Gentlewoman (and Modern Life) (1890–1926), subsequently merged with *Eve*, cost 6d., published weekly in London. Politically conservative, aiming at an upper-middle-class readership of 'ladies' rather than 'women', reporting suffrage meetings, but satirising the idea of the woman voter. Included articles on art and fashion, a children's 'salon', correspondence pages and serious pieces. [B, O]

Girl of the Period Almanack (1869), ran to only one annual edition. It was published in London and like the *Girl of the Period Miscellany** was edited by 'Miss Echo'. It cost 3d. and included engravings, cartoons and a social calendar for 1870. [*WD*]

Girl of the Period Miscellany (March 1869–November 1869), cost 6d., published monthly in London. Conservative in tone, it was edited by the fictional 'Miss Echo' and her female assistants, and pitted against the nascent suffrage movement by suggesting that its successes might lead to the destruction of the female character and the derogation of her domestic duties. Subjects included courtship and weddings, with poems directed against the infractions of the 'modern' girl and satirical cartoons. [BLC, *WD*]

Girl's Own Paper (1880–1908, then various titles until 1950), cost 1d., published weekly in London by the Religious Tract Society. Edited by Charles Peters (1880–1908), the price never changed, then from 1908 with Flora Klickman it became a 6d. monthly. Conservative and evangelical, offering advice on dress, behaviour and occupations, serial fiction, information and a regular correspondents' page. Less rigid in format and moving with the times, *GOP* regularly outsold *BOP*. [BLC, O, R]

Girl's Realm (1898–1915), cost 1d., published in London by Cassell. A domestic magazine politically conservative and respectable. [B, BLC]

Grant's London Journal (1840–1), edited by London publisher James Grant. [BLC]

Home and Foreign Review (1862–4), cost 6s., published quarterly in London. Affiliated with the Roman Catholic Church and politically liberal. [A, BLC]

Home Chat (1895–1958), cost 1d., published weekly in London by Harmsworth. While conservative, aimed at middle and lower classes, it suggested home duties could display management skills and competency. It was bright, interesting and practical. [B, BLC, CW]

Home Circle (1849–53), cost 1d. or 1½d. with illustrations, published weekly in London by W. S. Johnson and edited by Pierce Egan. Politically conservative, it aimed at an upper-middle-class readership offering fiction, crochet and needlework patterns, correspondents' page (titled 'intercommunication'), children's pages and articles of general interest. [BLC]

Household Words (1851–9), cost 2d., published weekly in London by Bradbury and Evans. Founded and edited by Charles Dickens, with W. H. Wills as sub-editor, it was designed as a family magazine focussing on matters of social concern, education and information, with serials, short fiction and poetry. [BLC, S]

Howitt's Journal of Literature and Popular Progress (1847–8), cost 1½d., published weekly in London. Founded and edited by William and Mary Howitt, former Quakers, and politically radical-progressive. Aimed at an artisan and lower-middle-class readership, offering occasional pieces, aesthetic descriptive essays, reviews, political commentary, poetry and short fiction, most articles and contributions were signed. Format identical to *The People's Journal**. [BLC]

Humanitarian [or Humanity: a Journal of the Humanitarian League] (1895–1919), cost 1d., published weekly in London by W. Reeves. Edited by H. S. Satt and designed to combat cruelty to animals, its focus was the ethics of 'humaneness'. [*WD*]

Illustrated London News (1842–1988), cost 6d. (1860), published weekly in London. Founded by Herbert Ingram, a Nottingham compositor and newsagent, it was politically liberal-conservative and innovative in offering miscellaneous pictorial journalism, privileging news events until the 1880s when it began to include serial fiction. [A, AE, S, VPR]

Judy, or the London Serio-comic Journal (1867–1907), cost 2d. (1892), published weekly in London by the Dalziels. Politically conservative, editors included C. H. Ross. An illustrated comic paper containing social and political commentary modelled on its successful rival, *Punch**. [BLC, *VPVS*]

Knowledge: an Illustrated Magazine of Science (1881–1917), published in London. Edited by R. A. Proctor, merged with *Illustrated Scientific News* in 1904, edited by Major B. Baden-Powell and E. S. Grew. A popular science journal offering articles on history, science, the woman question, education and public health, with a correspondents' page revealing a lively scientific readership. [*VPVS, WD*]

Lads of the Village, a Magazine of Universal Recreation (1874 only), cost 1d., published weekly in London by the Provident Printing and Publishing Co. Founder, publisher and editor William Watkins offered a miscellany of topics including sports and lads who became famous, and serial fiction.

Lady's Magazine (1770–1847), cost 6d., published monthly in London by J. Page. Offering entertainment and instruction to a conservative, upper-middle-class readership. An earlier series is dated 1756 but the BLC notes its records are imperfect. [BLC, CW]

Lady's Magazine and Museum of Belle Lettres (1832–7), cost 6d., published monthly in London by Dobbs & Page. A continuation of the *Lady's Magazine**, with the same mix of offerings and the same conservative social and political position. [CW]

Lady's Monthly Museum (1798–1828), published in London. Politically conservative but advocating improved female education, while stressing the primacy of household duties. It offered articles of general interest and fiction. [CW]

Leisure Hour. Family Journal of Instruction and Recreation (1852–1905), cost 1d. (1860) and published weekly in London by the Religious Tract Society, publishers of *GOP** and *BOP**. Politically conservative and evangelical, and designed for family reading. It offered articles of general interest, short stories and poems, notably focussing on outposts of the empire. [A, AE, BLC]

Literary World. A Journal of Popular Information and Entertainment (1839–40), published in London. Edited by John Timbs, offering fiction, reviews and articles. [BLC]

London Review (1860–9), cost 3d., published in London by Saunders and Otley, then Simpkin, Marshall & Co. Politically liberal, focussing on the literary and philosophical. Incorporated with the *Examiner* in 1869. A standard review and under pressure from competitors. [AE, BLC]

Magazine of Domestic Economy (1836–44), cost 6d., published monthly in London by Orr & Smith. Politically conservative, focussing on the domestic but offering a miscellaneous range of reviews and articles that included pieces on outposts of empire, the United States and Europe. [BLC]

Metropolitan Magazine (1831–50), cost 3s.6d., published in London by Saunders & Otley (1836–47). Politically conservative, briefly edited by Thomas Campbell but under Frederick Marryat's proprietorship and editorship (1832–6) considered to have pioneered serial fiction in Britain. [BLC, S]

National Review (1855–64), cost 6s. (1860), published quarterly in London, produced by a small Unitarian group. Edited by R. H. Hutton and W. Bagehot with the usual review articles addressing topical political and social questions. [AE, BLC]

New Monthly Magazine (1814–84), cost 3s.6d. (1860), published monthly in London by founder Henry Colburn, the prototype of the monthly miscellanies. Originally focussing on current affairs, with Thomas Campbell's editorship (1820–30) it shifted to literary reviews, short stories, articles and poetry. Politically liberal-conservative, with Bulwer Lytton (1831–3) it advocated reform. Sold to Harrison Ainsworth who was editor and proprietor 1845–70. [AE, BLC, S, VPR]

Nineteenth Century (1877–1950), published in London by Henry S. King, then Kegan Paul until 1891, then Sampson Low. From 1900 the words *and After* added to the title. Edited by architect James Knowles. Politically liberal with no specific affiliations, and influential in its reviewing, abandoning anonymity in favour of signed articles. [BLS, *W*]

North British Review (1844–71), cost 6s. (1860), published in Edinburgh and London by W. P. Kennedy and others. Short-term editors included David Welsh (1844–5), A. C. Fraser (1850–7) and W. G. Blaikie (1860–3). Evangelical at outset, by the 1860s tended to be non-sectarian, offering sound literary and scientific articles to a predominantly Scottish readership. [AE, VPR, *W*]

Once A Week. An Illustrated Miscellany of Literature, Art, Science and Popular Information (1859–80), cost 3d. (1860), published weekly in London by Bradbury & Evans opposing Dickens's *All the Year Round**. Politically liberal, illustrated by the artists employed on *Punch** and edited by Samuel Lucas, acquired by James Rice after Lucas's death in 1865 and bought by Manville Fenn (1873). It offered a miscellany of literary reviews, criticism and general information. [AE, S, *VPVS*]

Pall Mall Gazette (1865–1923), cost 2d., published daily in London by the proprietors. Initially liberal-conservative then more radical under John Morley's editorship (1880–3) assisted by W. T. Stead, subsequently editor until 1889. Stead championed women's suffrage among other campaigns. Sold in 1892 to Lord Astor, a Conservative, then purchased by Davison Dalziel (1915) and incorporated with his *Evening Standard* (1923). [AE, BLC, EC]

People's and Howitt's Journal (1849–51), published in London by John Saunders and identical in layout, content and politics to *People's** and *Howitt's**. Saunders won the court case brought by the Howitts and, although their name is in the title, they never contributed to it. [BLC]

The People's Journal (1846–8), cost 1½d., published in London by W. Lovett, edited by John Saunders. Mary and William Howitt, prolific contributors, fell out with Saunders over money and began their own journal *Howitt's**, in opposition. Aimed at keeping the working class informed, it advocated restraint through terms like 'duty' and 'home'. Many contributions were signed. [BLC]

Photographic News (1858–1908), published weekly in London by Cassell. A special interest publication edited by Sir William Crooks, the first devoted to photography. [BLC]

Punch, or the London Charivari (1841–1992), cost 3d. (1860), published weekly in London by Bradbury & Evans. Edited by Mark Lemon (1841–70) who established its format of cartoons and short comic items. Politically liberal, with a conservative middle-class readership. At times misogynist and anti-feminist, it nevertheless addressed the woman question with some sympathy and provides insight to contemporary politics through its aggressive cartoons and witticisms. [AE, EC, S]

Quarterly Review (1809–1942), cost 6s. (1860), published in London by John Murray. Politically Tory and edited by William Gifford (1809–24), whose winning format of unsigned, intellectually demanding articles meant it outsold its nearest rival, the *Edinburgh**. Other long-term editors included John Gibson Lockhart (1826–53) and William Smith (1867–93). [AE, VPR, *W*]

Quiver (1861–1926), published weekly in London by Cassell. Edited by John Cassell, it was designed for the advancement of religion but offered fiction serials as its principle item. After Cassell's death in 1865 the religious tone eased significantly and it offered illustrations, Doré's among them. [S, *VPVS*]

Rational Dress Society Gazette (1888–9), cost 3d., published in London by Hatchards. A radical instrument for amending women's dress, it was forced to modify its approach for a more contemporary and conservative middle-class readership but failed nevertheless. Constance Wilde was secretary of the Rational Dress League and one of its anonymous correspondents. [BLC, VPR]

Review of Reviews (1890–1936), published monthly in London. Designed and edited by W. T. Stead as a digest of the major late-century British and foreign periodicals illustrated with woodcuts and photographs. Stead embraced the causes of the day, in particular women's suffrage. [BLC, EC, *VPVS*]

St. James's Magazine (1861–82), cost 1s., published monthly in London by Kent & Co. Designed to rival the *Cornhill**, offering short articles on domestic and colonial matters, as well as fiction. First edited by Anna Maria Hall (1861–2), a later editor and part-proprietor was novelist Mrs J. H. Riddell. [BLC, S]

Saint Pauls Magazine (1867–74), cost 1s. (1870), published monthly in London by James Virtue, then Alexander Strahan, then Henry S. King.

Modelled on the *Cornhill**, it was edited by Anthony Trollope (1867–70). The lack of women readers, which Strahan tried to remedy, probably contributed to its brief run. [BLC, S, T]

Saturday Review (1855–1938), cost 6d. (1860), published weekly in London. Founded by A. J. Beresford-Hope to compete with the *Athenaeum** and the *Spectator**, and edited by John Douglas Cook (1855–68). Politically conservative, offering decided opinions in reviews and on contemporary issues. [AE, BLC, S, VPR]

Savoy (1896 only), cost 2s.6d., published quarterly in London by Frank Cass. An illustrated magazine initiated by Leonard Smithers, designed and illustrated by Aubrey Beardsley and edited by poet Arthur Symons. It was very modern and had censorship problems, a boycott by W. H. Smith, booksellers, contributing to its early demise. [BLC, S]

Shafts (1892–1900), published in London, and edited by Margaret Sibthorpe. Politically feminist, it was a radical journal supporting women's suffrage and featuring noted feminist writers. Its motto was 'Light comes to those who dare to think'. [EC]

Sharpe's London Magazine: A Journal of Entertainment & Instruction for General Reading (1845–70), cost 1s., published monthly by T. B. Sharpe. Early editors included Frank Smedley (1847–9) and Anna Maria Hall (1852). It offered fiction serials, articles on people and places, translations from the German and French and fiction reviews. Its contributors featured a significant number of women.

Spectator (1828–ongoing), cost 9d. (1855), published weekly in London. Founding editor Robert Rintoul was responsible for its independent, liberal politics, mostly maintained by subsequent editors and proprietors like Hutton and Townsend. Offering well-written political and literary articles and reviews, including scientific and religious matters, it participated in contemporary social and political reforms. [AE, S, VPR]

Sylvia's Journal (1878–91), published in London, a continuation of Samuel Beeton's *Young Englishwoman*. Politically conservative and domestic, primarily edited by women, Miss Graham (early 1880s), Rosamond Marriott Watson and Mrs. Tomson privileging domestic management over fashion. [BLC, O, VPR]

Tait's Edinburgh Magazine (1832–61), cost 2s.6d. (1834), published monthly in Edinburgh by William Tait until 1846, then John Sutherland and James Knox. Edited by William Tait, it was politically radical and liberal. Merging with *Johnstone's Edinburgh Magazine* (1834), the price was reduced to 1s., making it the first of the shilling monthlies. Christian Isobel Johnstone became half-share proprietor and principal editor until 1846, the period of its greatest success, offering reviews, short stories, articles and poems. She was politically feminist and gave prominence to women's writing both in reviews and in items accepted for publication. [BLC, O, *W*]

Temple Bar. A London Magazine for Town and Country Readers (1860–1906), cost 1s. (1865), published monthly in London by Ward Lock, then Bentley, then Macmillan. Devised by John Maxwell and edited by G. A. Sala, who purchased it in 1862. Edited by Edmund Yates until 1867, it was purchased by Richard Bentley (1866), and edited by George Bentley. Liberal and bohemian, it offered serialised sensation fiction, chit-chat and articles of general interest. [AE, S, VPR]

Time: a Monthly Miscellany of Interesting and Amusing Literature (1879–1901), published monthly in London and edited by Edmund Yates until 1884. Liberal conservative, offering fiction, poetry, general interest articles and biographical pieces on prominent people. [S]

Tinsley's Magazine (1867–92), cost 1s. (1870), published in London by Tinsley Bros. Liberal conservative and edited by Edmund Yates until 1869, when he fell out with William Tinsley who took over the editorship. Designed as a general family magazine offering fiction, reviews and general articles, it had only limited success. [BLC, S]

Tit-Bits (1881–1920), cost 2d., published weekly in London by George Newnes, editor until 1891. Aimed at commuting readers of the upper working and lower middle classes. Exemplar of the 'New' journalism with sensational advertising and competitions with exciting prizes, its correspondence columns were a feature. [BLC, *NCM*]

Train. A First-Class Magazine (1856–8), cost 1s., published monthly in London by Richard Bentley as a rival to *Punch**. Edited by Edmund Yates, the all-male contributors offered mostly fiction and poetry with a racy, undergraduate style, but it was not successful. [BLC, E]

Universal Review (1888–90), published in London by S. Sonneschein, was edited by Harry Quilter with a focus on literature and the visual arts. [*VPVS*]

Victoria Magazine (1863–80), cost 1s. (1865), published in London by the Victoria Press, founded by Emily Davies and Emily Faithfull to succeed the *English Woman's Journal* * espousing many of that journal's platforms, including social reform and education for women, with standard offerings on literature, art and science. First edited by Emily Davies, financially it was the most successful of the three Langham Place publications. [BLC, O, VPR]

Waverley Journal (1855?–7), annual cost 10s.2d., published fortnightly in Edinburgh 'by ladies' and edited by Eleanor Duckworth. Literary offerings included fiction and articles on Protestant philanthropy. Bessie Parkes and Isa Craig joined the staff (1857), and Parkes was offered the editorship, producing her first number in July 1857. Negotiations for its purchase by Barbara Leigh Smith collapsed and she and Parkes then established the *English Woman's Journal**. [JR, O]

Welcome Guest. A Magazine of Recreative Reading for All (1858–64), cost ½d., published weekly in London. Politically liberal this illustrated journal was edited by George Sala, offering fiction, poetry, articles on current affairs and reviews, often with a comic slant. [*VPVS*]

Westminster Review (1824–1914), cost 6s. (1860), published quarterly in London, the radical voice of the triumvirate of quarterlies and the *Quarterly** and *Edinburgh**'s nearest rival. Founded by James Mill, funded by Jeremy Bentham, John Stuart Mill was editor (1836–40) and despite changes of ownership it remained radical. Purchased by John Chapman in 1851, he remained editor until 1894. George Eliot served as sub-editor (1851–3), and continued reviewing for it until 1856. As a free-thinking, intellectual journal it supported national education and women's suffrage. [AE, EC, *W*]

Wheeling (1884–1901), cost 1d. (1894), published in London by F. Percy Low. Strictly a special interest publication with news about bicycles and tricycles. [*WD*]

Windsor Magazine. An Illustrated Monthly for Men and Women (1895–1939), published in London by Ward Lock. A popular illustrated magazine, co-founded by Flora Klickman, later editor of the *Girl's Own Paper**. Politically conservative, even reactionary and anti-feminist, it carried fiction serials, short stories, poetry and articles, many by women. [BLC, O, *VPVS*]

Woman (1890–1912), cost 1d., published weekly in London, founded and first edited by Fitzroy Gardiner. Arnold Bennett was assistant editor from 1893 and editor from 1896. Male editors assumed female pseudonyms. Politically liberal, it carefully avoided a feminist label, offering domestic journalism aimed at an upper-middle-class readership. [B, CW, O]

Woman at Home. Annie S. Swann's Magazine (1893–1917), published in London by Hodder & Stoughton, was conservative, domestic and anti-suffrage. Founded and edited by Sir William Robertson Nicoll, with Jane Stoddart, succeeded by Alice Head. Novelist and journalist Annie S. Swann was the main contributor and contents included short fiction, articles on people and places, and a regular editor to readers column titled 'Over the Teacups'. Illustrated, it included articles on sport and employments for women. [N]

Woman's Life: An Illustrated Weekly for the Home (1895–1934) thence *Woman's Own*, cost 1d., published in London by George Newnes, a popular illustrated magazine describing itself as modern, 'latest, up-to-datest', offering interviews with notable women, fiction, articles on careers for women, women's sport and general knowledge. [B]

Woman's Penny Paper, & the Woman's Herald (1888–93), cost 1d., published in London, founded and edited by Henrietta Müller. Politically feminist and linked to the Suffragist Women's Liberal Association and Temperance. It focussed on key contemporary educational and social questions and was taken over by the *Woman's Signal**. [O, VPR]

Woman's Signal (1894–9), cost 1d., published in London. Pro-suffrage with links to the Women's Christian Temperance Union. Originally edited by Isobel Somerset, Florence Fenwick Miller, a highly experienced journalist, became unpaid proprietor/editor in 1895 popularising the journal by making it less aggressive. Nevertheless, it remained propagandist rather than commercial. [EC, O]

Woman's Tribune (1906–7), published in London by the Women's Franchise Declaration Committee, founded and directed by Lady Christiana

Herringham. From November 1906 to June 1907 continued as *Women and Progress*. [EC]

Woman's World (1887–90), originally *The Lady's World. A Magazine of Fashion and Society*, renamed and edited by Oscar Wilde (1887–9). Published monthly in London by Cassell, it featured predominantly female contributors, offering quality illustrations with fiction, poetry, general interest articles, literary and fashion notes. [BLC]

Working Man's Friend, and Family Instructor (1850–2), published in London by John Cassell with a politically and socially diametric readership. It offered short stories, poems, advice, and a significant proportion of articles on British colonies and emigration, focussing on instruction rather than entertainment. [BLC]

Yellow Book (1894–7), cost 5s., published quarterly in London by Bodley Head. Avant-garde, supporting young experimental writers including Ada Leverson, and airing socially and sexually progressive subject matter. It became more conservative following Aubrey Beardsley's departure as art editor. [B, *VPVS*]

Young Man. A Monthly Journal and Review (1887–1915), then combined with *Young Woman** as *Young Man and Woman*, cost 3d., published monthly in London by Horace Marshall, focussing on British supremacy with a Christian bias. First edited by Frederick A. Atkins, offering short stories, serials, interviews with famous names, recommended reading, as well as a regular readers' column. [BLC]

Young Woman. An Illustrated Monthly Magazine (1892–1915) then combined with *Young Man** to become *Young Man and Woman*, cost 3d. (1894), published in London by S. W. Partridge. A conservative publication with low church affiliations and egalitarian aims to cross class boundaries and reach a more serious-minded female readership. Edited by Frederick A. Atkins, like its male counterpart it offered fiction, interviews, general information articles and a regular readers' column, followed by correspondents' pages. [BLC, CW]

*appear elsewhere in the index

Bibliography

'Address'. *The Home Circle* 1 (1849): iii–iv.
'Address'. *Magazine of Domestic Economy* 7 (1842): iii–iv.
'Advertisement'. *Edinburgh Review* 1 (1802): iii–iv.
'Advertisement'. *Literary World* 1 (1839): i.
Ainsworth, Harrison. 'Preliminary Address'. *Ainsworth's Magazine* 1 (1842): i–iv.
Althusser, Louis. 'Ideology and Ideological State Apparatuses', *Lenin and Philosophy and Other Essays*. Trans. Ben Brewster. London: New Left Books, 1971.
Altick, Richard D. *The English Common Reader: a Social History of the Mass Reading Public, 1800–1900*. University of Chicago Press, 1957.
  Writers, Readers, and Occasions: Selected Essays on Victorian Literature and Life. Columbus: Ohio State University Press, 1989.
Amateur Sewersman. 'A Gloomy Ramble'. *Boy's Own Paper* 3 (1880–1): 817–18.
Anderson, Patricia. *The Printed Image and Transformation of Popular Culture 1790–1860*. Oxford University Press, 1991.
'Answers to Correspondents'. *Englishwoman's Domestic Magazine* 4 (1861–2): 191.
'Answers to Correspondents'. *Englishwoman's Domestic Magazine* 5 (1862): 191.
'Answers to Correspondents'. *Young Woman* 5 (1896–7): 118.
Armstrong, Isobel and Joseph Bristow, with Cath Sharrock, eds. *Nineteenth-Century Women Poets*. Oxford: Clarendon Press, 1996.
Armstrong, Nancy. *Desire and Domestic Fiction: a Political History of the Novel*. New York: Oxford University Press, 1987.
Arnold, Matthew. 'Up to Easter'. *Nineteenth Century* (1887): 638–9.
Ashdown, Dulcie M., ed. *Over the Teacups*. London: Cornmarket Reprints, 1972.
'Australia'. *North British Review* 4 (1845–6): 281–312.
'Australia. II. – Its Gold-Fields'. *Leisure Hour* 1 (1852): 513–17.
Bagehot, Walter. 'The First Edinburgh Reviewers', *The Collected Works of Walter Bagehot*. Ed. Norman St John-Stevas. 15 vols. London: The Economist, 1965–86.
Ballaster, Ros, Margaret Beetham, Elizabeth Frazer and Sandra Hebron. *Women's Worlds. Ideology, Femininity and the Woman's Magazine*. London: Macmillan, 1991.
Baudelaire, Charles. *The Painter of Modern Life and Other Essays*. Ed. and trans. Jonathan Mayne. London: Phaidon, 1964.

Baudrillard, Jean. *The Consumer Society: Myths and Structures.* London: Thousand Oaks, New Delhi: Sage Publications, 1998.

Beck, S. William. 'A Treatise on Hoops.' *Woman's World* 1 (1888): 59–64.

'Gloves Old and New.' *Woman's World* 2 (1889): 86–9.

Beerbohm, Max. 'A Defence of Cosmetics.' *Yellow Book* 1 (1894): 65–82.

'A Note on George the Fourth.' *Yellow Book* 3 (1894): 247–69.

Beetham, Margaret. *A Magazine of Her Own? Domesticity and Desire in the Woman's Magazine, 1800–1914.* London: Routledge, 1996.

'Towards a Theory of the Periodical as a Publishing Genre'. *Investigating Victorian Journalism.* Ed. Laurel Brake, Aled Jones and Lionel Madden. New York: St. Martin's Press, 1990.

Beeton, Samuel. [Editorial Preface]. *Englishwoman's Domestic Magazine* n.s.1 (1860): iii.

Bennett, Arnold. *Journalism for Women. A Practical Guide.* London: John Lane, 1898.

Bevington, Merle Mobray. *The Saturday Review, 1855–1868.* New York: Columbia, 1941.

'A Bewailment from Bath: or, Poor Old Maids.' *Blackwood's Edinburgh Magazine* 55 (1844): 199–201.

Bhabha, Homi K. *The Location of Culture.* London and New York: Routledge, 1994.

Bird, Christopher. 'Introduction.' *British and Foreign Review* 1 (1835): 5–16.

Bird, Isabella L. 'Australia Felix. IX. – Victoria and Victorian Progress.' *Leisure Hour* 26 (1877): 469–72.

Bivona, Daniel. *Desire and Contradiction. Imperial Visions and Domestic Debates in Victorian Literature.* Manchester University Press, 1990.

Black, Clementina. 'A Working Woman's Speech.' *The Nineteenth Century* (1889): 667–71.

'A Blast Against the Monsterous Regimente of Womene.' *Tait's Edinburgh Magazine* 2 (1835): 707–14.

Boardman, Kay. '"A Material Girl in a Material World": the Fashionable Female Body in Victorian Women's Magazines.' *Journal of Victorian Culture* 3 (1998): 93–110.

Bodichon, Barbara Leigh Smith. 'Middle-Class Schools for Girls.' *English Woman's Journal* 6 (1860): 168–77.

Bonnell, Marilyn. 'The Power of the Pedal: the Bicycle and the Turn-of-the-Century Woman.' *Nineteenth-Century Contexts* 14 (1990): 215–39.

'Book of the Seasons.' *Athenaeum* (1831): 147–9.

'Books We Do Not Review.' *Eliza Cook's Journal* 10 (1853–4): 216–17.

Booth, Robert M. 'Aubrey Beardsley and *The Savoy*.' *Ayelseford Review* 8 (1966): 71–85.

'A Boy's Account of the Coming-of-Age Dinner.' *Boy's Own Paper* 22 (1899–1900): 218.

'A "Boy's Own" Artist at the Royal Academy.' *Boy's Own Paper* 2 (1879–80): 697.

'A Boy's Sermon.' *Children's Friend* 25 (1885): 183.

Brake, Laurel. 'Endgames: the Politics of *The Yellow Book*, or Decadence, Gender and the New Journalism.' *The Ending of Epochs*. Essays and Studies. The English Association. Ed. Laurel Brake. London: D. S. Brewer, 1995.

A. Jones and Lionel Martin, eds. *Investigating Victorian Journalism*. New York: St Martin's Press, 1990.

Bill Bell and David Finkelstein. *Nineteenth-Century Media and the Construction of Identities*. Houndsmill: Palgrave, 2000.

Subjugated Knowledges: Journalism, Gender and Literature in the Nineteenth Century. Basingstoke: Macmillan, 1994.

'The *Westminster* and Gender at Mid-Century.' *Victorian Periodicals Review* 33 (2000): 247–72.

Brantlinger, Patrick. *The Reading Lesson: The Threat of Mass Literacy in Nineteenth-Century British Fiction*. Bloomington: Indiana University Press, 1998.

Rule of Darkness: British Literature and Imperialism, 1830–1914. Ithaca: Cornell University Press, 1988.

Bristow, Joseph. *Effeminate England: Homoerotic Writing After 1885*. Buckingham: Open University Press, 1995.

'Sterile Ecstasies: the Perversity of the Decadent Movement', *Essays and Studies* 48 (1995): 65–88.

Brown, Julia Prewitt. *Cosmopolitan Criticism: Oscar Wilde's Philosophy of Art*. Charlottesville: University of Virginia Press, 1997.

Brown, Lucy. *Victorian News and Newspapers*. Oxford: Clarendon, 1985.

Brown, Thomas. 'Opie's Poems.' *Edinburgh Review* 1 (1802–3): 113–21.

Buckle, Thomas Henry. 'The Influence of Women on the Progress of Knowledge.' *Fraser's Magazine* 57 (1858): 395–407.

Burdett, Osbert. *The Beardsley Period: an Essay in Perspective*. London: John Lane/The Bodley Head, 1925.

Butler, Judith. *Gender Trouble: Feminism and the Subversion of Identity*. New York: Routledge, 1990.

'Critically Queer.' *GLQ: a Journal of Lesbian and Gay Studies* 1 (1993): 17–32.

Campbell, Kate ed. *Journalism, Literature and Modernity: from Hazlitt to Modernism*. Edinburgh University Press, 2000.

Carey, Rosa Nouchette. *Twelve Notable Good Women of the Nineteenth Century*. London: Hutchinson, 1899.

Chadwick, Edwin. 'Physical Training.' *English Woman's Journal* 6 (1860): 262–5.

Chambers, Iain. *Border Dialogues. Journeys in Postmodernity*. London: Routledge, 1990.

'Narratives of Nationalism. Being "British"'. *Space and Place. Theories of Identity and Location*. Ed. Erica Carter, James Donald and Judith Squires. London: Lawrence and Wishart, 1993.

'Character of a Good Colonist.' *Colonist* 1 (1848): 29–31.

'Cheap Reading.' *Eliza Cook's Journal* 1 (1849): 2–3.

Childe-Pemberton, Harriet L. 'Women of Intellect. Jane Austen.' *Girl's Own Paper* 3 (1881): 378–9.

'China. No. VIII. Condition of Women in China.' *Saturday Magazine* 11 (1837): 38–40.

Christ, Carol T. 'The Hero as Man of Letters.' *Victorian Sages and Cultural Discourse: Renegotiating Gender and Power*. Ed. Thais Morgan. New Brunswick, N.J.: Rutgers University Press, 1990.

Clarke, William. 'Is Britain on the Down Grade?' *Young Man* 13 (1899): 181–5.

'Is Britain on the Down Grade? A Remarkable Series of Letters from Leaders in Thought and Action.' *Young Man* 13 (1899): 222–7.

Clayforth, Anya. '*Woman's World*: Oscar Wilde as Editor.' *Victorian Periodicals Review* 30 (1997): 84–101.

'Clever Women.' *Chambers' Edinburgh Journal* 1 (1832): 281.

Cobbe, Frances Power. 'The Indigent Class – their Schools and Dwellings.' *Fraser's Magazine* 73 (1866): 143–60.

'What Shall we do with Our Old Maids?.' *Fraser's Magazine* 66 (1862): 594–610.

Cohen, Monica F. *Professional Domesticity in the Victorian Novel: Women, Work and Home*. Cambridge University Press, 1998.

Collins, Wilkie. 'The Unknown Public.' *Household Words* 18 (1858): 217–22.

Cook, Eliza. 'A Word to My Readers.' *Eliza Cook's Journal* 1 (1849): 1.

'Best Rooms.' *Eliza Cook's Journal* 2 (1850): 73–4.

'The Englishman.' *Eliza Cook's Journal* 4 (1851): 40.

'The "House of Lords" and the "House of Commons".' *Eliza Cook's Journal* 6 (1851–2): 97–9.

'To My Readers.' *Eliza Cook's Journal* 3 (1850): 65.

Corbett, Mary Jean. *Representing Femininity. Middle-Class Subjectivity in Victorian and Edwardian Women's Autobiographies*. Oxford University Press, 1992.

Corelli, Marie. 'Shakespeare's Mother.' *Woman's World* 2 (1889): 435–38.

'Correspondence.' *Boy's Own Paper* 13 (1890–1): 592.

'Courting Extraordinary.' *The Lady's Museum* 1 (1831): 241.

Crawford, Emily. 'Women as Journalists.' *Review of Reviews* (1893): 289.

'Women Wearers of Men's Clothes.' *Woman's World* 2 (1889): 283–6.

'Dandyism.' *Lady's Magazine*. Improved Series, 136 (February 1831) np.

'Daniel Deronda.' *Edinburgh Review* 144 (1876): 442–70.

D'Arcy, Ella. 'Irremediable.' *Woman's World* 1 (1894): 87–108.

Darling, J. J. 'Liberal Newspapers – Effects of the Reduction of Stamp-Duty.' *Tait's Edinburgh Magazine* n.s.3 (1836): 685–92.

Davies, Emily. 'The Influence of University Degrees on the Education of Women.' Repr. *Thoughts on Some Questions Relating to Women, 1860–1908* [1910]. New York: Kraus Reprint, 1971.

Debord, Guy. *Society of the Spectacle*. Detroit: Black & Red, 1983.

Demoor, Marysa. *Their Fair Share: Women, Power and Criticism in the* Athenaeum, *from Millicent Garrett Fawcett to Katherine Mansfield, 1870–1920*. Aldershot: Ashgate, 2000.

Dennis, John. 'Literary Criticism and Biography.' *Fraser's Magazine* n.s. 26 (1882): 509–20.

Dixon, Robert. *Writing the Colonial Adventure. Race, gender and nation in Anglo-Australian Popular Fiction, 1875–1914*. Cambridge University Press, 1995.

Djikstra, Bram. *Idols of Perversity: Fantasies of Feminine Evil in Fin-de-siècle Culture*. Oxford University Press, 1986.

Doane, Mary Ann. 'Film and the Masquerade: Theorising the Female Spectator.' *Screen* 23 (1982): 74–88.

'Domestic Man.' *Chambers's Edinburgh Journal* 1 (1832): 385.

Eccles, Charlotte O'Conor. 'Are Pretty Women Unpopular?' *Windsor Magazine* 2 (1895): 737–41.

'How Women Can Easily Make Provision for their Old Age.' *Windsor Magazine* 1 (1895): 315–18.

Dowden, Edward. 'Hopes and Fears for Literature'. *Fortnightly Review* n.s. 45 (February 1889): 166–83.

Eckley, Sophia May. 'To Emily Faithfull.' *Victoria Magazine* 20 (1872): frontispiece.

'Editing.' *Contemporary Review* 29 (1877): 517–20.

'The Editor's Address to His Readers.' *Chambers' Edinburgh Magazine* 1 (1832): 1–2.

'Education in the Colonies and in India.' *Eliza Cook's Journal* 7 (1852): 124–5.

Eliot, George. 'John Ruskin's *Modern Painters, Vol. III*.' Repr. *George Eliot: Selected Essays, Poems and Other Writings*. Ed. A. S. Byatt and Nicholas Warren. London: Penguin, 1990.

'The Natural History of German Life.' *Westminster Review* 66 (1856): 51–79.

'Prospectus.' *Westminster Review* 57 (1852): iii–vi.

'Silly Novels by Lady Novelists.' Repr. *George Eliot: Selected Essays, Poems and Other Writings*. Ed. A. S. Byatt and Nicholas Warren. London: Penguin, 1990.

'Woman in France: Madame de Sablé.' Repr. *George Eliot: Selected Essays, Poems and Other Writings*. Ed. A. S. Byatt and Nicholas Warren. London: Penguin, 1990.

Eliot, Simon. *Some Patterns and Trends in British Publishing, 1800–1919*. London: Bibliographical Society Occasional Papers, 1993.

Elise, Madame. 'Women Writers' in 'Ladies' Pages.' *Bow Bells* n.s. 3 (1865): 139.

'Elizabeth and Victoria: From a Woman's Point of View.' *Victoria Magazine* 3 (1864): 97–103.

Ellegård, Alvar. *The Readership of the Periodical Press in Mid-Victorian Britain*. Göteborgs: Göteborgs Universitets Arskrifft, 1957.

Elliott, Bridget. 'Sights of Pleasure: Beardsley's Images of Actresses and the New Journalism of the Nineties.' *Reconsidering Aubrey Beardsley*. Ed. Robert Langenfeld & Simon Wilson. Ann Arbor: UMI Research Press, 1989.

Ellis, Mrs [Sarah Stickney]. *The Women of England, their Social Duties and Domestic Habits*. London: n.p., c1840.

Elwell, Stephen. 'Editors and Social Change: a Case Study of Once a Week (1859–80).' *Innovators and Preachers. The Role of the Editor in Victorian England*. Ed. Joel H. Wiener. Westport, Conn.: Greenwood, 1985.

'The Emigrant in Port Phillip.' *Eliza Cook's Journal* 1 (1849): 193–5.

'Emigration.' *Chambers' Edinburgh Journal* 1 (1832): 149–50.
'Emigration and the Sexes.' *Tait's Edinburgh Magazine* NS25 (1858): 509–15.
'English Girls.' *Saturday Review* 5 (1858): 239.
'English Journalism.' *Fraser's Magazine* 34 (1846): 631–40.
'Englishwoman's Conversazione.' *Englishwoman's Domestic Magazine* 1 (1860): 48.
'Englishwoman's Conversazione.' *Englishwoman's Domestic Magazine* 4 (1861–2):
    48, 96, 284.
'Englishwoman's Conversazione.' *Englishwoman's Domestic Magazine* 5 (1862): 192.
'Englishwoman's Conversazione.' *Englishwoman's Domestic Magazine* 7 (1863): 144.
'Englishwoman's Conversazione.' *Englishwoman's Domestic Magazine* 8 (1863–4):
    192.
'Epigraph.' *The Magazine of Domestic Economy* 1 (1836): n.p.
Ernstrom, Adele M. 'The Afterlife of Mary Wollstonecraft and Anna Jameson's
    Winter Studies and Summer Rambles in Canada.' *Women's Writing* 4 (1997):
    277–96.
Esler, Mrs. E. Rentoul. 'Between Ourselves. A Friendly Chat with the Girls. Mrs.
    Oliphant.' *Young Woman* 5 (1896–7): 473–4.
'Etiquette for "Our Brothers"'. *Girl's Own Paper* 4 (1882): 74–5.
Evans, Eric. 'Englishness and Britishness: National Identities, c.1790–c.1870.' *Unit-
    ing the Kingdom? The Making of British History*. Ed. Alexander Grant and
    Keith J. Stringer. London: Routledge, 1995.
Faithfull, Emily. 'The Progress of Women: In Industrial Employment.' *Universal
    Review* 2 (1888): 637–43.
    'Victoria Press.' *English Woman's Journal* 6 (1860): 121–6.
'Farewell Banquet to Miss Faithfull.' *Victoria Magazine* 21 (1873): 252–64.
Fawcett, Millicent Garrett. 'The Progress of Women in Political Education.'
    Universal Review 2 (1888): 289–94.
    'Woman's Suffrage.' *Woman's World* 2 (1889): 9–12.
Faymonville, Carmen. '"Waste Not, Want Not": Even Redundant Women Have
    Their Uses'. *Imperial Objects. Essays on Victorian Women's Emigration and the
    Unauthorized Imperial Experience*. Ed. Rita S. Kranidis. New York: Twayne,
    1998.
Felski, Rita. *The Gender of Modernity*. Cambridge, Mass.: Harvard University Press,
    1995.
Feltes, N. N. *Literary Capital and the late Victorian Novel*. Madison: University of
    Wisconsin Press, 1993.
'Female Authorship.' *Fraser's Magazine* 33 (1846): 460–6.
'Female Employment. II. Educated Workwomen.' *Leisure Hour* 9 (1860): 53–5.
'Feminine Suffrage and *The Pall Mall Gazette*.' *Victoria Magazine* 11 (1868): 211–21.
Fetterley, Judith. *The Resisting Reader: a Feminist Approach to American Fiction*.
    Bloomington: Indiana University Press, 1978.
'A Few Words to our Readers.' *Family Economist* 1 (1848): 217.
Fisher, Judith L. 'Thackeray as Editor and Author: the Adventures of Philip and
    the Inauguration of the *Cornhill Magazine*.' *Victorian Periodicals Review* 33
    (2000): 2–21.

Fleming, George. 'On a Certain Deficiency in Women.' *Universal Review* 3 (1888): 401–6.

Flint, Kate. *The Woman Reader 1837–1914*. Oxford University Press, 1993.

Forbes, A. S. 'Dandyism.' *Temple Bar* 88 (1890): 527–34.

'Foreword.' *Windsor Magazine* 1 (1895): 1–3.

Foucault, Michel. *The History of Sexuality*, vol 1. Trans. Robert Hurley. New York: Pantheon Books, 1978.

Fowler, Roger. *Language in the News. Discourse and Ideology in the Press*. London and New York: Routledge, 1991.

Fraser, Hilary, with Daniel Brown. *English Prose of the Nineteenth Century*. London: Longman, 1997.

Froude, James Anthony. 'England and her Colonies.' Repr. in *Short Studies on Great Subjects*. London: Longmans, Green, 1911.

Frykstedt, Monica. *Geraldine Jewsbury's 'Athenaeum' Reviews*. Uppsala University Press, 1986.

Gagnier, Regenia. *Idylls of the Market Place: Oscar Wilde and the Victorian Public*. Aldershot: Scolar, 1986.

Gallienne, Richard Le. *The Romantic Nineties*. London: Putnam & Co., 1951.

Garnett, Lucy M. J. 'Reasons for Opposing Woman Suffrage.' *Woman's World* 2 (1889): 306–10.

Garvey, Ellen Gruber. *The Adman in the Parlor: Magazines and the Gendering of Consumer Culture, 1880s to 1910s*. New York: Oxford University Press, 1996.

Gaskell, Elizabeth. *The Life of Charlotte Brontë*. Ed. Alan Shelston. London: Penguin, 1975.

George, Rosemary Marangoly. *The Politics of Home. Postcolonial Relocations and Twentieth-Century Fiction*. Cambridge University Press, 1996.

Graham, Walter. *English Literary Periodicals* [1930] New York: Octagon, 1966.

Grahame, Kenneth. 'The Headswoman.' *Yellow Book* 3 (1895): 22–47.

Greg, W. R. 'Mary Barton.' *Edinburgh Review* 89 (1849): 402–35.

'The Newspaper Press.' *Edinburgh Review* 102 (1855): 470–98.

'Why Are Women Redundant?' *National Review* 14 (1862): 434–60.

Green, Stephanie. 'Oscar Wilde's *Woman's World*.' *Victorian Periodicals Review* 30 (1997): 84–101.

Hampton, Mark. 'Journalists and the Fragmentation of Knowledge: Professional Identity, Anonymous Journalism and the Public Sphere in Late-Victorian Britain.' *Scholarship in Victorian Britain*. Leeds Working Papers in Victorian Studies Volume 1. Leeds: Trinity and All Saints/ Leeds Centre for Victorian Studies, 1998.

Harland, Henry. 'A Birthday Letter. From "The Yellow Dwarf".' *Yellow Book* 9 (1896): 11–22.

'Dogs, Cats, Books, and the Average Man. By "The Yellow Dwarf".' *Yellow Book* 10 (1896): 11–23.

Harmsworth, Alfred. 'Answers to Correspondents.' *Answers* 13 (1895): 220–6.

Harrison, Fraser, ed. *The Yellow Book: an Illustrated Quarterly: an Anthology*. London: Sidgwick & Jackson, 1974.

Harrison, Frederic. 'A Word for England' [1898]. Repr. *Memories and Thoughts.* London: Macmillan, 1906.

'The Regrets of a Veteran Traveller' [1887]. Repr. *Memories and Thoughts.* London: Macmillan, 1906.

Hassam, Andrew. *No Privacy for Writing. Shipboard Diaries 1852–1879.* Melbourne University Press, 1995.

Haweis, H. R. 'The Mannish Girl.' *Young Woman* 5 (1896–7): 332–4.

Hazlitt, William. '*Life and Times of Salvator Rosa,* by Lady Morgan.' *Edinburgh Review* 40 (1824): 316–19.

'The Periodical Press.' Ed. P. P. Howe. *The Complete Works of William Hazlitt.* 21 Vols. London: Dent, 1930–4.

Helsinger, Elizabeth K., 'Consumer Power and the Utopia of Desire: Christina Rossetti's "Goblin Market".' *Victorian Women Poets: Emily Bronte, Elizabeth Barrett Browning, Christina Rossetti.* Ed. Joseph Bristow. New York: St. Martin's Press, 1995.

Robin Lauterbach Sheets and William Veeder. *The Woman Question: Society and Literature in Britain and America 1837–1883,* 3 vols. Vol 1. University of Chicago Press, 1983.

Hemans, Felicia. 'The Homes of England.' *Saturday Magazine* 1 (1832): 224.

'The Homes of England.' *Youth's Instructer and Guardian* 14 (1840): 106–7.

Hepworth-Dixon, Ella. 'Women on Horseback.' *Woman's World* 2 (1889): 227–33.

Heraud, J. A. 'Oliver Yorke's Epistle to the Reading Public.' *Fraser's Magazine* 5 (1832): 1–5.

Herstein, Sheila R. 'The *English Woman's Journal* and the Langham Place Circle: a Feminist Forum and its Women Editors.' *Innovators and Preachers. The Role of the Editor in Victorian England.* Ed. Joel H. Wiener. Westport, Conn.: Greenwood, 1985.

Hogarth, Janet. 'The Monstrous Regiment of Women.' *Fortnightly Review* 68 (1897): 926–36.

Homans, Margaret and Adrienne Munich. *Remaking Queen Victoria.* Cambridge University Press, 1997.

'Home Circle.' *Home Circle* 1 (1849): 8–9.

'The Hon. Mrs. Caroline Norton.' *Eliza Cook's Journal* 10 (1853–4): 39–41.

Hopkins, J. Castell. 'Mr. Goldwin Smith.' *Westminster Review* 141 (1894): 539–52.

Houghton, Walter E. *et al.,* eds. *The Wellesley Index to Victorian Periodicals 1824–1900.* 5 vols. Toronto and London: University of Toronto Press and Routledge & Kegan Paul, 1987.

'Household Duties and Operations.' *Magazine of Domestic Economy* 1 (1836): 4–7.

'The House of Business Young Lady.' *Girl of the Period Miscellany* 1 (1869): 43.

'How Women May Earn a Living. XV. – As a Short Story Writer.' *Woman's Life* 2 (1896): 85–6.

Howitt, Mary. Manuscript Letters Ht/1/1/180/1&2, Ht/1/1/181, Ht/1/1/184, Ht/1/1/196, and Ht/1/1/356, The Howitt Collection (ACC 1280), Box 1, Mary Howitt to Anna Harrison, 1820s–1840s Ht/1/1/1–196 and Box 2, Mary Howitt to Anna Harrison, undated Ht/1/1/341–356. Hallward Library, University of Nottingham, Department of Manuscripts and Special Collections.

'Woman's Mission.' *Bow Bells* n.s.3 (1865): 235.

Howitt, William. 'Letters on Labour to the Working Men of England. Letter First. On the True Dignity of Labour.' *People's Journal* 1 (1846): 208–10.

'The People's Portrait Gallery. Harriet Martineau.' *People's Journal* 1 (1846): 141–3.

Howitt, William and Mary. 'The Weekly Record of Facts and Opinions Connected with General Interests and Popular Progress.' *Howitt's Journal* 1 (1847): 1–2.

'William and Mary Howitt's Address to their Friends and Readers.' *Howitt's Journal* 1 (1847): 1–2.

Hughes, Clair. 'Daisy Miller: Whose Girl of the Period?' *Australasian Victorian Studies Journal* 6 (2000): 113–21.

Hughes, Linda K. 'History in Focus. 1870.' *A Companion to Victorian Literature and Culture.* Ed. Herbert F. Tucker. Oxford: Blackwell, 1999.

and Michael Lund. *The Victorian Serial.* Charlottesville: University Press of Virginia, 1991.

Hyde, Michael W. 'The Role of "Our Scottish Readers" in the History of *Tait's Edinburgh Magazine.*' *Victorian Periodicals Review* 14 (1981): 134–40.

Hyde, Michael W., and Walter E. Houghton. 'Tait's Edinburgh Magazine, 1832–1855', vol. 4. *The Wellesley Index to Victorian Periodicals 1824–1900,* 5 vols. Toronto and London: University of Toronto Press and Routledge & Kegan Paul, 1987.

'Idea of an English Girl.' *Chambers' Edinburgh Review* (12 July 1834): 185.

'Important Notice.' *The Lads of the Village* 2 (1874): 223.

'Influence of Sex on Mind: Cranial Contours' [Letter 47]. *Knowledge* 3 (1881): 78–9.

'Introduction.' *Magazine of Domestic Economy* 1 (1836): i–ii.

'Introduction.' *Saint Pauls* 1 (1867–8): 1–7.

'Irony of the Situation.' *Girl of the Period Miscellany* 1 (1869): 33–4.

Israel, Kali. *Names and Stories: Emilia Dilke and Victorian Culture.* Oxford University Press, 1999.

Jackson, Revd. George. 'Some Manly Words for Boys by Manly Men. 1. – True Manliness, and How to Get it.' *Boy's Own Paper* 20 (1897–8): 127.

Jackson, Holbrook. *The Eighteen Nineties: A Review of Art and Ideas at the Close of the Nineteenth Century* [1929]. London: Jonathan Cape, 1931.

James, Henry. 'Death of the Lion.' *Yellow Book* 1 (1894): 7–52.

James, Louis. *Fiction for the Working Man 1830–50: a Study of the Literature Produced for the Working Classes in Early Victorian Urban England* [1963]. Harmondsworth: Penguin, 1974.

'The Trouble with Betsy: Periodicals and the Common Reader in Mid-Nineteenth-Century England.' *The Victorian Periodical Press: Samplings and Soundings.* Ed. Joanne Shattock and Michael Wolff. Leicester University Press, 1982.

Jeffrey, Francis. 'Felicia Hemans.' *Edinburgh Review* 50 (1829–30): 32–7.

Jeffries, Richard. 'Hope on Household Furniture.' *Edinburgh Review* 10 (1807): 478–86.

Jeune, Lady. 'The Ideal Husband.' *Young Woman* 3 (1895): 23–5.
   Viscountess Harburton & Mrs Norman. 'What is the Best Cycling Dress for Women? I; II; & III.' *Woman at Home* 5 (1895–6): 619–23.
Johnstone, Christian Isobel. 'A Page for the Lasses.' *Tait's Edinburgh Magazine* 2 (1835): 128–9.
   'What Shall We Do with Our Young Fellows?.' *Tait's Edinburgh Magazine* n.s.1 (1834): 527–30.
   'Women of Business.' *Tait's Edinburgh Magazine* n.s.1 (1834): 596–7.
Johnstone, Mrs. 'The Latest Fashions.' *Woman's World* 2 (1889): 465–9.
King, Andrew. 'A Paradigm of Reading the Victorian Penny Weekly: Education of the Gaze and the *London Journal*.' *Nineteenth-Century Media and the Construction of Identities*. Ed. Laurel Brake, Bill Bell and David Finkelstein. Houndmills: Palgrave, 2000.
Kingsley, Charles. 'The Wonders of the Shore.' *North British Review* 22 (1854): 1–56.
Kingston, W. H. G. 'How the Unemployed May Better their Condition.' *Colonist* 1 1 (1848): 3–6.
Kipling, Rudyard. 'A Song of the English.' *Rudyard Kipling's Verse. Inclusive Edition 1885–1926*. London: Hodder & Stoughton, 1927.
Klancher, Jon. *The Making of English Reading Audiences, 1790–1832*. Madison: University of Wisconsin Press, 1987.
Kranidis, Rita S. *Subversive Discourse: the Cultural Production of Late Victorian Feminist Novels*. New York: St. Martin's Press, 1995.
   The Victorian Spinster and Colonial Emigration. Contested Subjects. New York: St. Martin's Press, 1999.
   'Introduction.' *Imperial Objects. Essays on Victorian Women's Emigration and the Unauthorized Imperial Experience*. Ed. Rita S. Kranidis. New York: Twayne, 1998.
Lacey, Candida Ann, ed. *Barbara Leigh Smith Bodichon and the Langham Place Group*. New York: Routledge, 1987.
Langland, Elizabeth. 'Nation and Nationality: Queen Victoria in the Developing Narrative of Englishness.' *Remaking Queen Victoria*. Ed. Margaret Homans and Adrienne Munich. Cambridge University Press, 1997.
Lawrence, Arthur H. 'Chat with Mrs. Sarah A. Tooley.' *Young Woman* 5 (1896–7): 441–7.
Layard, George Somes. *Mrs. Lynn Linton: Her Life, Letters, and Opinions*. London: Methuen, 1901.
'Letter from Sydney.' *Athenaeum and Literary Chronicle* 106 (4 November 1829): 685–7.
Levine, Philippa. *Victorian Feminism 1850–1900*. London: Century Hutchinson, 1987.
Lewes, George Henry. 'The Condition of Authors in England, Germany, and France.' *Fraser's Magazine* 35 (1847): 285–95.
   'A Gentle Hint to Writing Woman.' *Leader* 1 (1850): 189.
Lewis, Gifford, ed. *The Selected Letters of Somerville and Ross*. London: Faber and Faber, 1989.

Lewis, Reina. *Gendering Orientalism. Race, Femininity and Representation*. London: Routledge, 1996.

'Liaceloga'. 'A Dip into the Editor's Correspondence.' *Girl's Own Paper* 4 (1882): 582–3.

Liddle, Dallas. 'Salesmen, Sportsmen, Mentors: Anonymity and Mid-Victorian Theories of Journalism.' *Victorian Studies* 41 (1997): 31–68.

Linton, Eliza Lynn. 'Feminine Affectations.' *Saturday Review* 25 (1868): 776.

   The Autobiography of Christopher Kirkland, 3 vols. Vol II. London: Richard Bentley & Son, 1885.

   'The Girl of the Period.' *Saturday Review* 25 (1868): 339.

   'Mistress and Maid on Dress and Undress.' *Modern Women and What is Said of Them*. Ed. Lucia Gilbert Calhoun. New York: J. S. Redfield, 1868, 262–71.

   'Partisans of the Wild Women.' *Nineteenth Century* 31 (1892): 455–64.

   'Pushing Women.' *Saturday Review* 25 (1868): 578.

   'The Wild Women as Social Insurgents.' *Nineteenth Century* 30 (1891): 596–605.

   'The Wild Women, No.1, "As Politicians".' *Nineteenth Century* 30 (1891): 79–88.

'Literary Women.' *London Review* 8 (1864): 328–9.

'Literature of the Day: – The New Magazine.' *The Metropolitan: a Monthly Journal of Literature, Science, and the Fine Arts* 1 (1831): 17–22.

Loeb, Lori Anne. *Consuming Angels. Advertising and Victorian Women*. Oxford University Press, 1994.

Macaulay, Thomas Babington. 'Life and Writings of Addison.' *Edinburgh Review* 78 (1843): 193–8.

Mackay, Jane and Pat Thane. 'The Englishwoman'. *Englishness, Politics and Culture 1880–1920*. Ed. Robert Colls and Philip Dodd. London: Croom Helm, 1986.

Mackenzie, John A. *Propaganda and Empire. The Manipulation of British Public Opinion, 1880–1960*. Manchester University Press, 1984.

Maginn, William. 'Desperate System. Poverty, Crime, and Emigration.' *Fraser's Magazine* 1 (1830): 635–42.

   'Gallery of ILLUSTRIOUS Literary Characters. No.X. Mrs. Norton.' *Fraser's Magazine* 3 (1831): 222–3.

   'Gallery of ILLUSTRIOUS Literary Characters. No.XLII. Miss Harriet Martineau.' *Fraser's Magazine* 8 (1833): 576–7.

   'Our "Confession of Faith".' *Fraser's Magazine* 1 (1830): 1–7.

Maidment, Brian. 'Domestic Ideology and its Industrial Enemies: the Title Page of *The Family Economist* 1848–1850.' *Gender Roles and Sexuality in Victorian Literature*. Ed. Christopher Parker. Aldershot: Scolar, 1995, 25–54.

   'Magazines of Popular Progress and the Artisans.' *Victorian Periodicals Review* 17 (1984): 83–94 and frontispiece.

   'Victorian Periodicals and Academic Discourse.' *Investigating Victorian Journalism*. Ed. Laurel Brake, Aled Jones and Lionel Madden. New York: St. Martin's Press, 1990.

Makower, Stanley V. 'Three Reflections.' *Yellow Book* 12 (1897): 113–37.

Marchand, Leslie A. *The Athenaeum: a Mirror of Victorian Culture*. Chapel Hill: University of North Carolina Press, 1941.

Marks, Patricia. *Bicycles, Bangs and Bloomers: the New Woman in the Popular Press.* Lexington: University Press of Kentucky, 1990.

Maurer, Jr., Oscar. 'Froude and *Fraser's Magazine*, 1860–1874.' *Texas Studies in English* 28 (1949): 213–43.

Mayo, Isabella Fyvie. 'The Other Side of the World.' *Girl's Own Paper* 3 (1881–2): 145–8; 257–9; 289–91.

Mays, Kelly J. 'The Disease of Reading and Victorian Periodicals.' *Literature in the Marketplace: Nineteenth-Century British Publishing and Reading Practices.* Ed. John O. Jordan and Robert L. Patten. Cambridge University Press, 1995. 165–94.

McClintock, Anne. *Imperial Leather: Race, Gender and Sexuality in the Colonial Context.* London: Routledge, 1995.

McLaren, Lucy M. J. 'The Fallacy of the Superiority of Man.' *Woman's World* 1 (1888): 9–12.

'Melaia and Other Poems.' *Athenaeum* 582 (1838): 914.

Mill, John Stuart. 'Periodical Literature.' *Westminster Review* 1 (1824): 505–41.

Miller, Florence Fenwick. 'Character Sketch: Olive Schreiner.' *The Woman's Signal* 4 (1895): 1–2.

'Editor's Farewell Address.' *The Woman's Signal* 12 (1899): 1.

'How I Made My First Speech.' *The Woman's Signal* 1 (1894): 4–5.

Miller, Hugh. 'Periodicalism'. *Leading Articles on Various Subjects.* Edinburgh: William P. Nimmo, 1870.

Mills, Sara. *Discourse.* London: Routledge, 1997.

'Gender and Colonial Space.' *Gender, Place and Culture* 3 (1996): 125–47.

'Miss Burdett Coutts' Experiment.' *Victoria Magazine* 13 (1869): 81–4.

Mitchell, Sally. *The Fallen Angel. Chastity, Class and Women's Reading.* Bowling Green University Popular Press, 1981.

Mix, Katherine. *A Study in Yellow.* Lawrence: University of Kansas Press, 1960.

'Modern Periodical Literature.' *Dublin Review* 51 (1862): 275–308.

Morell, B. de Montmorency. 'The Umbrella', *Woman's World* 2 (1889):149–55.

'Mrs Humphry ("Madge," of "Truth").' *Woman's Life* 3 (1896): 301–2.

Nestor, Pauline. "A New Departure in Women's Publishing: *The English Woman's Journal* and *The Victoria Magazine*.' *Victorian Periodicals Review* 15 (1982): 93–106.

'A New Year's Family Party.' *Judy; or the London Serio-Comic Journal* 18 (1875–6): 117–18.

Nightingale, Florence. *Cassandra and other Selections from Suggestions for Thought.* Ed. Mary Poovey. London: Pickering & Chatto, 1991.

'Nights at the Round Table.' *Train* 1 (1856): 59–64.

Noble, E. 'Readers and Writers.' *Colburn's New Monthly Magazine* n.s.3 (1877): 34.

Noble, James Ashcroft. 'The Phantasies of Philarete.' *Yellow Book* 5 (1895): 195–225.

'Note.' *Woman* (17 Jan 1894): 5.

'Notes on a Residence in Van Diemen's Land.' *Simmonds's Colonial Magazine and Foreign Miscellany* 2 (1844): 170–3.

'Notices of New Works.' *Eliza Cook's Journal* 2 (1850): 219–21.

'Notices of New Works: The Fourth Estate.' *Eliza Cook's Journal* 3 (1850): 381–2.

Oliphant, Margaret. 'The Condition of Women.' *Blackwood's Edinburgh Magazine* 83 (1858): 139–54.

Onslow, Barbara. *Women of the Press in Nineteenth-Century Britain*. Basingstoke: Macmillan, 2000.

'On the Effeminacy of Some of the Male Sex.' *Lady's Magazine* (June 1738): 82–3.

'On the Establishment of a Reading Society, or Book Club.' *Magazine of Domestic Economy* 1 (1836): 134–7.

'On National Economy. No. III. Miss Martineau's "Cousin Marshall" – "The Preventive Check".' *Fraser's Magazine* 6 (1832): 403–10.

'On the Social Position of Women.' *Magazine of Domestic Economy* 7 (1842): 271–5.

'Open Council.' *English Woman's Journal* 2 (1858): 141–2.

'Our Portrait Gallery. Eliza Cook.' *Bow Bells* n.s.1 (1865): 18

'Our Sisters in China. Native Estimate of the Sex.' *Leisure Hour* 12 (1863): 199–201.

Owens, J. B. 'Life in Australia.' *Leisure Hour* 2 (1853): 214–5; 231–4; 253–5; 280–3.

Parker, Christopher. *Gender Roles and Sexuality in Victorian Literature*. Aldershot: Scolar, 1995.

Parkes, Bessie. 'A Review of the Last Six Years.' Repr. Candida Ann Lacey. Ed. *Barbara Leigh Smith Bodichon and the Langham Place Group*. New York: Routledge, 1987.

   'Opinions of John Stuart Mill.' *English Woman's Journal* 6 (1860): 1–11, 193–202.

   'Sanitary Lectures.' *English Woman's Journal* 6 (1860): 47–54.

   'A Year's Experience in Woman's Work.' *English Woman's Journal* 6 (1860): 112–21.

Pattison, E. F. S. 'John Ruskin, *Lectures on Art and Catalogue of Examples*.' *Academy* 1 (1870): 305–6.

'The Payment of Women.' *Victoria Magazine* 23 (1869): 84–5.

Pearce, Lynne. *Feminism and the Politics of Reading*. London: Arnold, 1997.

'Periodicals.' *Eliza Cook's Journal* 1 (1849): 182.

Peterson, Linda H. 'Mother-Daughter Productions: Mary Howitt and Anna Mary Howitt in *Howitt's Journal, Household Words*, and Other Mid-Victorian Publications.' *Victorian Periodicals Review* 31 (1998): 31–54.

Phillips, C. S. M. 'Miss Strickland's *Queens of England*.' *Edinburgh Review* 89 (1849): 435–62.

Phillips, Maurice. 'Famous Editor and Journalist. A Chat with Mr. P. W. Clayden.' *Young Man* 13 (1899): 93–6.

'Platonic Friendship.' *Woman at Home* 5 (1895–6): 359–61.

'A Poor Woman's Work.' *Victoria Magazine* 3 (1864): 396–9.

Poovey, Mary. *Making a Social Body: British Cultural Formation, 1830–1864*. University of Chicago Press, 1995.

   The Proper Lady and the Woman Writer: Ideology as Style. University of Chicago Press, 1984.

   Uneven Developments: The Ideological Work of Gender in Mid-Victorian England. University of Chicago Press, 1988.

'Portrait Gallery of Contributors to the *Girl's Own Paper.' Girl's Own Paper* 20 (1898–9): between 320–21.

Pratt, Mary Louise. 'Conventions of Representation.' *The Taming of the Text: Explorations in Language, Literature and Culture*. Ed. Willie van Peer. London: Routledge, 1989.

'Preface.' *Dublin Penny Journal* 1 (1832–3): iii–iv.

'Preface.' *The Magazine of Domestic Economy* 1 (1836): iii–iv.

'Preface.' *Rational Dress Society Gazette* 1 (1888): 1.

'Preface.' *Welcome Guest* 1 (1858): iii–iv.

Probyn, Elspeth. *Sexing the Self: Gendered Positions in Cultural Studies*. London: Routledge, 1993.

'Programme.' *Review of Reviews* 1 (1890): 14–20.

'Prospectus.' *The British and Foreign Review* 1 (1835): 1–4.

Psomiades, Kathy. *Beauty's Body: Femininity and Representation in British Aestheticism*. Stanford University Press, 1997.

Pykett, Lyn. 'Reading the Periodical Press: Text and Context.' *Victorian Periodicals Review* 22 (1989): 100–8.

'The Queen as a Woman of Business.' *Time* 1 (1879): 40–7.

Reed, David. *The Popular Magazine in Britain and the United States, 1880–1960*. University of Toronto Press, 1997.

'Remarks on the Periodical Criticism of England – in a letter to a friend.' Translated from the German of Von Lauerwinkel. *Blackwood's Edinburgh Magazine* 2 (1817–18): 670–9.

Rendall, Jane. '"A Moral Engine"? Feminism, Liberalism and the *English Woman's Journal.' Equal or Different. Women's Politics 1800–1914*. Ed. Jane Rendall. Oxford: Blackwell, 1987.

'The Reviewer of the Period.' *Tinsley's Magazine* 2 (1868): 617–22.

Richards, Thomas. *The Commodity Culture of Victorian England: Advertising and Spectacle, 1815–1914*. Stanford University Press, 1990.

Rigby, Elizabeth. 'Lady Travellers.' *Quarterly Review* 76 (1845): 98–137.

'Modern Painters I–III.' *Quarterly Review* 98 (1856): 384–433.

Rivière, Joan. 'Womanliness as a Masquerade.' *Psychoanalysis and Female Sexuality*. Ed. Hendrik M. Ruitenbeek. New Haven: College and University Press, 1966.

'Robina Crusoe, and her Lonely Island Home, 1.' *Girl's Own Paper* 4 (1882): 184–5.

Robinson, F. Mabel. 'Fans.' *Woman's World* 2 (1889): 115–19.

Robinson, Solveig. '"Amazed At Our Success": the Langham Place Editors and the Emergence of a Feminist Critical Tradition.' *Victorian Periodicals Review* 29 (1996): 159–72.

Robson, Ann P. and John M. 'Private and Public Goals: John Stuart Mill and the *London and Westminster.' Innovators and Preachers. The Role of the Editor in Victorian England*. Ed. Joel H. Wiener. Westport, Conn.: Greenwood, 1985.

Rose, Jonathan. 'How Historians Study Reader Response: or, What did Jo think of Bleak House.' *Literature in the Marketplace: Nineteenth-Century British Publishing and Reading Practices*. Ed. John O. Jordan and Robert L. Patten. Cambridge University Press, 1995.

Rosenberg, Sheila. 'The "Wicked *Westminster*": John Chapman, His Contributors and Promises Fulfilled.' *Victorian Periodicals Review* 33 (2000): 225–46.

Ruskin, John. 'Preface'. *Munera Pulveris*, vol. XVII. *The Works of John Ruskin*, 39 vols. Ed. E. T. Cook and Alexander Wedderburn. London: Allen, 1905.

'Lecture 1. Inaugural', vol. XX. The works of John Ruskin, 39 vols. Ed. E.T. look and Alexander Wedderburn. London: Allen, 1905.

Salmon, Edward G. 'What Girls Read.' *Nineteenth Century* 20 (1886): 524.

Sanders, Valerie. *Eve's Renegades: Victorian Anti-Feminist Women Novelists*. Basingstoke: Macmillan, 1996.

'"I'm your Man": Harriet Martineau and the *Edinburgh Review.*' *Australasian Victorian Studies Journal* 6 (2000): 36–47.

Schmidt, Barbara Quinn. *Epistemology of the Closet*. London: Penguin, 1994.

'In the Shadow of Thackeray: Leslie Stephen as the Editor of the *Cornhill Magazine.*' *Innovators and Preachers. The Role of the Editor in Victorian England*. Ed. Joel H. Wiener. Westport, Conn.: Greenwood, 1985.

Seed, John. '"Commerce and the Liberal Arts": the Political Economy of Art in Manchester, 1775–1860.' *The Culture of Capital: Art Power and the Nineteenth-Century Middle Class*. Ed. Janet Wolff and John Seed. Manchester University Press, 1988.

Shattock, Joanne. *The Oxford Guide to British Women Writers*. Oxford University Press, 1993.

Politics and Reviewers: The Edinburgh *and the* Quarterly *in the Early Victorian Age*. London: Leicester University Press, 1989.

and Michael Wolff, eds. *The Victorian Press: Samplings and Soundings*. University of Toronto Press, 1982.

'She Took Out the "If".' *Children's Friend* 25 (1885): 182.

Shevelow, Kathryn. *Woman and Print Culture: the Construction of Femininity in the Early Periodical*. New York: Routledge, 1989.

Shires, Linda M. 'Maenads, Mothers and Feminized Males: Victorian Readings of the French Revolution.' *Rewriting the Victorians: Theory, History and the Politics of Gender*. Ed. Linda M. Shires. London: Routledge, 1992.

Shirreff, Emily. 'College Education for Women.' *Contemporary Review* 15 (1870): 55–66.

Showalter, Elaine. *Sexual Anarchy: Gender and Culture at the Fin de Siècle*. New York: Viking, 1990.

'Our Past and Our Future.' *Fraser's Magazine* n.s.20 (1879): 1–12.

Skelton, John. 'Sketches of Irish Character.' *Fraser's Magazine* 4 (1831): 100–12.

Smiles, Samuel. 'Industrial Schools for Young Women'. *Eliza Cook's Journal* 1 (1849): 81–2.

'Men and Women – Education of the Sexes.' *Eliza Cook's Journal* 4 (1851): 97–9.

Smith, Goldwin. 'Imperialism.' *Fraser's Magazine* 55 (1857): 493–506.

Smith. W. Jardine. 'Wanted – A Career! A Colonist's Advice to Certain British Fathers.' *Saint Pauls* 11 (1872): 738–48.

Snodgrass, Chris. 'Decadent Parodies: Aubrey Beardsley's Caricature of Meaning.' *Fin de Siècle, Fin du Globe: Fears and Fantasies of the Late Nineteenth Century*. Ed. John Stokes. Houndsmill: Macmillan, 1992.

'Some Boys who Constantly Write to the Editor.' *Boy's Own Paper* 3 (1880–1): 128.

Somerset, Isobel. 'Our Policy.' *Woman's Signal* 1 (1894): 1–2.

'The Song of the Train.' *Train* 1 (1856): 59.

Spence, Catherine Helen. 'An Australian's Impressions of England.' *Cornhill Magazine* 13 (1866): 110–20.

Stanley, H. M. 'Our Contributors' Club.' *Young Woman* 3 (1895): 25.

Stead, W. T. 'The Future of Journalism.' *Contemporary Review* 50 (1886): 663–79.

'Government by Journalism.' *Contemporary Review* 49 (1886): 653–74.

Stephen, Fitzjames. 'Journalism.' *Cornhill Magazine* 6 (1862): 52–63.

Stephen, Leslie. 'Some Early Impressions – Journalism.' *National Review* 42 (1903): 420–36.

Stewart, Garrett. *Dear Reader: the Conscripted Audience in Nineteenth-Century British Fiction*. Baltimore: Johns Hopkins University Press, 1996.

Stocking, George W. Jr. *Victorian Anthropology*. London: Macmillan, 1989.

Stopes, Charlotte Carmichael. Unpublished Correspondence with Constance Wilde. British Library Add.58454, ff.1–38.

Sutherland, John. *The Longman Companion to Victorian Fiction*. London: Longman, 1988.

'Trollope and *St. Pauls* [sic] 1866–70.' *Anthony Trollope*. Ed. Tony Bareham. London: Vision, 1980.

Swan, Annie S. 'Life and Work at Home. Over the Teacups.' *Woman at Home* 1 (1894): 62–4.

'Swells.' *Belgravia: A London Magazine* 1 (1867): 39.

Symons, Arthur. 'Stella Maris', *Yellow Book* 1 (1894): 129–31.

Tasma (Jessie Couvreur). 'Iftar in a Harem.' *Temple Bar* 92 (1891): 395–406.

Thackeray, William Makepeace. 'Roundabout Papers – No. I. On a Lazy Idle Boy.' *Cornhill Magazine* 1 (1860): 124–8.

'Roundabout Papers.—No. IX. On a Joke I Once Heard from the Late Thomas Hood.' *Cornhill Magazine* 2 (1860): 752–60.

Thomas, William Beech. *The Story of the Spectator 1828–1928*. London: Methuen, 1928.

'To a Male Scold.' *Punch or the London Charivari* (1889): 21.

'To Fathers. The Duty of Provident Investments.' *The Home Circle* 1 (1849): 9–10.

'To Our Friends.' *Woman's Signal* 1 (1894): 1.

'To Our Readers.' *Sharpe's London Magazine* 4 (1847): 409.

'To the Readers of "The Quiver"'. *Quiver* n.s.1 (1866): 832.

'Treatment of Women.' *Eliza Cook's Journal* 5 (1851): 225–7.

Trollope, Anthony. 'Introduction.' *Saint Pauls* 1 (1867–8): 1–7.

Turner, Mark. 'Defining Discourses: the *Westminster Review, Fortnightly Review*, and Comte's Positivism'. *Victorian Periodicals Review* 33 (2000): 273–82.

Tyrrell, Alex. 'Samuel Smiles and the Woman Question in Early Victorian Britain.' *Journal of British Studies* 39 (2000): 185–216.

Uffelman, Larry K., Lionel Madden and Diana Dixon. *The Nineteenth-Century Periodical Press in Britain: a Bibliography of Modern Studies*. Toronto: Victorian Periodicals Review, 1992.

Vann, J. Don, and Rosemary T. VanArsdel, eds. *Victorian Periodicals and Victorian Society*. University of Toronto Press, 1994.

'Victoria Discussion Society.' *Victoria Magazine* 26 (1870): 99–113.

Vincent, David, *Literacy and Popular Culture, England 1750–1914*. Cambridge Studies in Oral and Literate Culture 19. Cambridge University Press, 1989.

Violette. 'Paris Fashions.' *Woman's World* 2 (1889): 470–3.

Warren, Lynne. 'Women in Conference: Reading the Correspondence Columns in *Woman* 1890–1910.' *Nineteenth-Century Media and the Construction of Identities*. Ed. Laurel Brake, Bill Bell and David Finkelstein. London: Palgrave, 2000, 122–34.

Waugh, Arthur. 'The Auction Room of Letters.' *Yellow Book* 6 (1895): 257–65.

'What are we to Expect?.' *Fraser's Magazine* 35 (1847): 244–52.

'What it Means to be a Lady Journalist.' *Young Woman* 7 (1899): 93–4.

'What Will Our Spinsters Do? or, What Shall We Do With Our Spinsters?.' *New Monthly Magazine* n.s.34 (1832): 273–6.

'What Will You Do?.' *Children's Friend* 13 (1873): 43.

'What Will You Write for the Magazine?.' *Eliza Cook's Journal* 5 (1851): 351–2.

White, Caroline Alice. 'A View of the Dwellings of the Working Classes, Taken from a Back Window.' *The Home Circle* 1 (1849): 217–19.

White, Cynthia. *The Women's Periodical Press in Britain, 1946–1976*. London: H. M. S. O., 1977.

Wilde, Constance. 'Muffs.' *Woman's World* 2 (1889): 174–8.

Wilde, Oscar. *The Picture of Dorian Gray*. 1891. London: Penguin, 1984.

   Selected Letters of Oscar Wilde. Ed. Rupert Hart-Davis. Oxford University Press, 1962.

   'The Critic as Artist', repr. *Complete Works*. Ed. Vyvyan Holland. London: Collins, 1966.

   'A Fascinating Book.' *Woman's World* 2 (1889): 53–6.

   'A Note on Some Modern Poets.' *Woman's World* 2 (1889): 108–112.

   'Some Literary Notes.' *Woman's World* 1 (1888): 389–92.

   'Some Literary Notes.' *Woman's World* 2 (1889): 221–4.

   'The Soul of Man Under Socialism', repr. *Complete Works*. Ed. Vyvyan Holland. London: Collins, 1966.

Williams, Raymond. *Keywords. A Vocabulary of Culture and Society*. London: Fontana, 1983.

Williams, Robert, F. 'Female Character.' *Fraser's Magazine* 7 (1833): 591–601.

Wilson, E. D. J. 'The Colonial Empire of England.' *Dark Blue* 1 (1871): 770–80.

Winter, John Strange [Henrietta Eliza Vaughan, Mrs. Arthur Stannard, also 'Violet Whyte']. 'The Ideal Husband.' *Young Woman* 3 (1895): 119–20.

Wolff, Janet. *Feminine Sentences: Essays on Women and Culture*. Cambridge: Polity, 1990.

Wolff, Michael, John S. North and Dorothy Deering. *The Waterloo Directory of Victorian Periodicals 1824–1900*. Waterloo: Wilfred Laurier Press, 1976.

Wolfreys, Julian. *Being English. Narratives, Idioms, and Performances of National Identity from Coleridge to Trollope*. New York: State University of New York Press, 1994.

'Woman: Her Position and Influence.' *Home Circle* 1 (1849): 56.

'Woman in Domestic Life.' *The Magazine of Domestic Economy* 1 (1836): 65–8; 129–31.

'Woman's Proper Place in Society.' *Temple Bar* 33 (1871): 168–78.

'Woman's Rights. By a Weak-Minded Female.' *Time* 2 (1880): 114–18.

'Women of the Day.' *Saint Pauls* 2 (1868): 302–14.

Woolf, Virginia. *To the Lighthouse*. Ed. Margaret Drabble. Oxford University Press, 1998.

    A Room of One's Own, Three Guineas. Ed. Morag Shiach. Oxford University Press, 1992.

    'Professions for Women.' *Collected Essays of Virginia Woolf*. Ed. Leonard Woolf. 4 Vols. London: Hogarth, 1966–7.

'A Word or Two About Women.' *Train* 2 (1856): 181–5.

'A Word to Little Girls.' *Children's Friend* 13 (1873): 42.

'A Word to Those who are Willing to Help.' *Review of Reviews* 1 (1890): 53.

'A Word with Our Readers.' *Leisure Hour* 1 (1852): 8–10.

Yates, Edmund. 'Preface.' *Tinsley's Magazine* 1 (1867–8): iii.

Yonge, Miss [C.M.]. 'Children's Literature, Part III: Class Literature of the Last Thirty Years.' *Macmillan's Magazine* 20 (1869): 453.

'Young Women as Journalists.' *Girl's Own Paper* 12 (1890): 305–6 [Signed 'G.H.P.'].

'Young Women in the Colonies.' *Eliza Cook's Journal* 6 (1851–2): 241–3.

Zedlitz, Baroness von. 'A Chat with Madame Sarah Grand.' *Woman's Life* 3 (1896): 501–2.

    'An Interview with Miss Mary Kingsley.' *Woman's Life* 1 (1896): 431–2.

Žižek, Slavoj. *The Sublime Object of Ideology*. London and New York: Verso, 1989.

Index

CAMBRIDGE STUDIES IN NINETEENTH-CENTURY
LITERATURE AND CULTURE

General editor
Gillian Beer, *University of Cambridge*

Titles published